DEGREES O

Arab Higher Education in the Global Era

Presenting an analysis of higher education in eight countries in the Arab Middle East and North Africa, *Degrees of Dignity* works to dismantle narratives of crisis and assert approaches to institutional reform. Drawing on policy documents, media narratives, interviews, and personal experiences, Elizabeth Buckner explores how models of apolitical external reform become contested and modified by local actors in ways that are simultaneously complicated, surprising, and even inspiring.

Degrees of Dignity documents how global discourses of neoliberalism have legitimized specific policy models for higher education reform in the Arab world, including quality assurance, privatization, and internationalization. Through a multi-level and comparative analysis, this book examines how policy models are implemented, with often complex results, in countries throughout the region.

Ultimately, *Degrees of Dignity* calls on the field of higher education development to rethink current approaches to higher education reform: rather than viewing the Arab world as a site for intervention, it argues that the Arab world can act as a source for insight on resilient higher education systems.

ELIZABETH BUCKNER is an assistant professor in the Department of Leadership, Higher, and Adult Education at the Ontario Institute for Studies in Education, University of Toronto.

ELIZABETH BUCKNER

Degrees of Dignity

Arab Higher Education in the Global Era

UNIVERSITY OF TORONTO PRESS
Toronto Buffalo London

ISBN 978-1-4875-2894-2 (cloth)   ISBN 978-1-4875-2897-3 (EPUB)
ISBN 978-1-4875-2895-9 (paper)   ISBN 978-1-4875-2896-6 (PDF)

Library and Archives Canada Cataloguing in Publication

Title: Degrees of dignity : Arab higher education in the global era /
Elizabeth Buckner.

Names: Buckner, Elizabeth, author.

Identifiers: Canadiana (print) 20210313676 | Canadiana (ebook) 20210313781 |
ISBN 9781487528959 (softcover) | ISBN 9781487528942 (hardcover) |
ISBN 9781487528973 (EPUB) | ISBN 9781487528966 (PDF)

Subjects: LCSH: Higher education and state – Arab countries. | LCSH:
Education, Higher – Arab countries. | LCSH: Arabs – Education (Higher)

Classification: LCC LC179.5 .B83 2022 | DDC 379.1/2140956–dc23

This book has been published with the help of a grant from the Federation
for the Humanities and Social Sciences, through the Awards to Scholarly
Publications Program, using funds provided by the Social Sciences and
Humanities Research Council of Canada.

University of Toronto Press acknowledges the financial assistance to its
publishing program of the Canada Council for the Arts and the Ontario
Arts Council, an agency of the Government of Ontario.

**Canada Council   Conseil des Arts
for the Arts   du Canada**

ONTARIO ARTS COUNCIL
CONSEIL DES ARTS DE L'ONTARIO
an Ontario government agency
un organisme du gouvernement de l'Ontario

Funded by the   Financé par le
Government   gouvernement
of Canada   du Canada

Canada

For Simo, who made this book possible

Contents

Tables and Figures

Acknowledgments

I have many people to thank for inspiring this book and supporting me over the past five years in writing it: John Meyer, Chiqui Ramirez, and Evan Schofer nurtured my interest in globalization while I was a graduate student at Stanford, and taught me how to think about the role of the global in education. Lina Khatib, formerly the head of the Program on Arab Reform and Democracy at Stanford University's Center on Democracy, Development, and the Rule of Law, gave me opportunities to explore my interest in the Arab world. Garnett Russell, my friend and colleague, planted the idea of writing this book during a seemingly ordinary walk in Central Park, New York City. Natasha Ridge, at the Al Qasimi Foundation, provided the vision and support for a Visiting Professorship in Education in the Middle East at Teachers College, where I began to bring my ideas together into arguments and eventually chapters. Thanks go to Sue Kippels, Cait Mullan, Hanadi Mohammed, and Brian Chung for welcoming me to Ras al-Khaimah; to Mary Mendenhall, who first sent me to Beirut to study educational policy; and to Hana El-Ghali, who welcomed me back and facilitated my research at the American University of Beirut. At Teachers College, I am thankful to the students in my class on higher education in the Middle East, whose ideas deeply influenced my own. And I still feel lucky to have met Sarah Shedeed, the most detail-oriented research assistant I could have hoped for.

When I moved to the University of Toronto, I found the institutional support I needed to bring this book into print. Glen Jones, dean of the Ontario Institute for Studies in Education, understood my vision and gave me the support to conduct additional fieldwork. Nina Bascia, my most supportive chair, made sure I had extra time to write. Lobna Mahdi helped me expand my sources and deepen my historical arguments through her research assistance. Meg Patterson, at the University of Toronto Press, believed in this book project from the beginning and guided me through every step of publishing process. I am also deeply indebted to the three anonymous reviewers, who made my arguments more nuanced and my facts more grounded.

Beyond the academic, material, and logistic support, writing this book has been deeply personal. It has been my opportunity to reflect on over fifteen years of travelling, studying, and living inside and outside of the Arab world. There are innumerable conversations, comments, and memories from which I have learned. Many of them have made their way into this book. They may not realize their indelible impact on me, but I would like to thank Abdelhay Moudden and Farah Cherif D'Ouezzan for starting my journey at the Center for Cross-Cultural Learning in Rabat; Nader Kabbani for welcoming me at the Syrian Trust for Development and again at the Brookings Institution in Doha; Khaled Gudah, Bara'a Abdessalam, Ayman Mohammad, and Dua'a Yousef at the Modern Arabic Language International Center in Amman; and Saba Khawas for facilitating my fieldwork in Jordan.

For a decade of learning from and with others, I thank my scholar friends: Charis Boutieri and Rebecca McClain Hodges for pushing me to think more like an anthropologist, and Kristen Kao for pushing me to think more like a political scientist.

Over the past four years Rohaan has been my partner through this writing journey, and I thank him for his patience, love, and unwavering support. He understands what this book means to me, and, for that, I feel profoundly lucky. I must thank my family: my mother for inspiring my interest in the Middle East, and Alayna for a lifetime of inspiration and insight as well as her remarkable responsiveness to my urgent requests for wordsmithing assistance.

I dedicate this book to Simo Taoufik and Zahra Oukharro, my two great teachers, for welcoming me into their family and becoming mine for ten years. Much of what I know and have been able to put into words in this book is thanks to them.

DEGREES OF DIGNITY

Introduction

In 2016, I spent a summer in Beirut, the capital of Lebanon. At the time, due to political gridlock the country had been without a president for over two years. Meanwhile Beirut was in the middle of a garbage crisis: the authorities had closed the city's main landfill and given residents no alternative disposal, so trash was literally piling up on the streets. Every day I would walk the length of the city centre from my apartment in Mar Mikhael, an artistic, gentrifying neighbourhood in the east, to the American University of Beirut (AUB), a symbol of elite higher education overlooking the Mediterranean in the western part of the city. As I wound through the narrow streets, I passed crumbling colonial-era buildings that had not been rebuilt after the end of the civil war in 1990; garbage heaps, a symbol of current government dysfunction; and churches and mosques side by side, testifying to the country's sectarianism. I then passed through the ostentatious, empty downtown, which had been rebuilt with luxury boutiques to cater to the wealthy, a neighbourhood-sized manifestation of the country's crony capitalism.

Along the way I was greeted by Beirut's infamous street art: walls, bollards, and construction sites that were all covered in murals and graffiti, serving as public commentary on political issues. Scrawled behind a pile of trash was the phrase "The government is trash," and on a wall leading into the new downtown was the phrase, in English, "When injustice becomes law, rebellion becomes duty." On the ad hoc barriers of a construction site was the phrase, in Lebanese colloquial Arabic, "We are the country. We are the voice." You simply cannot walk the streets of Beirut without seeing a city marked visibly by the spirit and creativity of its people, demanding more from their government.

Eventually I would make it to the university, which seemed to shimmer in comparison. Its historic ivy-covered buildings were spotless, and its campus filled with majnouneh vines and their bright pink

flowers and with shady groves of banyan, cypress, and olive trees. Vis-
itors were greeted by a banner proudly celebrating the university's one
hundred and fiftieth anniversary: "AUB 150 – We Make History." On
its business school façade another banner celebrated its position on the
QS World University Rankings by Subject in 2015: "Among the elite we
rank, leading the Arab world."

The contrast was clear: outside these gates there was a complicated and politicized Lebanon, but inside there was a private, elite,
English-speaking, world-class institution devoted to providing a
non-sectarian, liberal education. Throughout its history AUB has been
a symbol of prestige, educating generations of the region's political and
cultural elites and promising to be a bastion of liberal values in an illib-
eral region. And yet, as I entered its iconic main gate, I could not help but
see the stark contrast between these two worlds as reflecting the most
pressing issues facing Arab higher education today – the seeming inability of the government to meet its citizens' needs; the divide between the
public and the private; economic inequalities and the role of language
in perpetuating them; tensions between serving a local community and
pursuing global status; and, fundamentally, the university's isolation
from or integration into the political and social life beyond its gates.

While in Beirut, I met with Dr. Adnan El Amine, director of the
Lebanese Association for Educational Studies and an expert on Arab
higher education. Dr. El Amine reflected on his life's work to improve
higher education in the region, much of it focused on the topic of quality assurance. He explained: "After the Arab Spring, I thought about
all our work on improving quality. But now, I don't think that quality
is the problem. The more pressing questions are: What is the role of
higher education in creating civic values? What is the university doing
to promote the stability and social cohesion of the society?"

His questions proved remarkably prescient. Three years later Lebanon
witnessed unprecedented nationwide protests, which started in October
2019 and upended society over the next few months. These spontaneous
protests called for an end to the government's crippling sectarianism
and corruption and ultimately led to the prime minister's resignation.
University students and professors were important players in this
movement; they took to the streets, calling for change and demanding
a better future. Higher education policy was also on the reform agenda,
with protesters calling for the government to address graduate unemployment and grant the Lebanese University greater autonomy.

Lebanon's 2019 demonstrations were only the latest in a string of
protests throughout the region that have defined much of the decade since the Arab Spring, the term coined to describe the various

people-led demonstrations and revolutions in the Arab world that began in late 2010. Starting in December 2010, Tunisians of all backgrounds took to the streets to outcry at economic stagnation and regime corruption. Peaceful protests then spread to Egypt in early 2011 and led to more violent revolutions in Bahrain, Yemen, Libya, and Syria (L. Anderson, 2011). In academic circles and the popular media the Arab Spring's call for "bread, freedom, and dignity" has been understood as a demand for economic and political justice, motivated by inequality, poverty, unemployment, repression, and corruption. Young people and their discontents have been central to understandings of the outbreak of the Arab Spring, and they continue to be protagonists in ongoing protests in the region.

In the wake of the Arab Spring, higher education in many parts of the region has been indelibly changed. Conflicts in Iraq, Libya, Syria, and Yemen have resulted in attacks on universities, in scholarly flight, and in the fragmentation of national academic communities (Dillabough et al., 2018). Civil conflict in Syria and the rise of the Islamic State of Iraq and Syria have displaced millions, mostly within the region, including hundreds of thousands of university-age refugees in Turkey, Jordan, Lebanon, Iraq, and Egypt (Barakat & Milton, 2015). Crackdowns on academic freedom have occurred in Egypt and the United Arab Emirates (UAE), signalling rising authoritarianism occurring across many parts of the region (Holmes & Aziz, 2019). Meanwhile, university students and professors in Algeria, Morocco, Tunisia, and Lebanon have staged large-scale strikes and boycotts to protest low-quality employment or high rates of unemployment among university graduates, proposed austerity measures, and privatization.

Yet conversations about the causes and consequences of the Arab Spring have barely touched on the role of education generally, or of higher education in particular, in shaping young people's lives and opportunities. Scholars of Middle Eastern politics have tended to focus on who holds power and how they maintain it, largely ignoring what they do with their power to shape social policies such as those on education. In the decade after the Arab Spring their interest focused on explaining the region's return to authoritarianism. Meanwhile, international development agencies, such as the World Bank, have much to say about education: they draw on economic theories of labour productivity to criticize higher education in the region as inefficient and ineffective. Technical and policy reports suggest, and subsequently fund, a host of reforms based on generic best practices in international development, frequently with little consideration of the specific national context or the reasons such reform efforts often fail.

Even worse, policy discussions of higher education in the region often adopt a neocolonial or orientalist gaze that casts the region's educational systems as failures, largely because they lack the financial resources of systems in Europe and North America. When a lack of resources cannot be blamed, some critiques resort to cultural accounts, suggesting that the region's "traditional" values are incompatible with modernity or that the region's Islamic heritage stymies intellectual inquiry (Lavergne, 2004; Sukarieh, 2017). A recent article in the *Financial Times* offers a typical assessment of education in the region, stating that "stultifying rote learning is overlain with a narrow-minded religiosity that stifles curiosity, critical thinking, originality and self-expression" (Gardner, 2017). These discussions of higher education in the Arab world are then linked to broader discourses on youth disenfranchisement, regional instability, and terrorism (Chaaban, 2009; Chakir, 2008; Fuller, 2003; Hendrixson, 2003; Street, Kabbani, & al-Oraibi, 2006).

Clearly, higher education policy in Arab societies is a dynamic arena that invokes both normative questions and contentious policy debates. However, as long as political scientists largely ignore education, and economists ignore its social and political aspects, important questions regarding higher education reform in the Arab Middle East remain largely unaddressed. There is a pressing need for more nuanced conversations about higher education in the Arab Middle East that view higher education as a socio-cultural and politically consequential institution, while also fully rejecting stereotypes of Arab societies as inherently lacking.

This book critiques technical and universalizing prescriptions and instead brings a comparative perspective to analyse contemporary higher education in the Arab Middle East and North Africa. It asks why countries adopt certain policies and what their effects are. I document how the entrenchment of particular discourses in development, namely the knowledge economy and neoliberalism, has resulted in the legitimation of certain policy models for higher education reform that have dramatically shaped the nature of educational reforms in the Arab world. Through multilevel and comparative analysis, I examine how globally circulating discourses map onto specific national contexts across the region, to identify the diverse ways in which reform is occurring and the ways in which external reform models are contested and undermined by different actors. Ultimately I argue that higher education in the Arab world is a socio-political institution that links the fates of students and states, and discussions of reform must recognize the role and interests of local constituencies, the power and inertia of institutionalized

practices, and the inherently politicized nature of state-sponsored educational reform.

Higher Education and the Arab State in the Global Era

In the years before the Arab Spring, policy analysts expressed concern over the inability of Arab states to incorporate youth into socio-
economic life, and the region's many disaffected unemployed young
people were viewed as ripe for mobilization or radicalization (Assaad
& Roudi-Fahimi, 2007; Dhillon & Yousef, 2011; Sukarieh, 2017; Yusuf,
2008). For many observers, concerns over Arab youth came to fruition in
the Arab Spring. The story now told about the Arab Spring characterizes
it as a movement led primarily by young people connected by mobile
phones and social media. Anecdotal evidence suggests that many of the
protesters in Tunisia, Egypt, Jordan, Morocco, and Yemen were young
people dissatisfied with their lack of opportunities for political and economic participation (al-Momani, 2011; L. Anderson, 2011). University
students and professors helped organize anti-regime protests in Tunisia
and Egypt in 2011, often marching from campuses to public squares
(Kohstall, 2015; Slama, 2013), and campus demonstrations have been
integral to ongoing protest movements in the region (L. Anderson, 2012;
Dorio, 2017). Yet, this narrative also erases the significant roles that others, including religious movements, labour unions, and political parties,
have played, and it places undue blame on young people for the repression and violence that has followed (Sukarieh, 2017).

Young people cannot become the scapegoats of the instability that
the region faces. Yet, their discontents were real then and remain important today. The problems that Arab states face are not only those of
non-representative political systems, heavy-handed militaries, or high
rates of corruption; in fact, these are manifestations of low levels of state
legitimacy linked to the perceived lack of social and economic opportunity (Cammack et al., 2017; Guazzone & Pioppi, 2012; Weipert-Fenner &
Wolff, 2015; Zemni, 2017). Political scientists have argued that one of
the underlying causes of the Arab Spring was the "breakdown" of
"the social contract in which the autocratic regimes had offered limited socioeconomic benefits in exchange for loyalty" (Weipert-Fenner &
Wolff, 2015, p. 3). Echoing this sentiment, Abdelwahab Alkebsi, the former director of the Middle East division at the National Endowment for
Democracy, a US-based non-profit foundation that seeks to strengthen
global democracy, stated in 2012 that the "uprisings were not just
a rejection of leaders. They were a rejection of an archaic and dys-
functional social contract that left citizens dependent on their states"

(Buckner, Beges, & Khatib, 2012, p. 8). The inability of Arab states to provide their young people with economic opportunity, social mobility, and a sense of progress continues to undermine their legitimacy.

Discussions of state legitimacy are closely related to higher education. A country's higher education system establishes both material and ideological links between young people and the state. Commenting on an earlier wave of social unrest, the social theorist Immanuel Wallerstein (1969) stated: "the government needs the university, as it needs the church, as it needs the arts, as it needs the major political and economic structures ... to say over and over that it is worthy of support" (p. 32). As the most easily recognizable and legitimated source of knowledge and advanced training, the university has been a catalyst of state- and nation-building for over two hundred years (Herrera, 2006; Mazawi, 2005). In the period after independence, universities in the Middle East became symbols of social mobility, national unity, and economic development, playing their part in the larger efforts to consolidate power under a centralized state, strengthen the political legitimacy of the ruling regime, and educate civil servants for an independent post-colonial nation state. Yet, in the wake of the Arab Spring, it has become clear that higher education systems are no longer fulfilling popular aspirations for opportunity and mobility. Wilkens and Masri (2011) explain that young people have "deep frustrations with the existing status quo – not least of which is the failure of the social contract for advancement that should be offered by higher education" (p. iii). One reason for this seeming disconnect is that the world has changed. In the era of globalization, national university systems are being called upon to fulfil a new mandate: to produce highly educated and entrepreneurial workers for a globally competitive and mobile economy. This shift involves new models for how to provide, govern, and fund higher education, which have had profound impacts on young people's pathways to adulthood.

The Limits of Technical Approaches

The shift from higher education for nation-building to higher education for global competitiveness is no easy undertaking. By many accounts, the Arab world is failing. John Waterbury, who previously served as president of AUB and adviser to the government of Abu Dhabi on higher education, begins his recent book, *Missions Impossible: Higher Education and Policymaking in the Arab World* (2020), by stating that "a premise of this study, so widely held that I doubt it would arouse any dissent, is that Arab higher education has been and remains in a state of structural crisis" (p. xii). Similarly, among international development experts and national governments alike, a constant stream of reports decries the problems of higher education in the region – admissions, financing, governance, quality assurance, and scientific research.

Within development studies, critiques of the region's higher education systems are typically rooted in human capital theory, which argues that formal education makes labour more productive and hence more economically valuable. For decades economists have argued that educational institutions in the region are of low quality and are not preparing youth with the knowledge and skills needed for productive employment (Chaaban, 2008; Kabbani & Kamel, 2007; World Bank, 2008b). Within policy studies, scholars have focused on issues of poor governance (Waterbury, 2020). In international development, studies focus on the inputs and outputs of the higher education system. People are rarely mentioned, except to the extent that they undermine effective implementation when they are unable or unwilling to carry out policies fully. To reduce the higher education system to its numbers – budgets, admission rates, quality assurance indicators, and research productivity (as technical approaches do) – is to largely ignore the reality of the everyday lived experiences of people as they navigate higher education systems and structures. The varied reasons for which young people attend university, including social status, parental pressure, boredom, and marriage, are largely ignored.

Moreover, reform approaches tend to look for quick-fix technical solutions in the form of privatization, public-private partnerships, quality assurance mechanisms, or the wholesale importation of international best practices or foreign university campuses. Waterbury (2020) laments the fact that not only is much of the empirical research on higher education in the Arab world carried out by donors and international governmental organizations, but it is overwhelmingly prescriptive, focusing on what *should* be done, with little contextualization of *how* such reforms could be accomplished. Andre Mazawi (2005) has similarly criticized the narrow focus on issues of management or policy, arguing that "scant research attention is given to the social, cultural, and political underpinnings" of higher education in the region (p. 133). For decades, scholars in the region have pushed back against the idea of quick-fix technical reforms. In 1997, A. Halim stated that "the World Bank propose[d] to 'reform' our education to open the country to a modern, competitive economy, while not recognizing the role of education in forming either the character of students, or their national identity" (Emran, 1997, p. 6). Yet, large-scale, foreign-funded reform projects continue.

In contrast to dominant technical approaches, anthropologists and qualitative researchers have made important contributions to the study of education in the Arab world, shedding light on the ways in which educational systems socialize young people as loyal national citizens and gendered subjects or sort them into different life paths (Adely, 2012; Boutieri, 2016; Cantini, 2016; Cohen, 2004; Vora, 2018). Their studies are based on in-depth analyses of young people's lived experiences within particular educational institutions and communities. Development actors, however, rarely engage with these studies. In general, qualitative accounts of young people's lives seldom seem to inform pressing policy debates in higher education development. Moreover, despite their important insights, given their focus on particular local contexts, ethnographic studies rarely explicitly compare countries, leaving many important and policy-relevant questions unanswered, such as how and why higher education systems in the region vary.

In short, current approaches to studying education in the region tend to be either one-size-fits-all, grounded in universalizing economic theories, or localized ethnographic accounts. Despite a few notable exceptions (see Mazawi, 2005, 2007, 2009; Ridge, 2014; and Waterbury, 2020), there have been few studies that draw on the theoretical and conceptual tools offered by comparative education to examine how global trends and local dynamics intersect to affect Arab higher education systems in different ways. This book draws on a comparative and multilevel analysis to examine how global models intersect with national political factors to shape higher education in the Arab world, while also exploring how individuals are navigating the changing policies and opportunity structures in their own lives.

A Multilevel and Comparative Approach

To move beyond the technical and universalizing perspectives that dominate the development literature, a new approach is needed. This book adopts a multilevel and comparative perspective to analyse higher education systems in the region. Its starting premise is that higher education systems are inherently social and political institutions. In line with this view, neither higher education reform nor its implementation is a purely technical process of determining what works and just doing it, but rather they occupy what Mazawi (2005) calls "contested terrain" (p. x). In taking this approach, I draw on Bartlett and Vavrus (2014) who argue that education policy must be viewed as "a deeply political process of cultural production engaged in and shaped by social actors in disparate locations who exert incongruent amounts of influence" (p. 132). This socio-cultural perspective calls attention to the role of powerful ideas, institutions, and actors in shaping policy reform and implementation.

In my multilevel approach I draw on a long-standing tradition in comparative education that situates educational systems within global, national, and local contexts. Scholars of comparative education have shown how global actors, processes, and institutions affect national higher education policies throughout the world (McNeely, 1995; Mundy, Green, Lingard, & Verger, 2016). Those writing from the perspective of sociological neo-institutionalism and its application to global phenomena in the world society tradition have documented significant shifts in ideas about education over time that have filtered down and shaped reforms in diverse national contexts (Meyer, Boli, Thomas, & Ramirez, 1997; Ramirez, 2012). These global discourses and policy models are being adopted in Arab higher education systems that vary geographically, economically, and politically. The process of adaptation to the national level generates wide-ranging outcomes, and scholars of the region have argued that we must pay more attention to how global discourses and policy models interact with long-standing local structures to effect change, including how global models are adapted and resisted by local actors (Cantini, 2017; Guazzone & Pioppi, 2012). To understand and theorize local variation, I draw on the comparative method to examine how global discourses and policy models affect national education systems, why reforms do or do not take hold in a given context, and how they become modified in distinct national contexts.

The Global Arena in Education and Development

Over the past three decades a rich literature in comparative education has shown that even seemingly national policy domains such as higher education are affected by global processes. Scholars writing from the world society tradition in comparative education have shown that since the Second World War there has been an intensification and diffusion of particular cultural norms at the global level that emphasize ideals of human rights and commitments to progress through rationality, science, and development (Meyer, Boli, Thomas, & Ramirez, 1997). A central argument in the world society tradition is that the global cultural environment is imbued with, and circulates, particular scripts or models that serve as normative prescriptions. These models are powerful because they confer legitimacy to the actors who implement them, and serve as evidence that actors are in accordance with wider norms and standards (Meyer et al., 1997; Ramirez, 2012). Discussing how discourses are adopted in the Arab world in particular, Farag (2010) explains that alignment to global standards constitutes the proof that "rulers are willing to adapt societal realities to what seems to be rational and modern norms" (p. 288).

Changes in the global cultural environment have had a profound effect on educational systems. Throughout the world, states have legitimized geographic boundaries through claims to a common linguistic or cultural heritage (Zemni, 2017). Mass educational systems were used to inculcate and socialize citizens, and higher education systems were used to train elites to run modern states and economies in the name of modernization and development. In terms of policy, states' legitimacy has become increasingly linked to economic development and social welfare. Fourcade (2006) calls this the "reconstruction and rationalization of states as economic actors" (p. 165), in which "'acting' upon the economy was redefined as a normal and desirable expression of state power" (p. 162).

The fall of the Union of Soviet Socialist Republics (USSR) ushered in a new era of intensified global integration, spurred by the liberalization of trade and increased global mobility. Two of the most powerful ideas in current approaches to development are the knowledge economy and neoliberalism. Their rationales have become taken for granted to justify particular reforms in higher education. They have been diffused by powerful global actors, including the World Bank (WB), the United Nations, the Organisation for Economic Co-operation and Development (OECD) and donors such as the United States and the European Union, in the form of specific policy models, such as privatization and quality assurance (Dale, 2005; McNeely, 1995).

The knowledge economy discourse positions the creation and application of knowledge as central to national economic development (Robertson, 2005). Its idea is underpinned by the seeming consensus that knowledge is playing an increasingly important role in promoting economic growth (C.W. Jones, 2012; Powell & Snellman, 2004; Slaughter & Rhoades, 2004). While economists have long recognized the importance of human capital in the form of skilled labour in increasing economic efficiency, the idea that underpins the knowledge economy discourse is that knowledge itself supports economic growth by spurring innovations and technological progress. Economists have found that returns to knowledge-intensive industries have increased relative to other sectors such as manufacturing. Furthermore, economists of education have found that the pay-off to a university degree has increased relative to the pay-off to secondary education in countries around the world (Carnoy, Froumin, Loyalka, & Tilak, 2014). However, even while the knowledge economy has become a policy buzzword, there is actually no theoretically precise definition of a knowledge economy (C.W. Jones, 2012; Robertson, 2005).

Lack of definition notwithstanding, one of the most striking effects of the knowledge economy discourse is the idea that education at all levels, including higher education, is both possible and desirable for ever larger proportions of youth. This global commitment to access, grounded in a belief in education as a human right and a catalyst for development, has put pressure on most countries to expand access to higher education (Frank & Meyer, 2007; Schofer & Meyer, 2005). It has also had implications for the content of curricula and pedagogies and is associated with national reforms and initiatives at all levels of education. Specifically, knowledge economy discourses are associated with the need to develop particular individual traits, including achievement motivation and risk-taking. Scholars are interested in the extent to which education can promote particular outcomes, which are deemed important in helping countries prepare their young people to participate in competitive labour markets and knowledge-intensive industries; these attributes include the motivation to succeed and an interest in working in the private sector or in entrepreneurship (Hainmueller & Hiscox, 2006; Souitaris, Zerbinati, & al-Laham, 2007). Education in the knowledge economy is also associated with high rates of global labour mobility, which has put a greater emphasis on cross-cultural competencies (Nielsen, 2012).

The knowledge economy discourse has also put pressure on the university as an engine of development through its knowledge-production role (Frank & Meyer, 2007). Inter-governmental organizations, such as the WB and UNESCO, have encouraged national investment in research and development and pressured universities to prove their status as world-class institutions that are contributing to national and global development (World Bank, 2000). The knowledge economy discourse has been both powerful and contested in the Arab region (Mazawi, 2007, 2009). In Mazawi's (2007) critical take, the knowledge economy discourse cannot be divorced from "unequal power frameworks associated with Western colonialism and imperialism" that continue to affect knowledge production in the region (p. 255). Other scholars argue that at issue is not the knowledge economy discourse per se but rather a simplistic equation of abstract secular science with knowledge. They call for a reclaiming of the idea of the knowledge society within an Islamic epistemology, recognizing that knowledge and learning have always been important to Islam and Muslim-majority societies (Akdere, Russ-Eft, & Eft, 2006; Halstead, 2004).

A second powerful discourse that has dominated development thinking since the 1980s is neoliberalism. Neoliberalism is an ideology that extends principles from classical economic theory to broad domains of social life (Colclough, 1996; Harvey, 2007). It contends that social policies of all sorts, including education, should adopt market principles, including deregulation and consumer choice. Neoliberalism manifests in particular policy prescriptions, but also it has a broader impact on many domains of social life. In particular, it bases social policy on notions of competition, efficiency, and rational choice. This ideology has had an impact on both nation states and individuals. In terms of policy, neoliberalism has been associated with the deregulation of labour markets and the reduction of government spending. Programs that provided economic security have been dismantled as expensive and inefficient. In their place, workers are encouraged to compete with one another for positions in education and the labour market. In addition, nation states are increasingly portrayed as in competition with one another for resources, such as investments, jobs, and human resources. In education, rather than viewing themselves as purely or primarily national institutions, universities are engaged in international competition and comparison. Sociologist Gili Drori (2000) calls this perspective "public and political interest in international comparisons of educational performance" (p. 28).

Moreover, by relying on market-based conceptions of service delivery, neoliberal policies have resulted in commodification, thereby changing the relationships between students and their educational institutions – with students being increasingly viewed as "consumers" or "clients" in a global market for credentials. In the Arab world the embrace of neoliberal economic policies in higher education and the labour market has dismantled former sources of economic security and nation-building and left young people isolated and economically insecure (Cohen, 2004; Dhillon, Dyer, & Youssef, 2009). Additionally, neoliberal policies have been associated with growing socio-economic inequalities and raise concerns about the entrenchment of class hierarchies and social divisions through privatized spaces and services.

The entrenchment of neoliberal ideologies has also had well-documented consequences on individuals. Anthropologists and others have documented how neoliberal ideologies have changed state-citizen relations by extending market principles to social interactions (Sukarieh, 2016); individuals are expected to attain success through competition and self-reliance. In this conception, education becomes "recast as the individual's personal investment in his or her own future, rather than as a common or public good" (Nielsen, 2012, p. 2). In the Arab world, Mazawi (2007) argues that neoliberal education reforms have sought to "produce a civic identity associated with an autonomous, flexible, and economically productive citizen" (p. 263). Similarly, young people are framed as autonomous "choosers" who have greater choice over their education and labour-market paths (Adely, 2009). Competition is framed as inherently efficient, and, relatedly, the negative effects of competition, such as the creation of "winners" and "losers," are often ignored. The pervasive sense of competition is not always benign – young people are coming of age in societies, with greater economic insecurity and increasing anxieties about the future (Shirazi, 2020).

Reconstituting the Local

Global ideas and expertise often change national policies. Global ideas and actors, including international financial institutions that lend money to low- and middle-income countries, have the power to change policies, systems, and opportunity structures in societies worldwide, particularly in those low- and middle-income countries. In examining the power of international development on economic policies, Fourcade (2006) argues that foreign experts have the ability to "impose their own definition of reality – their norms, concepts, language, tools, and so on – to eventually engage in a profound reconstruction of the local economic setting" (p. 150). Despite Arab states' long histories of public commitments to individual opportunity and prosperity through education and public-sector employment, discourses of the knowledge economy and neoliberalism increasingly recast the purpose of education more narrowly as "work" and position individuals as carrying the primary responsibility for their fates (Mazawi, 2007).

Yet, changes to national and local systems are messy and impartial because global models are carried into contexts that have long-standing, distinctive, often contrasting traditions, and they frequently encounter groups whose interests are not compatible with desired reforms. Farag (2010) explains that global scripts must "work with, on, and around national histories and political constraints" (p. 289). Similarly, Cantini (2017) explains that while the discourses affecting higher education in the Arab world "are truly global" (p. 262), the outcomes are diverse and include "appropriation, mixing, rejection, and resistance" (Cantini, 2016, p. 61). Understanding why and how similar reform models result in different outcomes requires comparative analysis. In the chapters that follow, I examine specific policy domains across countries to understand how global policy models are reconstituted, negotiated, and resisted in local settings, and to shed light on the factors affecting the implementation of national policies.

Local Contestation, Power, and Privilege

Within their distinct country contexts, individuals interpret and navigate their changing higher education systems in various ways, with diverse goals and substantially different levels of resources at their disposal. Educational systems in the Arab region from pre-school to higher education, as around the world, are deeply unequal in terms of access, attainment, and outcomes (Assaad, Salehi-Isfahani, & Hendy, 2014; Salehi-Isfahani, Hassine & Assaad, 2014). Privileged groups, including upper classes and political elites, are able to take advantage of the expanding higher education systems and changing opportunity structures for their own benefit (Jackson & Buckner, 2016). They also have the resources to evade the consequences of academic failure that groups from lower classes likely do not. Part of the story of higher education reform in the Arab world, then, involves understanding how young people from different backgrounds understand, interpret, and differentially navigate their changing educational systems and societies. This includes bringing attention to the fact that educational opportunities and responses to changing environments vary across social classes.

In the chapters that follow, I weave together the complex and often contradictory stories of young people and their perceptions of opportunity, as they are shaped in and by experiences of higher education. I show how young people are acutely aware of the inequality of opportunity they face, and discuss both the many emotions that this situation generates, from frustration to anger, and the strategies that those studying and working in higher education use to navigate that changing opportunity structures.

In figure 0.1, I visualize the comparative and multilevel analysis that guides the book's analysis. The figure depicts the multiple scales and the myriad actors involved in higher education reform in the Arab world. At the global level, the figure highlights the powerful role of development discourses and organizations to generate specific policy models. At the national level, I outline various country characteristics, including demographic, economic, and political factors, that shape the adoption of these policy models in different countries in the region. Finally, at the individual level, I label the major stakeholders who then absorb and navigate such reforms, while also recognizing that there is great diversity within each group.

Figure 0.1. A Multilevel, Comparative Approach

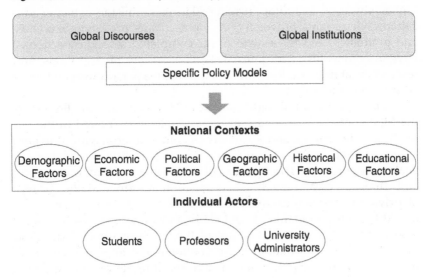

Data and Analysis

This book focuses on the Arab Middle East and North Africa, a multi-lingual, multi-ethnic, and geographically and religiously diverse region of the world. I concentrate on eight countries from three subregions where I have lived, studied, and conducted research over the past fifteen years: Egypt, Jordan, Syria, and Lebanon in the Middle East and Levant; Morocco and Tunisia in North Africa; and the United Arab Emirates and Qatar in the Arabian Gulf. Although these countries today use Arabic as an official language, and the majority of their citizens identify as Muslim, they also vary economically, culturally, politically, and geographically. Recognizing the region's diversity, I do not consider the peoples of the Arab Middle East and North Africa to have a common history, and I acknowledge the many divisions and ongoing political conflicts within the region. Nonetheless, in the post–Second World War era, the countries from Morocco to Iraq have been grouped together as a world region in the field of international development, and, not coincidentally, their approaches to education policy have many commonalities.

Over the past fifteen years I have studied the role of higher education in the Middle East and North Africa, inside and outside of classrooms – in lecture halls, formal and informal interviews, academic conferences, and campus visits. I have spoken to a broad range of stakeholders in higher education, including current and former ministers of higher education; civil servants; university presidents, deans, professors, students, and graduates; and those who never completed secondary school. I have also consulted with journalists, civil society organizations, and researchers at think-tanks to understand diverse perspectives on higher education in the region.

In 2006–8, I was a Fulbright scholar in Morocco, teaching English at the Mohammed V University in Rabat. In 2009–10, I lived in the old medina of Damascus and spent my evenings interviewing university-age students in Syria to understand their perceptions of higher education opportunity. Throughout 2013–14, I lived in Jordan, Morocco, and Tunisia, researching higher education reform and the growth of private higher education. In 2015–17, I was a visiting scholar at the Al Qasimi Foundation in the UAE, and in 2016, I was a visiting fellow at the American University of Beirut. In this book I draw on numerous sources of data including national and international statistics; media accounts; policy documents; and interviews with students, university professors and administrators, as well as higher education policymakers. I also draw on my own experiences living and travelling throughout the region; having countless informal daily conversations, including stories shared by taxi drivers, Arabic tutors, and family friends; and visiting public and private universities, sitting in on lectures, and teaching my own courses.

Organization of the Book

Although much of the research on higher education in the Arab world deals with individual countries, this book focuses on comparisons across countries. Each chapter addresses one of five key policy domains: access, quality, privatization, internationalization, and research. It first discusses how the issue is approached in international development, drawing on documents published by the WB, think-tanks, or other development agencies. It then reconsiders the technical approach by repositioning each policy issue as an arena of political and social contestation. I argue that hidden beneath each of these technical discussions are normative questions and contested visions of the role of the university, and the state, in its citizens' lives: Who should reap the benefits of higher education? What benefits should a university credential confer? Who should pay for or profit from young people's aspirations for higher education? What should the role of the university be in forging national unity? And what types of knowledge are valued?

Chapter 1 contextualizes subsequent discussions of higher education in the Arab world by providing a brief history of higher learning in the region and offering an overview of contemporary higher education in the book's eight focal countries. It prefaces later debates by arguing that higher education in the region has never been apolitical; rather, it has always been closely linked to the legitimacy of leaders.

The first debate in which I engage concerns the question of access: who gains admission and how do they do so? Chapter 2 argues that admissions systems in every country in the region reflect broader socio-political contracts between the state and society. It also shows how, in the global era, admissions systems are being contested or evaded through cheating and being manipulated through private tutoring or private higher education.

Next, I go inside the university to examine how countries have been reforming policies to improve quality. Chapter 3 deconstructs the "quality crisis" in the region and the way that development actors and foreign experts have pushed countries to adopt a particular model of quality assurance in the region. It argues that the technical literature, which focuses on quantitative indicators of the quality of higher education, ignores the relational and positional aspects of higher education, and that new definitions of quality are necessary. It calls for new ways of defining and conceptualizing higher education quality.

Chapter 4 addresses the rapid growth of private higher education in the region. Privatization is touted in much of the development literature as an apolitical approach to expanding access without additional public funding. Drawing on interviews with students and families, I argue that private higher education in the Arab world is, in fact, highly political. Private higher education is viewed as undermining commitments to public education in many Arab nations, while also allowing the wealthy and well-connected to profit from students' desires for education. Even in the countries where the private sector is not contested, it reflects and likely reproduces existing demographic divisions.

Chapter 5 focuses on the international dimensions of Arab higher education systems. The technical literature portrays internationalization as an imperative for systems around the world and as synonymous with high quality. I examine patterns of international student mobility and branch campuses in the region. I argue that current approaches to internationalization tend to associate prestige with Western models of higher education in ways that reinforce existing academic and geopolitical hierarchies.

Chapter 6 discusses the nature and implications of the university's role as a knowledge producer. The technical literature on research is highly critical of Arab academia – numerous reports detail the Arab world's lack of research and its low level of impact. This chapter argues that the discourse of productivity misses the fundamental and structural reality: research production is highly unequal globally. Moreover, because research involves defining and defending the truth, it can be threatening to those in power, and recent orientations towards neoliberalism and securitization have undermined academic research in the region.

The book concludes with a call to rethink current technical approaches to higher education development by asking not how the Arab world can improve its higher education system but how the field of higher education development can learn from the Arab world.

Towards a New Narrative

When I was twenty, I travelled to Morocco to study at the Center for Cross-Cultural Learning in Rabat. On my first day the centre's director, Dr. Abdelhay Moudden, told a room of eager students: "Americans are smart. Moroccans are also smart. They don't do things differently because they don't know better, but because their lives are different."

At the time I thought it was wholly unnecessary to remind us of our essential equality. After all, in the wake of 9/11 and the 2003 invasion of Iraq, we were the ones who had chosen to come to learn the Arabic language, experience a different culture, and live with Moroccan host families. But over the past fifteen years I often reflect on how rare, and profound, it was to remind ambitious American undergraduates that their ways of being and doing were not better or more rational than those in other parts of the world that seemed so distant and different.

As a scholar of comparative higher education, I continue to draw on Dr. Moudden's wisdom: deeper understanding must start with the rejection of implicit stereotypes about Western superiority, including the inherent rationality of Western higher education and the implicit assumption of irrationality in Arab higher education.

This book seeks to reframe the conversations on higher education in the Middle East that are occurring among think-tanks, development agencies, and donors located primarily in Europe and North America. One of the most harmful and pervasive stereotypes in development is the portrayal of the region's higher education systems as "lacking" or "in crisis." The sense of inferiority is perpetuated by a deficit orientation, which continues to view non-Western societies as underdeveloped or lacking in capacity and knowledge (largely because they are under-resourced), while continuing to reify European and North American universities as models for reform.

To begin a fundamentally different conversation, I propose an alternative narrative about higher education in the region: the Arab Middle East and North Africa has a long history of indigenous scholarship and an intellectual tradition that not only contributed to the Enlightenment but has continued and contributed to the resistance of colonization and invasion until the present day. Higher education institutions in the region have long been highly international and cosmopolitan, educating young people from around the world in Muslim teachings and, more recently, training them to become economic and political leaders. The national universities of the region are high-quality institutions that train the best and the brightest in their countries. Faculty members are as intelligent and talented as those working in North American universities, although they tend to have less access to resources and scholarship due to the exploitative practices of the contemporary publishing industry and the hegemonic power of the English language. Arab academia is full of dynamic and engaged academics who are active in print and social media, interested in influencing policy, and committed to solidarity with the communities they study. University leaders in the Middle East and North Africa are among important thought leaders in their countries. In response to global changes, Arab higher education systems have been adept at responding to the changing needs of their societies by introducing new degree programs and training their youth to be civically minded through participation in student activism and engagement. Moreover, rather than focusing exclusively on employment, Arab universities continue to educate young people to be well rounded and virtuous, to engage deeply with ideas about the nature of the world, and to understand inequalities in the contemporary global arena. Higher education institutions in the Arab world have, and continue to be, at the forefront of calling for change, and for that they deserve our respect.

Of course, this is only one side of the story. But how might conversations about higher education reform in the Arab world change with this as our starting point?

1
The University and the Arab World

For most of the twentieth century the Arab university was part of a larger state- and nation-building project that materially and symbolically linked individual opportunity for economic and social mobility to modernization and national development. Since the end of the Cold War and the concomitant rise of neoliberal globalization, however, it has been called upon to educate youth for a fundamentally different future – one of privatized opportunity and global awareness. Arab nations are not alone: higher education systems around the world have been urged to reorient their teaching and research to support national competitiveness for the twenty-first century. International development organizations frame higher education reform as a political and practical imperative. In response, Arab governments have adopted various globally circulating models of reform, including expansion, quality assurance, and privatization, fundamentally altering the region's higher education landscape.

This chapter provides a foundation for understanding higher education reform in the Arab world; it first outlines the historical legacies of higher education in the region and then examines the systems in the book's eight focal countries. In tracing their changes, I argue that institutions of higher education have never been simply sites of teaching and learning. Rather, as a socio-cultural and political institution, the university has been closely linked to other forms of cultural, economic, and political power throughout the region's more than one-thousand-year history. The cultural authority of universities, rooted initially in their religious knowledge and later in their promises of scientific progress, gives them the power to legitimate political rulers and confer prestige on individuals. At the same time, this cultural authority has also made them sites of broader transformations and contestations.

Early Models of Islamic Higher Education

As in Europe, Africa, and South Asia, the earliest institutions of higher learning in the Arab world were religious. In addition to being sites of worship, mosques were among the earliest institutions for teaching and learning and focused on religious instruction through explanatory circles (*halqa*, Arabic). In the tenth and eleventh centuries, the *madrasa* (meaning "place of study" in Arabic), a new institutional form, emerged and spread. Madrasas were locally established and supported by private endowments (*waqf*; plural, *awqaf*, Arabic) (Tamari, 2009, p. 40). Madrasas expanded on religious instruction to teach mathematics, medicine, natural sciences, philosophy, and the Islamic sciences, including theory, history, and Islamic jurisprudence (*fiqh*, Arabic) (Herrera, 2006; Perkin, 2007; Teferra & Altbach, 2003).

During the Umayyad (661–750) and Abbasid (750–1258) empires, both of which spanned large parts of the Arab world and beyond, madrasas also played an important role in preparing scholars to participate in state administration. Those educated in madrasas became judges, notaries, and religious functionaries (Hatina, 2003). More than sixty centres of learning were established to advance knowledge in diverse fields, including geometry, astronomy, geography, medicine, optics, physics, and philosophy. Madrasas developed into a "fully-fledged college and university system" (Nasr, 1987, p. 125). The most famous of these institutions include Zitouna (established in 737) in Tunis, Qarawiyyin University (859) in Fez, Morocco, and Al-Azhar (969) in Cairo (Herrera, 2006; Lulat, 2005). Throughout the medieval period these institutions created networks of scholars who read similar canonical texts and debated shared scholarly sources (Makdisi, 1981; Tamari, 2009).

For centuries, Al-Azhar occupied a pre-eminent position as the seat of Islamic education in Egypt and beyond. Despite its founding and ongoing role as the leading institution for Islamic education, Al-Azhar was never exclusively religious – various constituencies have always sought the legitimacy associated with Al-Azhar. During the Mamluk (1250–1517) and Ottoman (1517–1798) empires' rule over Egypt, the "military elite sought political legitimation from [Al-Azhar], while the common people looked to it for protection and representation during periods of economic and social upheaval" (Hatina, 2003, p. 51). During this era, Ottoman sultans and their appointed local rulers also invested in madrasas and endowed teaching posts (Tamari, 2009, p. 37). Given the importance of Al-Azhar in educating Islamic scholars, successive Ottoman rulers supported it as a centre of Islamic learning. During the sixteenth to eighteenth centuries, leaders increased funding to Al-Azhar, improved its facilities, and enhanced its prestige generally.

In the nineteenth century the Ottoman Empire undertook administrative reforms to modernize the state bureaucracy, economy, and military, which touched all domains of life, including education and religion. Muhammad Ali (1769–1849), appointed governor of Egypt in the first half of the nineteenth century, introduced major changes to Egyptian society as part of a broader plan to separate from the Ottoman Empire and to found his own hereditary monarchy. To cement his power, he introduced a tax on institutional endowments. These endowments were common throughout the Islamic world and were a crucial source of funding for educational institutions, including Al-Azhar. In taxing them, Ali weakened the position of rival authorities, specifically the religious scholars, making Al-Azhar dependent on government funding and transforming it into a bureaucratic arm of the government that was tasked with training civil servants for a reformist and modernizing Ottoman Empire. Since that time, Al-Azhar has had a "more or less tight partnership with political powers" (Zeghal, 2007, p. 108). In partial response to European colonization and to competition from European-style institutions of higher education, many institutions of Islamic education, including Al-Azhar, underwent organizational and curricular reforms in the nineteenth century. These included the introduction of formal curricula, science, and other secular subjects, as well as the use of examinations, formally appointed faculties, and government-controlled budgets (Eickelman, 1978).

For decades, historians have characterized the period of the fourteenth to the nineteenth century as one of political, economic, and intellectual decline throughout the Islamic world, asking why, after centuries, Arab higher education experienced what Waterbury calls "centuries of intellectual torpor" (Waterbury, 2020, p. 55). More recent scholarship, however, has contested this narrative, pointing out that religious institutions flourished across North Africa until the fifteenth century and played an important role in the European Renaissance (Perkin, 2007). Others have traced the transformation of Al-Azhar over time, arguing that it represents not a sidelining in Egyptian society but the flexibility of the institution, and the enduring power of the religious leaders, or 'ulama (Zeghal, 2007). Fundamentally, the characterization of the Islamic world as lacking in knowledge portrays the Arab world's educational landscape as a vacuum that was ripe for European colonizers to fill. In so doing, it legitimized a vision of the Arab world that was devoid of local scholarship, and perpetuated a narrative that justified Western colonization in the name of modernization and development;

in so doing, it discounted the atrocities of colonization and their ongoing impact. Tamari (2009) argues that vestiges of this thinking persist in development discourse today. For example, the 2003 *Arab Human Development Report* states that it was largely the "communication with Western modernity" that lead to a reawakening and renaissance of Arab scholarly activity (UNDP, 2003).

The European Influence

Although institutions of higher learning in the Islamic and Arab world predate those in Europe by centuries, the university that we recognize today, with its focus on advanced training, secular knowledge, and scientific research, grew out of a European model. The English word *university* comes from the Latin word for "community of masters and scholars," and in its earliest sense the university was a "guild of scholars," not a physical place (Perkin, 2007). The European university had to navigate between the religious and cultural authority of the Catholic Church and the localized and fragmented political authority of feudal rulers. Scholars were sources of religious and cultural knowledge and could legitimize local rulers. To protect itself from the power of both the Church and feudal lords, the university began to institutionalize itself as a free-standing organization and to charter degrees recognized throughout Christendom. Between 1100 and the 1700s, universities were established in Britain, Italy, France, and Germany as rulers in Europe competed for legitimacy and power (Riddle, 1993). In the seventeenth and eighteenth centuries, as nation states were founded throughout Europe, universities expanded their curricular offerings to secular, professional, and scientific subjects and began to undertake empirical research (Perkin, 2007). These new national institutions came to play an important role in European nation-building.

During the subsequent period of empire building missionaries and colonizers carried the European model of the university throughout the globe. The colonization of the Arab world under the Spanish, French, and British signified the start of a new period for higher education in the region, as European nations sidestepped the existing institutions of religious learning to create their own parallel structures of higher education in the European model; they also imposed reforms on indigenous Islamic institutions (Eickelman, 1978). The effect of this sidelining of religious institutions was to undermine the role of Islamic universities in Arab societies and, more broadly, to drive a wedge between religious and secular knowledge, thereby creating fragmented and parallel university systems, with religious universities playing a different role than the nation-building role of secular universities.

This contact with Western European forces began to undermine the role and status of the Islamic institutions, including Al-Azhar in Egypt and Qarawiyyin in Fez. Many criticized Al-Azhar and the '*ulama* for their perceived rigidity and unwillingness to teach the modern sciences, while also recognizing their continued role in shaping the religious and cultural identity of the society. However, Malika Zeghal (2007) argues that religious universities are "far from being anachronistic institutions marginalized by the development of a modern educational system" but, rather, are part of "a complex sphere of symbolic production and social and political networks" (p. 109). Nonetheless, much of the authority and legitimacy that Al-Azhar and other religious universities of the region enjoy come from their claims to the maintenance and transmission of religious knowledge, while the region's secular, modern higher education systems derive their legitimacy from their links to the nation state. In this book I focus on these national higher education systems, recognizing that they are the ones that have been tasked with delivering on promises of economic, social, and political development.

The region's earliest European educational institutions were military colleges, founded during the late Ottoman era. Muhammad Ali, the reforming leader of Egypt, established a number of schools of engineering, medicine, pharmaceutics, mineralogy, agriculture, and translation to serve in his modernizing military and bureaucracy. Similarly, in 1840, a European-style military college was established in Bardo, Tunisia, by Ahmad I Bey, the ruler and a regent of the Ottoman Empire, as part of Westernizing reforms to train military officers for a modernizing army (Teferra & Altbach, 2003). Thirty-five years later, the institution was repurposed as Sadiki College, which would go on to educate a bilingual class of elite Tunisians and to incubate nationalist leaders.

Meanwhile, in the Levant, Christian missionaries were actively proselytizing Protestantism to the local Muslim and Orthodox populations. In 1866, Daniel Bliss, an American missionary, founded the Syrian Protestant College in what is today Beirut, Lebanon, based on the model of liberal arts at Harvard and Yale universities and Amherst College (B.S. Anderson, 2011). Amidst debates over how best to proselytize the local population, Bliss was convinced that education was the most effective form of spreading the Gospel. A similar missionary zeal led to the establishing of a number of religious colleges in the Levant and Egypt. French Jesuits founded the University of Saint-Joseph in Beirut in 1875; the American Protestant Mission founded Beirut

University College, for women, in 1885 (Nahas, 2011); and American Presbyterian missionaries founded the American University in Cairo in 1920. Similarly, the American Women's Protestant College, which would later become the Lebanese American University, was founded in 1928. These universities were the only providers of higher education in the Levant until after independence in 1943 (Bashshur, 1966).

The private colleges of the Levant provided not only a model but also early faculty members for a private, secular university in British-controlled Egypt. The Egyptian University in Cairo was championed by the country's local political and social elite in 1908 as an alternative to Al-Azhar. At its founding, the university struggled financially and found it difficult to enrol students and find qualified professors. By 1916, its student body had only four hundred members, compared to more than twelve thousand at Al-Azhar (Waterbury, 2020). However, in 1923, control over the Egyptian University was transferred to the state, and it became a public university three years later. Today it is one of the largest and most iconic universities in the Arab World: Cairo University.

In francophone North Africa, French colonizers were less explicitly religious, but their cultural project had no less missionary zeal. They conquered Algeria, taking it from the Ottomans in 1830, and stayed for more than 150 years. The French formally expanded their control to Tunisia in 1881, replacing Ottoman rule, and to Morocco in the early twentieth century, taking advantage of a country that had been weakened by the invasion of the Spanish in 1860 (Lulat, 2005). In 1912, Morocco was formally divided between Spain and France, and the French officially took control of most of the country, although many parts never fully came under their power. The French viewed education as part of a "civilizing mission" and were actively involved in the construction of schools and universities, while also destroying the financial base that had supported Islamic education (Eickelman, 1978). The imposition of the French model of education was disruptive, and its effects ongoing. Prior to French colonization, formal schooling had not been particularly linked to elite selection, social mobility, or wealth (Colonna, 2008). Colonization destroyed former social hierarchies and patterns, and in its wake formal, secular schooling became the key mechanism for training a national political, economic, and cultural elite.

Under the French government's assimilationist policies, higher education institutions in the Maghreb were treated as fully French universities with no distinctions being made simply because they were located outside of metropolitan France (Cohen, 2003). The University of

Algiers, the first French university founded in Algeria, was established in 1909 to educate the children of French civil servants and military officers (Teferra & Altbach, 2003). Moroccan universities were founded as annex campuses of the University of Bordeaux, offering the same academic programs, grading system, and language of instruction (Teferra & Altbach, 2003). These colonial-era universities sought to produce or reproduce French culture in line with the French secular education ideal. By the time the Arab nations had gained independence, after the Second World War, both the Levant and North Africa had the foundations of modern, national higher education systems that reflected the European model.

It is a great historical irony that the colonial-era universities, established to train local elites for a colonial bureaucracy, quickly became sites of critical intellectual movements and anti-colonial protest (Khan, 2011). For example, during the 1919 Egyptian anti-British revolution, students at Al-Azhar helped lead protests, and its campus was used as a meeting space where people of all ages, classes, and religions gathered to debate resistance strategies; this eventually led "nationalist leaflets to label the daily 'Azhar meetings as the 'Egyptian Congress'" (Fahmy, 2011, p. 148). Higher education campuses were also significant sites of anti-colonial resistance in francophone North Africa (McDougall, 2011). In Algeria the National Liberation Front frequently recruited youth from student groups and unions, including the Union Générale des Étudiants Musulmans Algeriens (General Union of Muslim Algerian Students) (Byrne, 2016). Meanwhile, in Jordan, university students, including those who had studied abroad in other Arab countries, became active in anti-Israel protests and established a Jordanian nationalist movement (L. Anderson, 2005).

University students and scholars helped lead their nations' independence movements, actively debating how to govern the new countries, and student activists were initially aligned with leftist and Arab nationalist movements. That said, for much of the nineteenth and the early twentieth century, the Arab university was still elite, was located primarily in urban capitals, and enrolled only small proportions of young people. Unsurprisingly, in the post-colonial era, greater proportions of youth demanded access to these privileged spaces and the opportunities they promised, leading to major changes in the region's higher education systems.

In contrast to the Levant and North Africa with its elite, activist, European-style universities, throughout the nineteenth and most of the twentieth century the Arab Gulf states were still primarily Bedouin communities that provided a traditional Islamic education. The Arab

Gulf states, which include Saudi Arabia, the UAE, Qatar, Bahrain, Oman, and Kuwait, emerged from a number of traditional tribal sheikhdoms situated on the Arabian Peninsula. Although the Portuguese, French, and Dutch all established early colonial outposts in the Arabian Gulf and the Indian Ocean, the British were the primary colonial influence and maintained hegemonic power between 1820 and 1970. British interest was primarily related to the proximity of the Arabian Gulf region to its most lucrative colony, India. European colonization in the Arab Gulf states, unlike that in the Levant and North Africa, took the form of control over trade and security, with less missionary activity or cultural imposition. In 1820, after an attack on a ruling family, the British East Indian Company established exclusive control over the entrance to the Persian Gulf, and, in the Perpetual Maritime Treaty of 1853, ruling families surrendered their right to wage war against Britain in return for protection from other external threats to their rule. In the UAE, British influence was formally codified in 1892 through a treaty that granted authority over designated territories to local leaders and created formal truces between warring sheikhdoms, including Dubai, Abu Dhabi, Sharjah, Ajman, Umm al-Quawain, Ras al-Khaimah and later, Fujairah. Collectively, these sheikhdoms were called the Trucial States by the British. Unlike the UAE, Qatar was part of the Ottoman Empire into the twentieth century. In the wake of the empire's collapse, due to the First World War, Qatar's leader, Abdullah Al Thani, entered into a protectorate of Britain in 1916, which was later cemented in a 1934 treaty.

The British agreed to leave the region in 1968, and the UAE was established as a federation of independent emirates in 1971, when six of the Trucial States unified. In 1972, Ras al-Khaimah joined as the seventh emirate. In the same year, Qatar was founded as an independent state, ruled by the Al Thani family, after receiving independence from Britain. The peoples of the Arabian Gulf maintained their tradition of community-based religious education until the middle of the twentieth century, living primarily as nomadic Bedouins or in small pearling and fishing villages along the coast. Traditional instruction involved memorizing the Qu'ran under the tutelage of a religious scholar, known colloquially as a *mutawwa*, meaning "volunteer" in Arabic, or studying at a religious school, known as a *katib* (plural, *katateeb*), which involved memorization of the Qu'ran, and the study of Islam, Arabic, and basic mathematics (Alhebsi, Pettaway & Waller, 2015). The first modern primary school in the UAE, Madrasa al-Qasimia, was founded in Sharjah in 1930. Until 1967, students completing secondary school would have to travel to Kuwait to take exams. It was only after independence that the Arab Gulf nations established university systems.

Independence and Nation-Building

After decades of colonial rule, newly independent Arab states staked their legitimacy in their ability to foster national development and improve citizens' standard of living (L. Anderson, 1987; Bashshur, 1966). Promises of social mobility and protections of social welfare were viewed as a way to incorporate working classes into the nation state and prevent more disruptive class struggles (Zemni, 2017). Arab governments began to reform their higher education systems in the name of modernization, development, and expanded opportunity. Relying on the dominant paradigm of the day, state-led development through manpower planning, Arab governments funded free public higher education for the best and brightest and created direct pathways from university to public-sector employment (L. Anderson, 1987). University graduates filled needed economic positions in industry and as future social and political leaders. In this era the university was simultaneously a symbol of both individual mobility and national economic and social development.

The provision of social services and the promise of social mobility were part of a larger political project to solidify political power under the ruling governments (Gherib, 2011; Zemni, 2017). In her analysis of middle-class youth in Morocco, Shana Cohen (2004) explains: "When the state provided a quality education and a job or successfully ensured enough economic growth to permit job creation in the private sector, the middle class generally tolerated or even supported the regime" (p. 14). Even those groups who opposed the regime, including Marxists and leftist movements, did so "as part of state-led modernization, not outside of it," in part because these debates occurred "within the discourse of national progress and reform" (p. 14).

Arab universities played a critical role in this nation-building project by moulding the identity of young peoples as citizens and consolidating their allegiances towards the modern nation state, away from more localized forms of religious or tribal authority. The university also became a symbol of a new era of progress and optimism. Anthropologist of the Arab world Linda Herrera (2006) explains that "independence and sovereignty would not be complete without a state university to symbolize them" (p. 412). For example, in Syria after independence in 1946, Damascus University "became a symbol of national pride, and was designated as the fountainhead of national guidance" (Bashshur, 1966, p. 456). Mazawi (2005, p. 159) cites a newspaper editorial published in *Al-Ahram Weekly*, a widely read Egyptian newspaper, which states: "The 'great universities' – Cairo, Alexandria, Ain Shams – symbolize the age of liberalism as well as liberation from colonial rule. They are considered by many to be truly 'national' institutions." As a result, "governments made it a priority to establish national universities, either by reorganizing and reforming already existing institutions – as was the case in Iraq, Tunisia, and Morocco – or by founding new universities from scratch, as occurred in Libya, Lebanon, Saudi Arabia and Jordan" (Waardenburg, 1966, p. 35). This expansion was clearly linked to nation-building and sought to establish the legitimacy of the political system (Farag, 2012).

Independence ushered in a wave of other reforms based on the idea of social mobility. Egypt was an early leader of education reform and set a precedent for other nations to follow. After the national revolution in 1952 the Nasser regime instituted a number of major educational reforms, including guaranteeing the admission of all secondary-school graduates to higher education, creating a national secondary-school exit exam, eliminating tuition fees, and guaranteeing public-sector employment for all university graduates (Arabsheibani, 1988; Cupito & Langsten, 2011; Howard-Merriam, 1979; Rugh, 2002). However, in many countries such commitments did not last long. Starting in the 1970s, with its economic opening program, known as Infitah in Arabic, Egypt began cutting public-sector work and opening the door to private-sector investment, which signalled a shift to greater alignment to the capitalist West.

In North Africa, language reform was an early priority. Arabic was elevated to replace French as the official language of public administration and education. Newly independent governments sought to Arabize all aspects of public life, including education, to move away from the French colonial model and to fill the states with freshly trained professionals to replace outgoing French bureaucrats. Arabization meant substituting French-language instruction and curriculum with their Arabic equivalent, as well as rewriting the national curriculum for the local context in order to move away from the French model as the basis for policies and strategies (Benrabah, 2013; Teferra & Altbach, 2003). Arabization is an ongoing and politicized process, one that is not supported by all groups in Algeria, Morocco, or Tunisia (Boutieri, 2016). While proponents of linguistic Arabization consider this process to be an important one that helps the Arabic language to reclaim its rightful place among the languages of scholasticism and intellectualism, opponents are often foreign educated and believe that the French language offers more benefits on the international stage than does the Arabic (Benrabah, 2013). In addition, declaring Arabic the country's official language has marginalized indigenous Berber populations (Errihani, 2008).

For the Arab Gulf states, the discovery of oil dramatically altered their course of development. Nation-building in the Arabian Gulf was occurring during a period of not only state consolidation and development but also tremendous social, cultural, and economic changes. Oil was discovered in the 1930s, leading to rapid and dramatic demographic and economic changes. The ruling families of the region started to amass significant wealth, and huge numbers of labour migrants began to arrive from South Asia. Arab Gulf states transformed from sparsely populated sheikhdoms to nation states with dense urban centres, large immigrant populations, and among the highest per capita income in the world. Given the wealth of their natural resources and the early influx of migrant labour, the social contract in the Arab Gulf states involves the direct redistribution of wealth towards citizens to assure their relative material comfort in exchange for political acquiescence and stability (Herb, 1999). This social contract stands in contrast to the more symbolic construction of meritocratic pathways of opportunity in the region's middle-income nations.

At the time of their independence, there were no universities in the Arab Gulf states. Ruling families invested significantly to rapidly develop national higher education systems. The emir of Abu Dhabi, Sheikh Zayed bin Sultan al-Nahyan, the visionary leader behind the unification of the UAE, and the first president of the country, stated: "The real asset of any advanced nation is its people, especially its educated ones, and the prosperity and success of the people are meaasured by the standard of their education" (UAECD, 2021). After their independence, both the UAE and Qatar made impressive commitments to expanding their public education system and establishing national universities. Qatar established a College of Education in 1973, which became Qatar University in 1977. The United Arab Emirates University was founded in 1976, followed by the Higher Colleges of Technology in 1988.

Two exceptions to the model of state-run public university systems in the Arab world are found in Lebanon and Palestine. In both countries, conflict contributed to political fragmentation and undermined the ability of the state to develop and maintain a centralized national higher education system. Although Lebanon did experience an era of nation-building in the 1950s–1960s, during which the Lebanese University was founded, its success was cut short by the outbreak of a sectarian civil war conflict in 1975. Today both Lebanon and Palestine have highly decentralized and privatized higher education systems.

The Global Era

The decline of the USSR in the late 1980s and early 1990s ushered in a new era of globalization, characterized by the entrenchment of market capitalism and the rapid flow of capital, technology, and ideas across borders. Starting in the 1980s, the USSR's decline led to a delegitimization of state planning, the rise of the free market, and the spread of neoliberal ideologies. Neoliberalism emphasizes the reduction of the role of the state in social and economic spheres, supporting both the privatization of public institutions and a shift towards viewing individual effort, entrepreneurship, and innovation as the source of progress (Bartlett, Frederick, Gulbrandsen, & Murillo, 2002; Stromquist, 2002).

In the 1980s, Arab middle-income nations experienced deep fiscal crises, and the WB and the International Monetary Fund (IMF) pushed structural-adjustment policies upon many Arab nations. The latter implemented economic reform and structural adjustment programs, which required greater openness to foreign investment, a reduction of state spending, "and the privatization of wide sectors of the economy, including in the field of higher education" (Mazawi, 2005, p. 161). Many Arab nations joined the World Trade Organization or signed bilateral or multilateral trade agreements with Western nations, which relaxed trade barriers and opened up markets to local and foreign investors and entrepreneurs (Momani, 2015). Arab states have simultaneously dismantled traditional structures of economic and social security. As a result, public spending in the region fell drastically, from roughly 23.6 per cent of the region's gross domestic product (GDP) in the 1980s to 22.1 per cent in the 1990s, to 17.2 per cent in the 2000s, which is the largest drop in public spending among lower- and middle-income countries in the world during that time period (Momani, 2015, p. 23).

In this new neoliberal model of development, young people are left to navigate their own paths through privatized education and deregulated employment systems. Scholars have argued that the implementation of neoliberal state policies in the region has left them less secure in the crucial domains of social life, including education, employment, and marriage (Cohen, 2003; Dhillon & Yousef, 2011). Cohen (2004) argues that a series of neoliberal economic reforms initiated in the early 1980s in Morocco "significantly eroded the capacity of the state to nurture the middle class." Over the past three decades, neoliberal policies have undermined the government's ability to ensure livelihoods through the public sector, have increased "unemployment, temporary employment, and economic insecurity" and income inequality, and have resulted in "conspicuous consumption among middle- and lower-income families" (Cohen, 2003, p. 170).

Globalization has meant dramatic changes for higher education around the world. In the Arab world, higher education systems that were once designed to educate a small proportion of elites for employment in the public sector are now being asked to orient their sectors towards economic development in a competitive global economy. Meanwhile, the changing bases of the economy – away from agriculture, industry, and manufacturing and towards knowledge-intensive sectors – have had important implications for education policy. As a critical source of human-capital development, higher education is now "deemed essential to the construction of the knowledge society" (Stromquist, 2002, p. xiii).

Expanding higher education is seen as an important means by which the Arab world will successfully integrate its workers into the global economy (Kabbani & Salloum, 2011; Mazawi, 2007; World Bank, 2008b). Enrolments in higher education have been growing rapidly even in countries that had historically restricted access. Explicit policy changes include tracking more youth into academic pathways that lead to university and introducing new university providers to accommodate expanding enrolments. At the same time, concerns over low youth employment have pressured governments in the region to improve the employability of their youth graduates by enhancing higher-education quality (Altbach & Peterson, 2007). Today, in the name of global economic competitiveness, Arab governments are being asked to simultaneously expand the access to, improve the quality of, and provide adequate funding to higher education. In the next section I discuss how various Arab countries have responded to these pressures.

Overview of Higher Education Systems

This section provides an overview of the contemporary higher education systems in each of the book's focus countries, classifying countries into three sub-groups based on shared characteristics (table 1.1).

Table 1.1. Overview of Higher Education Systems (2018, or most recent earlier year available)

Sub-region	Country	Pop. (millions)	GDP[1] per capita (USD)	Date first university founded	No. of universities[2]	GTER[3]	Private share (% total)	Public spending on tertiary, per student (% GDP per capita)[4]
Middle East	Egypt	96.4	2,444	969 / 1908[5]	57	35.2	19.9	—
	Jordan	10.0	4,312	1962	29	34.4	27.5	25.3
	Lebanon	6.8	8,025	1866	37	46.0	59.1	19.5
	Syria	16.9	2,033[6]	1923	28	40.1	3.3	49.4
Maghreb	Morocco	36.0	3,222	1957	23	35.9	7.3	82.1
	Tunisia	11.6	3,439	737 / 1960[7]	37[8]	31.7	11.5	54.7
Arabian Gulf	Qatar	2.8	65,908	1973	19	17.9	22.7	—
	UAE	9.6	43,839	1976	78	—	72.8	—

Sources: Data compiled from EACEA (2017c); MEHE (2021); MERIC (2019a, 2019b); MOE (2020); Mohamed, Skinner, & Trines (2019); SPHERE (2020a). Other data comes from UNESCO Institute of Statistics and is accessed through the WB Open Data module for Stata. Indicators SP.POP. TOTL (Population); NY.GDP.PCAP.CD (GDP); SE.TER.ENRR (GTER); SE.TER.PRIV.ZS (Private); SE.XPD.TERT.PC.ZS (Spending) (Azevedo, 2011)

Notes:

1 Gross domestic product.

2 Higher education institutions that grant bachelor's or graduate degrees and their equivalents. Tertiary education, used in many UIS statistics, encompasses both colleges and universities, meaning that it includes students enrolled in two-year diploma programs and their equivalents. In some countries a university is distinguished from an institute or equivalent in that it requires a minimum number of faculties.

3 GTER is calculated by dividing the total number of students enrolled in tertiary education, regardless of age, by the tertiary-age cohort, typically defined as the cohort of young people within five years of the official age of secondary school completion.

4 Most recent year available is Lebanon (2013), Syria (2009), Morocco (2009), and Tunisia (2015).

5 Al-Azhar was founded in 969, and the University of Cairo (now Cairo University) in 1908.

6 Data from 2007, the most recent year available.

7 Zitouna was founded in 737, and Tunis University in 1960.

8 Tunisia has 13 public universities, 24 higher institutes of technological studies, and 76 private higher education institutions that are not officially considered universities.

Egypt and the Levant (Jordan, Lebanon, and Syria)

Egypt and the Levant are the geographical heart of the Middle East. They vary significantly in terms of their size, demographic characteristics, and histories, but they share a common legacy of Ottoman rule and British control throughout much of the twentieth century, following French rule in Syria and Lebanon in the nineteenth century. Between 1985 and 2005, under pressure from the IMF and the WB, Egypt, Jordan, and Syria pursued policies to reduce public spending, expand privatized provision of education, and offset costs to students and families. Egypt and Jordan opened to foreign investment beginning in the 1980s; the civil war in Lebanon (1975–90) meant that its neoliberal turn coincided with its post-war reconstruction; and Syria's history of Ba`athist socialism and its stance against Western influence resulted in relative isolation from global institutions until the beginning of the twenty-first century. Nonetheless, by 2005, all four countries had signalled their tacit acceptance of neoliberal approaches to higher education, authorizing private universities and establishing new fee-charging programs in public universities (Abdel-Wahid, 2009; Mazawi, 2005).

EGYPT

Egypt is the largest country in the Arab world in terms of population, with roughly 96.5 million residents in 2018, most of whom live on the thin strip of fertile land along the Nile. With a GDP per capita of approximately USD 2,500, it is classified as a lower middle-income country. Its historic role as an educational and cultural hub has meant that Egypt was a model of reform for the region throughout the twentieth century. The country's oldest Islamic university, Al-Azhar, was founded in 969 and has been restructured and reformed numerous times throughout its more than one-thousand-year history; it was nationalized in 1961 in the wake of the Egyptian revolution. As mentioned earlier, the two other most prominent institutions in Egypt are Cairo University, founded in 1908, and the American University in Cairo (modelled on the American liberal arts college), founded in 1919 by an American Protestant missionary and offering instruction in English.

After independence, Egypt expanded its higher education system with the construction and funding of large public universities throughout the country as part of its broader nation-building aims. In 1992, Egypt passed a law to allow a for-profit private higher education sector (Law 101/1992). In 2006, it instituted a number of reforms that permitted cost-sharing in its public system (Fahim & Sami, 2011). As a result, public universities can charge small fees to students who have lower secondary-school exam scores (Fahim & Sami, 2011).

Today Egypt's higher education system is the largest in the region, with more than 2.9 million Egyptians in some form of post-secondary education, of whom more than 2 million are enrolled in one of twenty-six public universities and thirty-one private universities (Mohamed, Skinner, & Trines, 2019). In 2018, Egypt's gross tertiary enrolment rate was roughly 35.2 per cent, which includes the estimated 19.9 per cent of students who were enrolled in private institutions.

Egypt's higher education system falls under the control of the Ministry of Higher Education, which is composed of various sector-specific oversight bodies, including the Supreme Council of Public Universities and the Supreme Council of Private Universities (Mohamed, Skinner, & Trines, 2019). The National Authority for Quality Assurance and Accreditation in Education (NAQAAE), founded in 2007, is the body responsible for quality assurance. The government has implemented numerous initiatives in the name of improving higher education. In 2016 the country adopted a sustainable development strategy, *Egypt 2030*, that is tied to meeting its sustainable development goals (SDGs) (MPMAR, 2016). The strategy's goals include specific targets for higher education, in such areas as the ranking of Egyptian universities in the top five hundred globally, unemployment rates for university graduates, and the number of foreign students studying in Egypt. Egypt 2030 also commits to improving inputs by increasing public funding and reducing the number of students per faculty member. In line with this vision Egypt's president named 2019 "the year of education" and increased public spending on education by 8 per cent (Mohamed, Skinner, & Trines, 2019). Since the revolution in 2011, however, Egypt's higher education has also faced numerous challenges, many linked to broader instability in the country. For example, since 2013, the country has witnessed thousands of student protests, and security forces have maintained a presence on campuses (Hamzawy, 2017).

JORDAN

Jordan is a small monarchy of 10.0 million citizens, bordered by Palestine, Israel, and Syria. With a GDP per capita of approximately USD 4,300, it is classified as a middle-income country. The country's first university, the University of Jordan, was founded in Amman in 1962, which was followed shortly thereafter by Yarmouk University in Irbid, in the north. In the period of nation-building that followed, Jordan intentionally established a major public university in every governorate to build local capacity and provide a significant source of public-sector employment in rural regions.

As a small country with no natural resource wealth, Jordan has pursued ambitious higher education reform in the name of economic development and preparing youth for a knowledge economy. As of 2018, Jordan had twenty-nine universities, of which ten are public institutions and nineteen are private, as well as forty-four community colleges that have two-year courses focused on technical and vocational education (SPHERE, 2020a). In 2018 there were roughly 321,000 students enrolled in higher education in Jordan, representing 34.4 per cent of the relevant age cohort.

The first private university, Amman Private University, was founded in 1990 as part of a broader embrace of private higher education that started in the early 1990s. The policy shift to allow private universities was in response to both the demands of Palestinian Jordanians for greater access to university and the prevalence of Jordanian entrepreneurs, many of whom were returning to Jordan in the wake of the Gulf War in Kuwait and looking for investment opportunities. In 2018, roughly 27.5 per cent of all students were enrolled in private institutions.

Control over higher education falls under the Council of Higher Education and the Ministry of Higher Education and Scientific Research (MOHESR), with each being responsible for different domains including finances, students' admissions, and students' preparations for the labour market (SPHERE, 2020a). In 2007 an independent accreditation body was established, known as the Accreditation and Quality Assurance Commission for Higher Education Institution, which is responsible for quality assurance.

Recent higher education policy initiatives were outlined in the National Strategy for Higher Education in Jordan (2014–18), which focused on governance, admissions, and financing, among other domains. In addition, two laws, passed in 2018, seek to improve the competitiveness of the country's higher education system, with specific measures focused on improving support for research, providing technologically enabled learning, and securing international accreditations (SPHERE, 2020a).

LEBANON

Lebanon is a small upper-middle income (GDP per capita of USD 8,025) parliamentary republic of roughly 6.8 million citizens and, since 2012, roughly 1 million displaced Syrians. It has a history of both French and British colonization and experienced a devastating civil war that lasted from 1975 to 1990. Lebanon is home to a religiously diverse population, with eighteen officially recognized sects, including a large number of

Christians, Sunni Muslims, and Shia Muslims, as well as smaller religious groups such as the Druze. Its sectarianism is institutionalized into its constitution and government through a confessional system that ensures that the leadership positions, including the presidency and prime ministership, are held by members of particular sects. Given its extreme ethno-religious fractionalization and complicated history with Syria and Palestine, Lebanon is widely considered to have a weak central government, with significant power being held by the non-state political group Hezbollah.

Lebanon's higher education system was founded by religious missionaries and remains highly fragmented along sectarian and religious lines (el-Ghali, 2010). The first and only public higher education institution, the Lebanese University (LU), was established in 1951 as part of the same nation-building push occurring throughout the region. However, even as nation-building was sweeping the Arab world, the Lebanese state played a limited role in authorizing university degrees, and the country's major 1961 higher education law declared that only law degrees must carry government endorsement.

Lebanon's civil war was devastating to the country's public higher education system and resulted in the decentralization of the LU (Bashshur, 2006). Prior to the outbreak of the war, the university had only four faculties: Teaching and Social Sciences, Law, Engineering, and Agriculture. Due to students' restricted mobility caused by the conflict, the four faculties were separated into distinct campuses scattered around Beirut and had individual deans. A 1977 law (Decree 122) granted existing institutions the right to establish new locations outside their original campuses in order to offer their students and faculty safer options outside Beirut. As a result, branches of the LU were established in parts of the country that were less affected by the war, and existing private institutions also took advantage of the law to establish branches (Bashshur, 2006). By the end of the civil war there were nine universities across Lebanon, and the sole public university, the LU, had established forty-seven semi-autonomous branches throughout the country (Bashshur, 2006). In addition, the Taif Accords, which ended the civil war, enshrined confessionalism throughout Lebanese government and including the LU. Waterbury (2020) explains that senior posts at the university were distributed to particular sects, as were other government positions. Accordingly, the university president had to be a Shiite. Faculty appointments were similarly mapped onto sectarian quotas. The post-war period also coincided with the global embrace of neoliberalism and saw extensive expansion of the higher education system, primarily in the private sector.

Lebanon's gross tertiary enrolment rate is 46 per cent, one of the highest in the region, which is largely attributed to its diverse system and high rates of private investment at all levels of education (Nahas, 2011). In part due to its history of conflict and post-conflict trajectory, Lebanon has a highly privatized higher education system, with roughly 60 per cent of all enrolments being in the private sector (MERIC, 2019a). As of 2019, there were forty-nine higher education institutions in Lebanon, of which thirty-seven are universities (meaning they have three or more faculties), and the rest are classified as institutes or university colleges (MEHE, 2021). The LU remains the only public university, and today it has seventeen faculties and fifty branches located in all regions of the country (MERIC, 2019a; SPHERE, 2020b). In addition, a large number of Lebanese students study abroad, primarily in Europe and North America (Nahas, 2011).

Control over the higher education system is vested within the Ministry of Education and Higher Education, although Lebanon also has a council of higher education that plays a primarily consultative role. The LU, as a public institution, has a separate governance structure and is technically granted more autonomy. Legally, it enjoys administrative and financial autonomy; however, authority over many aspects of academic life, including faculty, decanal, and senior administrative appointments, is jointly held by the minister of higher education and the Council of Ministers (Waterbury, 2020). The minister of higher education selects the president from three candidates; in addition, the Council of Ministers approves the appointment of deans and the promotion of a faculty member to full professorship (Waterbury, 2020). Waterbury (2020) details the long history of political influence over appointments at the LU, which has resulted in many positions going unfilled. Research conducted by the AUB found that "independence of the Lebanese University" was among the twenty demands circulated in newspapers and online media, although it was not a priority of the October 2019 protests (AUB-IFI, 2019). In contrast, private universities are regulated by the Directorate General of Higher Education, a separate entity founded in 2002.

Recent reforms to higher education have include adoption of the French *licence-master-doctorat* (LMD) reforms within the LU in 2005, whose implementation was supported by the European Union's Tempus project. In 2014, Lebanon passed a new law (Law 285) to reform private-sector institutions, which included aligning the credentials from Lebanon's private universities to credentials offered in Europe (i.e., LMD) (MERIC, 2019a).

For over a decade many influential experts inside and outside Lebanon have sought to create an independent quality assurance agency (Scholz

& Maroun, 2015). They have gone so far as to draft a law and train experts in quality assurance with the support of the European Union. However, to date, the law to establish an independent agency has not been passed. In the absence of a rigorous national quality assurance agency, many private universities have sought international accreditations instead (SPHERE, 2020b). Additionally, the 2014 law asked private universities to initiate their own internal quality assurance practices.

SYRIA

Before the civil war in Syria, its population was approximately twenty-one million. Since 2010, the complex civil war has displaced roughly twelve million people, including five million refugees officially registered with the United Nations High Commissioner for Refugees and six million within Syria itself, making it one of the greatest humanitarian crises in the modern era. As a result, in 2018, Syria's population was roughly 17 million, and updated GDP per capita data is not available. The latest estimate of GDP per capita comes from 2007, when it was approximately USD 2,000.

The country's first university, the Syrian University (today known as Damascus University) was established as the Ottoman Medical School in 1901, under Ottoman control and with instruction in Turkish (Waterbury, 2020). When the Ottoman Empire ended after the First World War, Syria came under a French mandate, which lasted until de facto independence in 1946. The Syrian University was re-established as a public university in 1923 by the bringing together of two faculties, Medicine and Law. After independence, four faculties were added – Engineering, Sciences, Arts and Letters, and Education – and in 1958 a second university, the University of Aleppo, was founded in the country's second largest city. Expansion was modest in the 1970s and 1980s, with Syria following a Soviet model of prioritizing technical and vocational education rather than university education. That said, two additional universities were established in the 1970s. By the 1980s, roughly 15 per cent of all university-age Syrians were enrolled in university.

Syria has a long history with state socialism, which began when the Arab Socialist Ba`ath Party officially took power in 1963 and has remained the official rhetoric since the Assad regime took over in 1966. In the late 1990s, Syria initiated a transition to a market-based economy. Prior to the outbreak of its civil war, it was slowly liberalizing the economy and expanding the higher education system. As part of its larger economic transition, Syria implemented a number of educational reforms in 2001. The ministry opened a new public university, al-Furat, in 2006 and initiated a new program called Open Learning to allow previously excluded students to register for newly created degree programs in applied fields. Thanks to these Open Leaning programs, the number of full-time university students more than doubled between 1997 and 2007. In the 2009–10 academic year, 147,575 students were enrolled in fifteen Open Learning programs, accounting for roughly one third of all university students (Buckner, 2013). As of 2016, there were seven public universities in Syria (Immerstein & Al-Shaikhly, 2016). Although the country's higher education system has been negatively affected by conflict, in 2018 an estimated 40.1 per cent of the eligible age cohort was enrolled in some form of higher education. This represents a significant increase from 2008, when 24.0 per cent of the age cohort attended higher education. However, it is also possible that the 2018 estimate is the result of declines in the country's population due to the conflict.

As part of its broader liberalization reforms, Syria began to permit private universities to operate in 2001 (Waterbury, 2020). Its first two independent private universities were founded in 2003, and by 2010, fifteen private universities were operating. In 2011 a Presidential Decree (no. 48) permitted the establishment of non-profit private universities, and the total number of private universities reached twenty-one by 2019 (EACEA, 2017c; "Monitoring quality," 2019). Yet private enrolments remain small; in 2018 only 3.3 per cent of all tertiary enrolments were in the private sector.

Higher education remains under tight government control, although reforms in the early 2000s nominally gave universities more autonomy. Since 2011, there seems to have been a return to highly centralized decision making (EACEA, 2017c). Overall control and administration of the higher education system lies with the Council for Higher Education and the Ministry of Higher Education ("Monitoring quality," 2019). Members of the Council for Higher Education are appointed, but they are generally presidents of all public universities and some private universities, as well as student union representatives (EACEA, 2017c). Syria updated its higher education legislation in 2006 (Law 6), which ostensibly gave universities more autonomy over faculty promotions and appointments, but observers have been generally sceptical because decisions governing the curriculum must be approved by the national-level body (EACEA, 2017c; Waterbury, 2020). Quality assurance is carried out by the Center for Measurement and Evaluation in Higher Education ("Monitoring quality," 2019). However, no independent body exists for quality assurance in Syria, and the Council of Ministers can revoke an institution's licence at any time.

The Syrian civil war has taken an immeasurable toll on Syrians and the country's higher education system. After the rise of the Islamic

State in 2012, the Syrian civil war evolved into a proxy war between the United States, Iran, Russia, and Saudi Arabia, all seeking to advance their varied geopolitical interests. There is no doubt that higher education will play an important role in the rebuilding of Syria after the war ends. However, in this book I focus mostly on higher education reform in Syria that was carried out prior to the outbreak of the conflict.

Francophone North Africa (Morocco and Tunisia)

North Africa, also called the Maghreb (meaning "the west" in Arabic), is the westernmost part of the Arab world and is located in close proximity to Europe. Morocco, Tunisia, and Algeria were all influenced by French colonization and experienced similar post-independence nationalization reforms. Throughout the Maghreb, access to higher education is officially guaranteed to graduates of secondary school, and the right to free public higher education is enshrined in national law; this means that tuition fees are non-existent or minimal in all but a few competitive programs (Kohstall, 2012). Between 2005 and 2010, Morocco, Tunisia, and Algeria pursued large-scale reform modelled on Europe's Bologna Process; they restructured their degrees to align to the system of bachelor's and master's degrees and doctorates adopted in Europe, introduced new applied degree programs, and changed assessment practices (Zghal, 2007). An implicit goal of these reforms was to ensure pathways to studying, working, and living in Europe (Ferroukhi, 2009; Sedrine, 2009; Souali, 2009). Countries of the Maghreb have been slower than those of the Levant to permit private higher education, preferring instead to promote co-ordination between the higher education system and the labour market, although there are indications that this has been recently changing (Buckner, 2018; Ferroukhi, 2009).

MOROCCO

The westernmost country in the Arab world, Morocco is a geographic and cultural crossroads between Europe to the north, Africa to the south, and the Arab world to the east. Morocco is a hereditary monarchy of roughly thirty-seven million people, including a significant proportion with Amazigh heritage. With a GDP per capita of USD 3,222, it is considered to be a lower-middle-income country. Morocco was colonized by the French between 1912 and 1956, and its higher education system is modelled closely on that in France. Its first university, Mohammed V University, was founded in 1957 and at the time served only three hundred students; today more than one million Moroccans are enrolled in the country's expanded higher education system (WDI,

2021). In 2019 the country had twelve state-run public universities, five non-profit partnership universities, one public university under private management (i.e., al-Akhawayn), five purely private universities, and more than 150 private institutions, which offer specialized programs in business, engineering, technology, and other fields (ENSSUP, 2021; MERIC, 2019c).

The Moroccan system is divided into programs that are deemed open access, which serve about 80 per cent of all students and in which any secondary-school graduate may enrol; and programs with competitive admissions, including schools of medicine and higher institutes of management and technology. In 2018 an estimated 36 per cent of the relevant age cohort was enrolled in higher education, pointing to significant growth from 2008, when only 13 per cent of the age cohort was enrolled (UIS, 2019).

Starting officially in 2005, and in practice in 2011, Morocco began to permit new private universities, which were generally assumed to be for profit. The degrees they conferred were not immediately accredited or recognized by the state, which limited graduates' options for employment and post-graduate studies. However, since accreditation policies were put in place in 2012 (Decree 3061), a growing number of academic programs in private universities have received official accreditation. Nonetheless, the private share of enrolments remains low, at 7.3 per cent.

Morocco has also explicitly supported "partnership universities," which are non-profit and intended to support the broader internationalization efforts of the country (MERIC, 2019c, p. 11). For example, in 2017, Mohammed VI Polytechnic University was founded as a new non-profit public-private partnership in Ben Guerir, north of Marrakech. The university focuses on sciences and technology and positions itself as an internationalized university that aims to be a leader on the African continent.

The higher education system is managed by the Ministry of National Education, Vocational Training, Higher Education, and Scientific Research. It has been undergoing major structural reforms since 1999, when a national dialogue on education reforms was launched by the king. In 2004 Morocco rapidly adopted the LMD system to align its credentials to those adopted in Europe with the Bologna reforms. In line with the need to implement quality assurance, in 2014 Morocco created an autonomous agency to regulate quality, known as the National Agency for Assessment and Quality Assurance in Higher Education and Scientific Research (ANEAQ). More recently, in 2020, Morocco announced that it would begin shifting a university degree from a three-year undergraduate degree known as the *licence* in Europe to a four-year bachelor's degree that is more common in North America.

TUNISIA

Tunisia is a small nation on the Mediterranean Sea, nestled between Algeria and Libya, that has among the highest indicators of education and human development in the region. In 2018, its GDP per capita was roughly USD 3,440, classifying it as lower-middle income. When Tunisia gained independence from France in 1956, it pursued a short-lived version of Arab socialism. Although its commitment to state socialism waned in the late 1960s, its commitment to significant investments in social welfare has remained an enduring legacy (Harik, 1992). Tunisia's post-independence reforms were explicitly linked to modernity and progress through a focus on gender equality, and women's enrolments in higher education have been historically very high (Fryer & Jules, 2013). In late 2010, individual acts of protest over quality of life, inequality, and rampant corruption in the nation sparked what is now called the Tunisian Revolution and inspired people-led protests in other Arab countries in what we now call the Arab Spring. In January 2011, after twenty-eight days of civil protest, the long-term authoritarian leader of Tunisia, Zine el-Abidine Ben Ali, stepped down, which ushered in a somewhat rocky but, thus far, comparatively peaceful democratic transition.

Like those in Egypt and Morocco, the oldest institution of higher learning in Tunisia was Islamic. Zitouna, a religious institute of higher education, was founded in 737 and subsequently modernized in 1956 as a higher institute of theology. After its independence, Tunisia founded a university system modelled on that of France, with the first secular institution being the École Normale Supérieure, founded in 1956 and then incorporated as the University of Tunis in 1960 (Fryer & Jules, 2013). Over the next two decades Tunisia rapidly expanded the number of institutions in all parts of the country.

Tunisia has a large and predominantly public higher education system, also closely modelled on the French system. There are 13 public universities in Tunisia and an additional 203 public higher education faculties that provide specialized programs. In the 1990s Tunisia founded a network of 24 higher institutes of technological studies to strengthen links between education and employment in technology-based careers. These specialized schools and institutes are designed to offer a high-quality level of education and have student-faculty ratios below the national average (MERIC, 2019b). In 2018 there were roughly 272,000 students enrolled in higher education in Tunisia, which represents a steady decline in overall enrolments that has been occurring since 2010, when 370,000 students were enrolled in higher education (WDI, 2021). In 2018, approximately one-third of the relevant age cohort was enrolled in higher education.

Tunisia established a legal framework for the creation of private institutions in 2000, although there was a significant delay in implementation, and it was subsequently amended in 2008. That said, the number of private institutions operating in Tunisia has grown significantly. Private institutions are officially organized as limited companies and licensed as institutes, schools, or faculties, rather than comprehensive universities. Recently, however, a number of individual faculties have been grouped together to function as universities, with shared administrative and student services, and to call themselves universities for the purposes of branding and recruitment. The private sector has grown substantially over the past decade, and as of 2018 there were seventy-six private higher education institutions licensed by the Ministry of Higher Education, and an estimated 11.5 per cent of all students were enrolled in private universities (MESRS, 2019; WDI, 2021).

Higher education in Tunisia is closely regulated by the Ministry of Higher Education and Scientific Research (MESRS), which directly funds universities and regulates their spending. The country has a long history of international collaboration in higher education. In 2005, Zine el-Abidine Ben Ali launched an initiative known as Tunisia Tomorrow to encourage international scientific co-operation (Fryer & Jules, 2013). In 2006, Tunisia overhauled its degrees to align them to those in Europe as part of the Bologna Process. In 2008 a major reform was passed that permitted universities more autonomy over their governance and that formalized Bologna reforms. In 2011, after the Tunisian Revolution, the country undertook a new national university-reform initiative. In 2015, MESRS launched a ten-year tertiary-education development plan, known as the Strategic Plan for the Reform of Higher Education and Scientific Research, 2015–2025. In line with the goals of the plan, Tunisia established a national evaluation, quality assurance, and accreditation authority in 2017 to regulate quality according to international standards.

The Arab Gulf States (Qatar and the United Arab Emirates)

The Arab Gulf states share a number of important characteristics, including a history of British control, natural resource wealth, large expatriate populations, and kinship-based monarchical political systems. The distinction between national citizens and foreigners is an important social category in the region as national citizens constitute a small minority in both Qatar and the UAE. Nationals have access to subsidized housing and education and receive preferential treatment in the labour market through labour market nationalization policies known as Qatarization and Emiratization, respectively.

Throughout the sub-region, governments are investing heavily in education with the explicit goals of nationalizing their labour forces in order to rely less on expatriates and shifting their economies towards high-skilled service and technology sectors (Ridge, 2014). These reforms require long-term institutional change, and in the meantime most of the Arab Gulf states continue to provide their citizens with significant monetary benefits and public-sector jobs. The region's higher education policies are also marked by a striking openness to foreign expertise, and the Arab Gulf states are quick to adopt best practices that are popular with technical specialists and consultants (Donn & Manthri, 2010; Mazawi, 2005). As part of national development initiatives, many of the states have invited international universities to set up branch campuses in large-scale initiatives such as Doha's Education City, Dubai's Knowledge Village, and Sharjah's University City. In this book I focus on two Gulf states with high-profile education projects: Qatar and the United Arab Emirates.

QATAR

Qatar is a small but wealthy and resource-rich city-state nation, with a population of roughly 2.8 million, of whom only 12 per cent, or 330,000, are Qatari nationals. Thanks to its natural gas reserves, Qatar has one of the highest per capita incomes in the world (GDP per capita of USD 65,600). Qatar was under British control starting in 1915, and gained its independence in 1971.

Qatar's first national university was founded in 1973 as the College of Education and focused on training teachers for the growing public-school system. In 1977 three faculties were added, and the College of Education officially became Qatar University, which included schools of Humanities and Social Sciences; Sharia and Islamic Studies; and Science; in addition to Education (QU, 2021). Over the past five decades Qatar University has grown to have roughly twenty thousand students in ten faculties and to offer graduate degrees.

Overall, enrolments in higher education are higher for Qataris than non-nationals and exhibit a significant gender imbalance, in favour of females (Ridge, 2014). Data shows that in 2018 the gross enrolment in tertiary education was approximately 18 per cent of university-age students (WDI, 2021), but that figure includes the many, overwhelmingly male, foreign workers of university age in the country; a 2016 government report had shown that in 2015 the gross enrolment rate in tertiary education had been roughly 50 per cent for females, compared to only 6.9 per cent for males (MDPS, 2017).

Qatar's economic and education policies are explicitly framed around the need for an economic transition away from resource dependence and towards a diversified economy and knowledge-intensive sectors. As part of this vision, Qatar decided to diversify its higher education system by inviting branch campuses of foreign universities to operate within the nation. The Qatar Foundation, a private non-profit organization that was established by an Emiri decree in 1995 and supported by significant funding from the royal family, has supported the country's development objectives. In 2003 the country's rulers, the Al Thani family, founded Education City under the umbrella of the Qatar Foundation (Khodr, 2011; Romani, 2009). Education City, located in Doha, is an academic metropolis that spans fourteen kilometres and includes prestigious universities such as Northwestern, Carnegie Mellon, Texas A&M, Cornell, and Georgetown. Academic standards at these branch campuses are high, and only a small percentage of students qualify. In 2010 a Qatari university, Hamad Bin Khalifa University, was founded within Education City to offer primarily graduate-level programs. Despite significant global interest paid to Education City, it remains a small player in the overall higher education landscape, and Qatar University still enrols the vast majority of Qataris (Stasz, Eide, Martorell, Goldman, & Constant, 2007; Weber, 2014). Overall, an estimated 22.7 per cent of students are in the private sector, of whom roughly half are non-citizens (PSA, 2018).

Higher education is regulated by the Supreme Education Council and the Ministry for Education and Higher Education. Qatar University operates as a semi-autonomous institution, and control over campuses within Education City rests with the Qatar Foundation. Institutions outside Education City, including the Community College of Qatar and the University of Calgary–Qatar, are under the control of the ministry. Qatar has approved a number of other private and independent university programs, in addition to those in Education City, to operate in collaboration with international partners. As of 2018, the ministry had recognized twenty-six different university programs and nineteen universities (MOEHE, 2019). Education reforms are typically incorporated into broader development plans in Qatar, including National Vision 2030, which outlines long-term development goals and its medium-term National Development Strategies (GSDP, 2009). In 2018 Qatar announced its Second National Development Strategy (2018–2022), which includes specific targets for higher education, including increasing enrolments, particularly among male students; the number of graduates in science, technology, engineering, and mathematics (STEM); and the percentage of faculty who are Qatari (MDPS, 2018).

UNITED ARAB EMIRATES

The UAE is a high-income (GDP per capita of USD 44,000) federal state, composed of seven emirates, each with its own ruling sheikh. Today the UAE's population is more than ten million, roughly 80 per cent of which is non-national. More than half of the country's population live in its two largest and wealthiest emirates, Abu Dhabi and Dubai, while the other five emirates account for the rest of the country's residents. Since its independence in 1971 the UAE has transformed from having no universities to being home to more than one hundred universities today, including elite branch campuses such as those of the Sorbonne and New York University. The guiding vision for higher education in the UAE has always been primarily vocational, and higher education policy in public and private institutions is explicitly linked to training youth for both a future knowledge economy and the nationalization of the labour market, a policy known as Emiratization (Kirk & Napier, 2009).

There are three federal universities, which are funded by the federal government and provide free undergraduate education to all eligible nationals. The first federal university, United Arab Emirates University, was founded in al-Ain in 1976, five years after independence. Its language of instruction is primarily English, although certain courses are offered in Arabic. It has grown to offer programs at all levels and remains the only federal university offering doctorates. In 1988, the Higher Colleges of Technology (HCTs) were founded as a single but decentralized institution to provide primarily applied and vocational education. As of 2017, there were seventeen branches of HCTs throughout the country, which were all gender-specific, with nine branches for females and eight for males. In 1998 Zayed University was founded to be a more globally oriented university and has campuses in both Dubai and Abu Dhabi. Initially a female-serving institution, starting in 2010, Zayed began enrolling male students and also welcomes international students.

Given the UAE's federal system, higher education policy is decentralized, with different policies in place across different emirates. Each emirate sets its own policies governing private universities. One of the unique features of the Emirati higher education system is its free trade zones, which are home to a large, diverse, and ever-changing array of private higher education institutions of varying quality. Free trade zones for private universities currently exist in Dubai, Abu Dhabi, and Ras al-Khaimah. Initially, private universities operating in these zones had little to no regulation, although over the past few years all three emirates have been increasing regulation of the higher education institutions operating in the free trade zones. Owing to this supportive regulatory environment and its large population of non-citizens, who cannot study in public universities, the UAE has one of the most privatized systems in the region: nearly 73 per cent of all students in the UAE are enrolled in the private sector.

The Ministry of Higher Education and Scientific Research, which was established in 1993, is responsible for licensing higher education institutions and programs in the country. Starting in 1999, it founded the Commission for Academic Accreditation (CAA) as a fully independent body to accredit all degree programs of private universities operating outside of free trade zones. As in other countries, accreditation is required for the ministry to recognize degrees. Since the commission's founding, public university programs have been required to obtain accreditation, and many of the private universities in free trade zones have sought accreditation to validate their programming. As of 2018, roughly 950 programs in the UAE had been accredited by the CAA (CAA, 2019).

Global Models, Localized Approaches

Today the countries in the Middle East and North Africa region vary tremendously in terms of their size, national wealth, and historical legacies of higher education. Over the past thousand years, however, the peoples of the region have been subject to many similar influences. In the medieval era much of the area was part of successive Islamic empires that witnessed the development of the madrasa and higher institutions of Islamic learning. More recently the experience of European contact has left a lasting impact on national borders, societies, and higher education systems, including the creation and expansion of modern higher education systems modelled on the Western secular university that combines teaching and research. These education systems have long been influenced by external forces, including contact with Europe and exposure to regional models. Simultaneously, higher education reform has been subject to both internal contestation for authority – making it deeply political and linked to broader processes of political legitimation, cultural authority, and elite formation. In the current era of globalization Arab governments have been faced with similar pressures to expand access, improve quality, pursue equity, and generally transform their higher education systems so that they are responsive to changing and interconnected markets and societies. The following chapters discuss each of these policy domains in depth.

2

Sorting Students, Determining Fates

In many parts of the Arab world, as throughout the world generally, exit exam results make front-page news. In Jordan the release of exam scores is accompanied by gun-shots fired into the air in celebration – an illegal, but common, and occasionally deadly, practice. In Morocco, baccalaureate exam (known colloquially as Bac) results are the leading story on the evening news, and mothers are shown joyfully ululating as they see their children's names on the list of those who have passed. When I was living in Lebanon in June 2016, I received a notification on my cell phone from a major Lebanese newspaper, announcing that exam results were now available online – a testament to their "Breaking News" status. This national concern with exam scores and effusive nature of celebrations might seem surprising to those unfamiliar with the region, but it reflects the weight that these exams carry in young people's lives.

Around the world the shift to a knowledge-based economy means that higher education is closely linked to the goal of professional employment. Governments face pressures to expand access to higher education and have increased enrolments significantly. Yet, admissions systems in much of the Middle East and North Africa, like those in many post-colonial states, were created in an earlier era of elite access. They must now cope with increased pressures for enrolment. Critics argue that centralized and exam-based admissions are relics of an older era and should be updated in line with changing higher education needs. From an educational perspective, they argue that exit exams incentivize rote memorization instead of critical thinking or skill development. From an economic perspective, the high stakes incentivize corruption throughout the system, from teachers withholding instruction in order to encourage private tutoring, to ministry officials selling exam questions. One key policy recommendation is to reform the exams themselves, reorienting them away from memorization and towards a demonstration of the competencies that are rewarded by knowledge-intensive economies. Critics of centralized decision making advocate the devolution of decision-making power to the institutional level to give public universities more autonomy over how many students they can accept.

These recommendations, though important, ignore the reality that admission to higher education in the Arab world is not simply an educational or bureaucratic matter; it is political. National admissions policies are a highly visible instance of direct state intervention in young people's lives, and as a result they can be difficult and politically risky to alter. For the state, admission to university is not just a process of determining academic preparedness but also a process of gatekeeping and even social engineering (Reiter, 2002). For individual students and families, specific admissions decisions are even more consequential. A single test can sort students into future life paths and determine who receives the social status and economic power associated with a particular degree.

In this chapter I show how admissions systems reflect broader socio-political contracts between the state and society, classifying countries into three broad categories: centrally controlled admission based on the logic of meritocratic exit exams, found in Egypt, Jordan, Syria, Tunisia, and Morocco; open admissions based on a logic of capacity building, found in the Arab Gulf states; and institution-specific admissions based on the market mechanisms of supply and demand, found in Lebanon.

I argue that each model results from the institutionalization of historical patterns, which limit current reform options. In the case of exam-based systems, the logic of meritocracy has been undermined by structural inequalities, privatization, and politically motivated affirmative-action policies. And yet, official, if hollow, commitments to meritocracy through testing remain entrenched. In response, young people and their families are actively contesting the role of the state in dictating student futures and are reasserting agency over their lives by cheating extensively on exams, relying on informal networks to evade official policies, or paying to attend private universities.

Even in countries where admission is not based on competitive exit exams, including the Arab Gulf states and Lebanon, the structure of admission to higher education sheds light on important political calculations. In the Arab Gulf states, competency assessments allow all citizens who meet minimum criteria to study in some form of higher education. Under the logic of capacity building, even those who do not qualify for higher education can enrol in a pre-university academic bridge program that prepares them for university. This expectation-free social service forms part of a social contract that is premised on the distribution of natural resource wealth from rulers to nationals, and as a result it has been difficult for governments to eliminate it. In contrast, admissions decisions in Lebanon's highly privatized system, where students enrol directly in institutions, has permitted significant self-sorting by religious sect and social class. Although the lack of state involvement in young people's lives protects the government from being the target of students' anger, it also reflects and perpetuates a widespread lack of faith in the Lebanese state.

Access for All

Countries around the world are incorporating growing cohorts of young people into their higher education systems, and the Arab world is no exception. This trend towards greater access is part of broad global shifts away from viewing higher education as the domain of elites to seeing it as desirable and worthwhile for all. In earlier eras universities were designed to educate small cohorts of elites to be political and cultural leaders. In the post-colonial era, widespread cultural shifts at the global level entrenched the belief that education is both a fundamental right and a means to individual prosperity and national development (Ramirez, 2012; Schofer & Meyer, 2005). Access to higher education became linked to modernization and its possibilities of upward social mobility. The great promise of modernity is that individual humans have agency to determine their own life paths, rather than accept that their place in society is inherited and immutable. Meritocracy through the formal educational system has been central to the modernization project, by promising to reward hard work and intelligence.

In the twenty-first century, knowledge economy discourses have further advanced the belief that higher education is necessary and important for ever larger cohorts of youth. Higher education's role in supporting development was cemented in 2015 when countries around the world endorsed the United Nations Sustainable Development Goals (SDGs). SDG 4, the global goal for education, states that by 2030 all member states, including Arab nations, will "ensure equal access for all women and men to affordable and quality technical, vocational and tertiary education, including university" (UN, 2015, p. 21). The adoption of the SDGs has now tied access to higher education to global development objectives more closely than ever before.

These global shifts are actively endorsed by Arab governments and students alike, and the goal of expanded access to higher education is

rarely questioned. As a result, national governments must figure out
how to balance this demand for higher education with the competing
demands on national budgets, raising important questions over how to
regulate access. The pressure on Arab states to admit more students to
university, coupled with an intense burden on high-school students in
the region to achieve higher and higher marks, comes down to a simple
question of supply and demand: students versus seats.

Moreover, although the myth of meritocracy places great faith in the
ability of the educational system to produce upward social mobility,
nowhere in the world are educational systems truly meritocratic.
In reality, higher education maintains and reproduces inequalities,
rather than eliminating them. Sociologists point out that the middle
and upper classes are thought to have "superior material and cultural
assets" (Brown, 2013, p. 682). In the Arab world, as elsewhere, students
from wealthy families and urban centres have always had educational
and cultural advantages: they are more likely to have access to trained
teachers and well-resourced schools. They are increasingly likely to
have access to high-quality, expensive private schools and to those that
teach in Western languages or rely on foreign curricula, which gives
students an advantage on exit exams.

As access to higher education expands, previously excluded students have been able to enrol, including women; ethnic, religious,
and linguistic minorities; those from rural communities; and the poor.
Sociologists of education, however, have consistently shown that it is
the privileged classes that are in the best position to reap the benefits of
the expansion (Buchmann & Hannum, 2001). The wealthy not only disproportionately gain access to new seats in university but also obtain
qualitatively better forms of education, including prestigious degrees,
elite institutions, and competitive scholarships. More recently, they
have also been more likely to pursue advanced degrees. In other words,
despite rapidly growing enrolments in higher education, equality of
opportunity is not necessarily improving. These global trends of both
access and inequality have been borne out in the Arab world. In the following section I discuss how different countries in the region structure
their admissions to higher education and how the pressures to expand
access have played out.

The Exit Exam as Meritocracy

Admission to higher education in most Arab countries is based on
high-stakes, centrally co-ordinated, secondary-school exit exams
adapted from French and British models of the French baccalaureate

and British A levels. Countries including Egypt, Jordan, Syria, and Morocco use these exit exams to regulate the number of students entering higher education, by adjusting how many students qualify for admission. Their higher education admissions are based on a foundational logic of meritocracy, the idea that opportunities for social mobility should be based on the combination of academic ability and hard work, not on inherited or ascribed characteristics such as gender, race, or family wealth. In the theoretical literature, *merit* is often defined as the combination of ability and effort, although there are normative debates over whether *ability* should be defined as proven ability or potential ability (Stone, 2013).

In practice, in most Arab nations, merit is understood in a straightforward, if simplistic, way as performance on a nation-wide standardized exam. In their initial iteration these tests aimed to counter the colonialist legacies that reserved higher education for the wealthy and well-connected. Standardized exit exams were originally conceived of as allowing the best and the brightest throughout the country to access university education and public-sector positions (Cohen, 2004).

In 1952, Egypt's military leader, Gamal Abdel Nasser, staged a successful coup d'état, seizing power from the corrupt, spendthrift, and ineffective monarch, King Faruq, and setting in motion the process that transformed Egypt from a monarchy to an independent republic. Nasser's revolution was based on populist and nationalist ideals and promoted a vision of Arab nationalism that countered the highly unequal and corrupt colonial regimes. In line with these ideals, Nasser ushered in wide-ranging economic and social reforms that had "enormous ripple effects on all other institutions of the society and on the day-to-day lives of citizens" (Nagi & Nagi, 2011, p. 8). The 1956 constitution, passed by popular consent, guaranteed universal education and employment. The 1971 constitution stated: "Education is a right guaranteed by the State." State intervention in the economy was founded on a logic of state-led development and comprehensive economic planning. Article 23 of the 1971 constitution committed the country to organizing the national economy through a "comprehensive development plan which ensures the growth of the national income, fair distribution, higher living standards, elimination of unemployment, [and] the increase of job opportunities." By expanding opportunities for higher education and government employment, the public education system was crucial to meeting these aspirations. National secondary-school exit exams were established to determine placement in higher education institutions. Other important reforms included guarantees of admission to higher education for all secondary-school graduates, the elimination of tuition fees at all levels of education, and the guarantee of public-sector employment for all university graduates (Cupito & Langsten, 2011; Rugh, 2002). Admission to technical, vocational, and university education programs was also geared to key industries and economic needs.

As the most populous Arab nation, and the political home of the burgeoning Arab nationalist movement, Egypt served as a model for most Arab nations in the post-independence era, particularly in areas of social and economic policy. Admissions systems in many, but not all, Arab nations were based on the Nasser model, with strong commitments to free, universal higher education linked to public-sector positions, based on seemingly meritocratic exit exams.

Students' pathways through the education system reflect merit-based rationales, and each transition to a higher level is based on a standardized national examination. In Egypt, Jordan, Syria, and Morocco students sit for an exam at the end of preparatory school (i.e., grade nine), which determines upper-secondary-school track placement: either the academic track, which is a prerequisite for university, or the vocational track, where students specialize in occupationally oriented programs, such as commerce.

The number of students accepted into each track is set by the educational priorities of the day, with the ministries of education often imposing a fixed number of places available in the academic track. During the 1990s, roughly 50 per cent of students in Egypt were tracked into vocational education following the final exams in primary or lower secondary school (World Bank, 2008b). In recent years, as countries have focused on increasing access to higher education, the percentage of students attending academic secondary schools has risen – from about 45 per cent to 65 per cent in Egypt. In general, only students sorted into the general, or academic, track will have the opportunity to continue on to university. Vocational secondary schools are widely considered to be "second-class" schools, and the transition from a vocational secondary school to university is rare (Richards, 1992; World Bank, 2008b).

Within academic secondary schools, students are tracked into concentrations – typically, a mathematics and science track or an arts and humanities track – and some nations also have other tracks such as information technology (e.g., Syria) or a mixed pathway that includes both mathematics and science, and arts and humanities (e.g., Lebanon). In all Arab countries, the scientific and technical fields are considered to be more difficult and of higher status due to their difficulty of entry, which has reinforced hierarchies of majors and concentrations, with medicine and engineering at the top. In North Africa, tracking also maps onto linguistic differences. As scientific subjects are taught in French in university, and literary subjects in Arabic, the ability to succeed in scientific streams often requires near fluency in French (Boutieri, 2016).

At the end of upper secondary school, which lasts for three years (from grades ten to twelve), students in the academic track sit for an exit exam. In Egypt the official name for the exam is the Academic Secondary Certificate Examination, but it is commonly referred to as *thanawiya amma* ("general secondary," in Arabic). In Jordan the exit exam is known as the *tawjihi* ("orientation," in Arabic). In Syria and Lebanon and throughout North Africa the exam is referred to as the baccalaureate, or colloquially as "the Bac," after the French model.

These exams are not easy, and many teachers and parents have noted that they have become more difficult over time to restrict the number of students who can enter higher education and competitive careers. In 2012 only about 50 per cent of the students who sat for the tawjihi in Jordan passed the test; in the 2014 and 2015 summer sessions only 41 per cent of students passed (Adely, 2012). Similarly, slightly less than 50 per cent of Moroccan students passed the Bac in 2012 ("Résultats du Bac," 2012).

Performance on this secondary-exit examination determines the higher education options that are available to young people, and university placement involves a somewhat opaque process of matching university places with student preferences and student positions, in the distribution of the exit exam. In Jordan, Egypt, and Syria students are given a small number of options for universities and majors based on their score. In Tunisia, where students also take an exam known as the baccalaureate (*al-bakaluria*, Arabic), admissions decisions take into consideration both students' exit exam scores and their marks in their last three years of secondary school (el-Meehy, 2015). Students submit their top choices for their program of study, and are matched in waves based on their preferences and the field-specific quotas set by the ministry: those in the top wave are more likely to get their first choice, and subsequent waves are placed in less-in-demand programs and concentrations.

Gaining admission to prestigious or competitive programs is extremely difficult. In Jordan and Syria the public university system has strict requirements for admittance into each discipline, and prestigious programs such as medicine and engineering can require nearly perfect scores. Across the region those whose scores are not high enough for them to attend a university may be tracked into two-year intermediate institutes that provide training in an applied field such as informatics or bookkeeping.

One key difference between North Africa and the Levant (the historical region of greater Syria) is the idea of universal access. In North African systems, secondary-degree holders are legally guaranteed admission to university. In many cases promises of free and guaranteed access to higher education are built into national constitutions. In some countries, including Tunisia and Algeria, not only are students guaranteed admission and free tuition, but many also receive cost-of-living allowances. This is not the case in Jordan and Syria, where access to university is determined by exam score, and some secondary students graduate but do not meet the minimum scores to enter university (Malkawi, 2014). Jordanian admissions are also complicated by the country's demographics: there is unmet demand for higher education among urban Jordanians of Palestinian origin, for whom admission to the subsidized public sector is very competitive, a point discussed later in the chapter.

That said, the admission guarantees in most North African systems apply only to the more generalist and less prestigious programs. They are also regulated in various ways; for example, in Morocco the admission guarantee only extends to the student's home region. The more prestigious programs, with presumably better career prospects, require much higher scores on exams. For example, in Morocco admission to elite programs, such as medicine, also requires sitting for a separate program-specific entrance exam, known as the *concours*.

Despite the fundamental changes in Arab states and societies since Nasser's revolution (as described in chapter 1), the centrally coordinated, exam-based admissions system remains largely unchanged in many countries. In principle, access to higher education is meritocratic, with the highest achieving students tracked into the most needed or most rigorous professions. In practice, students from urban and upper-class backgrounds are much more likely to transition to university for both educational and economic reasons. Indeed, public education in the Arab world has always been stratified along class, ethnic, linguistic, and geographic lines, yet standardized testing remains justified in popular media on the basis of its practical and universalizing properties. For example, in 2001, Egypt's minister of higher education, Mufid Shebab, staunchly advocated for the examination system on both logistical and ideological grounds, stating that "the application system still has one significant virtue: equal opportunity" ("Crunching the numbers," 2001).

Criticisms of Exam-Based Admissions

Today, as countries in the region transition away from state-led development to neoliberal economic models, the logic of centralized admissions systems has come under intense scrutiny. Knowledge economy discourses that advocate lifelong learning have also called for expanded access and for second-chance programs that allow young people to continually upgrade their skills.

International development professionals have routinely criticized the region's centralized admissions systems, stating that they "promote memorization over investment in skills" (Dhillon & Yousef, 2011, p. 28). Similarly, in a 2013 Brookings publication on higher education in the region, the authors criticized the highly centralized nature of the process, noting that "student applications do not go to universities for consideration, but instead are sent to central government-run entities tasked with making decisions about which institution each applicant can attend" (Wilkens & Masri, 2011, p. 7). The authors recognized that admissions processes have social implications, including placing top students into sciences instead of liberal arts; they also criticized practices of accepting "unqualified students," which contribute to low completion rates and become a drain on government resources.

Additionally, the policy of guaranteed admission in North African systems has been widely criticized since at least the 1980s. One critic explained that despite difficulties for planners, "outright abrogation of this principle is politically risky. Student groups and others argue that this guarantee is essential for socioeconomic justice and have reacted quickly to proposals for its elimination" (M.T. Jones, 1981, p. 318). Interviews that I conducted in 2013 reflected a similar sentiment but a different rationale: given governments' fears over youth unrest in the wake of the Arab Spring, neither Morocco nor Tunisia was willing to increase tuition, limit enrolment, or decrease student aid.

Despite these criticisms, few feasible recommendations have been offered. Wilkens and Masri (2011) suggested that "more attention should be given to addressing the preparedness of secondary school graduates and applicants to universities" (p. 10). Possible efforts that they suggest include "the development of specialized exams, where appropriate, to assess language, reasoning, and thinking skills for admissions purposes" (p. 10). In other words, the key recommendation is "better tests," which seems to ignore the much broader social and political ramifications of admissions systems. In contrast, I interpret exit exams as a highly consequential domain of state involvement in students' lives.

The Many Social Consequences of Exams

The Rise of Private Tutoring

High-stakes exams have numerous unintended consequences. One very predictable and seemingly positive effect of high-stakes exams is that families will seek to obtain the best exam score for their children in the name of securing future opportunities. In practice, what this means is that in the Arab region, like the rest of the world, families make use of their financial and cultural resources to secure those opportunities, often through private schooling or private tutoring for their children.

Since the 1990s, rates of private schooling have rapidly increased throughout the Arab world. Many families are sending their children to private schools, particularly those that teach in foreign (i.e., Western) languages or those that allow students to avoid taking the dreaded national exam by securing a foreign credential instead. However, given their expensive tuition, these schools are viewed by many as "elitist institutions catering to the privileged few" (Farag, 2012, p. 81).

In addition, the use of private tutors has become ubiquitous throughout the region, a phenomenon that Sobhy (2012) calls "de-facto privatization" (p. 47) (see also Hartmann, 2008, 2013; Herrera, 2008). The rise of private tutoring is a global phenomenon and has been called "a shadow educational system" in the comparative education literature (Bray, 2006). In Egypt an estimated 75 per cent of all secondary-school students use private tutoring, and an additional 22 per cent continue to use tutors in university (Elbadawy, 2014; Waterbury, 2020). Farag (2012) argues that in Egypt the use of private tutors has been increasing rapidly despite the fact that the Ministry of Education views private tutors "with disdain" and considers them to be taking resources away from the public system (p. 81). Others have lamented the fact that private tutoring in Egypt, as in many countries, has become "an undeniable fact of life for students" (Sieverding, Krafft, & Elbadawy, 2019, p. 562). Scholars point to a number of primary drivers of private tutoring: on the demand side, students and families seek a competitive advantage on exams or perceive the schooling to be of low quality; on the supply side, teachers may encourage tutoring as a way to supplement their own incomes (Sieverding et al., 2019).

In my time travelling in numerous countries throughout the region, I found concerns over private tutoring to be widespread. In Egypt the teachers whom I interviewed explained that some public-school teachers do not teach material fully, in order to compel their students to pay them for tutoring. Prior research has found this to be a common practice in the region, along with more extreme forms of coercion such as threats of expulsion (Hartmann, 2013; Sieverding et al., 2019; Sobhy, 2012). In the seemingly reverse situation, where parental pressure drove private tutoring, in interviews conducted by my colleague and me in Jordan, secondary-school students expressed concern that they were covering official material for exams during the summer with their private tutors and then were less motivated or attentive during the school year (Buckner & Hodges, 2016). Alternatively, students might skip school to study with private tutors (Alayan, 2014).

The increasing reliance on private secondary education and private tutoring is a worrying trend because it may exacerbate inequalities and undermine the faith in and the quality of the public sector. Particularly when accompanied by declines in attention and in the quality of instruction in public schools, private tutoring has been called a "hidden cost" of ostensibly free educational systems (Sieverding et al., 2019). Given that families have various levels of resources to draw on to support their children, such practices invariably reproduce, and potentially exacerbate, socio-economic inequalities. Research in Egypt has found that rates of private tutoring increase with parental wealth and educational levels (Assaad & Krafft, 2015b; Elbadawy, 2009; Sayed & Langsten, 2014). Wealthy families also spend significantly more on private tutoring and ostensibly purchase "better" tutoring in the form of individualized rather than group lessons (Sieverding et al., 2019). Although concerns over private tutoring focus on its prevalence in primary and secondary schooling, its effects ripple through higher education systems because performance on exit exams determines admission to university. Research has found that throughout the region, students from wealthy families are much more likely to be found in higher education institutions overall, and particularly in prestigious fields that require high exam scores, such as medicine and engineering (Jackson & Buckner, 2016; Krafft & Alawode, 2018). Unsurprisingly, private tutoring has been called "an important barrier to equal opportunity in education" (Sieverding et al., 2019, p. 585).

Cheating and Connections

Another concerning consequence of high-stakes exams is the incentive to cheat, which is rampant in the Arab world, with cheating scandals frequently making national news. Prior research has found that cheating is common in the region. In a 2012 survey of 250 young people in the UAE, 78.0 per cent admitted to cheating, frequently facilitated by technology (Khan & Balasubramanian, 2012). Similarly, in a behaviour experiment, in which students were given the opportunity to cheat on a short and notably low-stakes quiz, C.W. Jones (2015) found that 48.8 per cent of high-school students in her sample cheated.

Cheating practices in the Arab world are similar to those used by young people elsewhere. Students bring in notes or exam answers written on clothing, water bottles, binders, desks, paper, or their skin. Some students receive answers by text message before or during the exam through mobile phones. There are also rumours of novel and extreme methods. In a 2013 interview that I conducted in Jordan, one young Jordanian man who admitted to cheating told me that some students are using a new method: getting a small incision behind the ear to hide an earphone. Regardless of whether such practices actually exist, the rumour illustrates the lengths to which young people will go to cheat on exams. Such rumours may also help young people to justify their own comparatively mundane cheating practices.

Cheating on high-stakes exit exams reflects the complicated web of structural constraints and cultural norms that youth must navigate: their own interests and abilities, family and social pressures, and the formal education system. Perhaps most surprising to those who believe that cheating is a moral failure on the part of students, in many Arab nations parents, families, and other adults frequently help students to cheat. Even though stories and editorials in Jordan and Morocco regularly lament the moral and institutional failures that cheating represents (Ait Hammou, 2012), cheating occurs in plain sight of adults – from parents who allow students to congregate in their living rooms with clandestine tests, to shopkeepers who knowingly permit students to make photocopies of tests – sometimes with their direct help.

The educational topography of Arab nations, which differentially values disciplines, may foster an environment in which parents feel justified in supporting cheating. High marks on the exit exam can lead to high-paying and high-prestige careers, while low scores lead to careers in fields such as Islamic law and Arabic literature, which have low economic returns in the local economy. Parents may decide to help their children cheat on the exit exam, even if it requires a small investment in buying exam questions, instead of paying more money later for private universities or parallel university programs.

Teachers and exam proctors are also blamed for, or at least are considered complicit in, cheating. Teachers in Jordan are widely accused of selling both copies of exams and correct responses, as well as simply providing answers during examinations. In an interview that my colleague and I conducted in Jordan, one young woman told me that, although she herself never cheated on an exam, during the administration of her exam the proctor leaned in and told her, "Make sure you fill in the A clearly," even though she had marked a B. Confused at first, she quickly understood that her teacher was telling her the correct answer. The role of teachers does not escape the notice of parents – even those who are critical of the culture of cheating. In another interview a Jordanian father of three said that the problem in schools was that teachers gave cigarettes to students, joked with them, and acted too informally: "If the teachers were clean, there wouldn't be any cheating. It's them who answer the questions and send answers to the students ... For material benefit they will sell their conscience. The teachers themselves are corrupt. It's cheap to cheat because the teachers are cheap." Teachers may benefit from cheating, either financially or socially, when large numbers of their students pass. Alternatively, some teachers may not want certain students to be in their classes again in the following year. The widespread involvement of adults in cheating schemes, however, suggests that there is a much larger socio-cultural fabric that shapes people's motivations, opportunities, and justifications for cheating.

Of course, not all students cheat: C.W. Jones (2015) finds that attitudes to cheating vary significantly based on gender, wealth, and the particular academic setting. Interviews that a colleague and I conducted with young people in Morocco and Jordan revealed that the ethical status of cheating was a grey zone. Although some young people claimed that all cheating was inherently wrong, most did not see cheating in black-and-white terms; they did not necessarily consider it *good*, but they also did not see is as *always* wrong or unfair. Instead, their ideas about fairness reflected complicated notions of what they perceived to be fair and unfair in the larger context of their lives. In both countries students explained that cheating was fair if larger social structures were unfair. For example, one female university student in Morocco told me: "I've never cheated, but I know why they do it. I don't judge them." Similarly, Abdullah, a young man from the south of Jordan, explained that cheating the formal bureaucratic system was fair if it allowed individuals who would otherwise fail to pass the test. He was adamant that he himself never cheated, but he did not think that it was necessarily wrong for others to do so if it was their only recourse for a better life.

Although the formal educational system claims that citizens are sorted into different life paths for the sake of national development, some young people whom I interviewed said that high-stakes exams are not a legitimate basis for sorting, given the significant inequalities in teacher preparation, educational resources, and exposure to foreign languages at the primary- and secondary-school levels, among other factors. For example, Thami, a young man from Morocco who admitted that he and most of his friends cheated, explained, "We didn't cheat the test. The test cheated us." When pressed, Thami explained that students were not well prepared to take the Bac, but then they realized that its results would determine their entire futures. The general perception of "being cheated" was particularly strong among those from rural areas and lower socio-economic classes, who felt they had not received a high-quality education. These justifications for cheating reflect the "hollowness" of the public educational project (Boutieri, 2012), in which state exams maintain a tight grip over young people's future lives, but schools are viewed as not fully preparing them for these exams.

Nonetheless, Abdullah made the crucial distinction that cheating was not fair if it was used to secure a higher score, obtain a seat in a prestigious university program, and thereby deprive another student of that university seat. In this case he considered cheating to be unfair because it had a direct, negative effect on someone else's life chances. Abdullah's insight suggests that cheating merely to get ahead individually is still not culturally justifiable. This kind of nuanced interpretation of fairness suggests that, for many young people, cheating is only interpreted as fair or acceptable when it is directed towards larger social structures perceived as unfair. Given the significance of the exams, which students, teachers, and parents routinely said "determine your fate" or "mean everything," cheating is one way that young people and their families attempt to reclaim agency over their lives.

Cheating clearly undermines the legitimacy of state-administered exams, which ultimately threatens the legitimacy of the education system itself and the state that is tasked with managing that system. Popular faith in testing, or lack thereof, reflects citizens' trust in the state as a fair arbiter of future opportunity. In my time of living in Morocco I often found that students and parents felt that grading was arbitrary – from the ministry's grading of Bac exams to university professors who had "power to pass or fail you based on nothing but their personal whims," as one interviewee stated. In conversations Moroccans rarely use the personal pronoun *I* to speak about the baccalaureate, such as saying, "I got ..." (*hasalt a'ala ...*). Instead, in colloquial Moroccan Arabic, they externalize the exam grades by stating, "They gave me" (*a'atawni*). This externalization implicitly undermines the idea that students earned their score. The linguistic difference feeds into larger perceptions that the scores one gets on the Bac are somewhat random. In interviews Moroccans explained that "sometimes graders make mistakes" and that if students did not agree with their exam scores, they could go to the district office and ask for another grader, and for yet another after that. The process by which a different group of graders raise or lower scores perpetuates students' lack of faith in the validity of grading. Boutieri (2016) notes that "the strategies of students, parents and teachers to circumvent the structural inequalities of the public education system through cheating, parallel lessons, and bribes reveal both their obligatory complicity ... and their contempt for government recommendations regarding the official rules of meritocratic promotion" (p. 38).

Given the importance of meritocracy as a cornerstone of the Moroccan education system, upholding the idea of fair grading is a priority for the Moroccan state, and the Ministry of Education has made public examples of cheaters. News accounts have reported students being arrested for cheating (Arbaoui, 2012). In 2012, in response to answers being leaked on Facebook, the Ministry of Education "issued a decision to consider invalid all the answers similar to those posted on Facebook" (Flah, 2012). If caught cheating, students can be barred from taking the Bac for up to five years or even face prison sentences of up to three years (Bin Tayyib, 2013). Meanwhile, those caught facilitating cheating, either through selling answers or leaking exam questions, face severe penalties: anywhere from six months to five years in prison, or fines of 5,000–100,000 Moroccan dirhams (USD 500–10,000) (Arbaoui, 2016).

In the days leading up to the 2016 Bac, news reports announced that the authorities had caught ninety-one people trying to leak answers to the Bac through social media sites. As a sign of the perceived seriousness of cheating, incidents are investigated as crimes by police, rather than simply being handled by educational officials. In June 2016 the Moroccan parliament passed a law to crack down on cheating, which was timed to align with the opening of that year's Bac. In announcing the law, Khalid Barjaoui, minister delegate to the minister of national education and vocational training, stated that its goal was to "anchor the values of fairness and equality of opportunity" (al-Youm, 2016). The ministry also claims to be taking a strict stance against cheating by publishing the names of students caught cheating, to "protect the creditability of the Moroccan Baccalaureate" (al-Youm, 2016). Many articles in national newspapers feature crackdowns on cheating in the days leading up to and during the examination period. I interpret these harsh penalties as the ministry's attempt to reassert the legitimacy of its exams and, in turn, itself.

Attempts to crack down on cheating are not restricted to Morocco but are widespread throughout the region. In 2016 the Lebanese Ministry of Education and Higher Education reported that it was reforming the testing system after 55 per cent of a sample of students confessed to cheating on exams in 2015 ("Cheating," 2015). Part of the reform measures included video-monitoring all exam rooms and decentralizing the examination process. Similarly, in 2016 the Egyptian government was embarrassed by a cheating scandal and in the following year introduced new exam booklets to prevent online cheating.

Not all countries have cracked down to the same extent, however. In ethnographic interviews conducted with young people in Jordan, Adely, Haddad, al-Husban, and al-Khoshman (2019) found that the students generally "accepted *tawjihi* results as a product of their own efforts rather than the quality of their education" (p. 81). Specifically, when students discussed their experiences of taking the tawjihi, they tended to emphasize their "own abilities and weaknesses as students, or personal and familial crises they faced while studying for the exam" (p. 88). Unlike in Morocco, interviews in Jordan revealed that the legitimacy of grading was not the primary issue; respondents stated that the "grading was fair" because it was done by ministry officials. Rather, concerns over cheating came to a head in the examination hall. According to Jordanian news reports, there is often an expectation that proctors will allow blatant cheating (even to the extent that some tribes have used a loudspeaker to read out answers near an examination centre) (al-Shawabke, 2012). Thwarted attempts at cheating have resulted in mass anger and violent outbursts. In the 2012 winter session of tawjihi exams in Karak, a city in the south of Jordan, a mob of two hundred students and family members attacked a police precinct with rocks after a man attempting to help students cheat was ejected from the school. At around the same time, a large group of students and parents in Amman attacked the car of one exam monitor who had not allowed cheating, and critically injured his wife (Azzeh, 2013).

In Jordan the use of violence in educational spaces is not unique to secondary schools. Tribal rivalries and affirmative-action policies are largely responsible for the widespread outbreaks of violence on Jordanian university campuses; these are particularly common in the more rural southern governorates and map onto a long-standing distinction between urban Palestinians and rural Jordanians. The young people I interviewed in Amman explained that students from tribal areas might be more likely to cheat because they were less prepared for the exam than were Palestinian-Jordanians living in urban areas, where secondary schools are of higher quality. Importantly, however, some with whom I spoke also thought of cheating because they felt entitled to the security promised by a degree and viewed the "right" to a certain number of university seats as a form of patronage. These impressions are overgeneralizations that rely on stereotypes about young people from rural areas being less educated or less academically motivated, which reflect the biases of many urban Jordanians. Yet, I mention them nonetheless to reflect accurately the opinions of the young people with whom I spoke and also to show how educational exams expose broader social and political divides. At least among some Jordanians, cheating is viewed as one way that tribal groups blatantly reject the formalized bureaucracy that would deny them opportunities.

As the Jordanian monarchy's power depends critically on its support by tribes, efforts to combat cheating are officially codified, yet superficial in practice. A 2012 investigation into cheating on the tawjihi found "no wrong-doing," and the report stated that ministry officials carried out their duties to the best of their ability. It also denied the participation of ministry officials and called on reporters to release the names of the officials who had leaked questions, thus shifting the burden of proof to civil society. According to one newspaper, the investigative committee "acknowledged that some people had used loudspeakers outside examination halls to help students cheat, but said the ministry was not responsible for preventing this and that only security forces had the authority to do so" ("Investigation," 2012). By dividing authority through multiple branches, the government largely excuses itself from controlling cheating. Such evasive tactics suggest that the centralized government is avoiding a more direct engagement with cheating in tribal areas.

The absence of severe crackdowns and the general leniency in punishing cheating in Jordan is noteworthy. In 2015 the Jordan Teachers Association received several complaints of cheating, which were promptly and forcefully denied by the Ministry of Education. In fact, the ministry warned that such campaigns to shed light on cheating "hamper[ed] the reputation of the exam and spread confusion" ("Teacher syndicate," 2014). Ostensibly, cheating on the tawjihi in Jordan is illegal, and students who are caught with any devices for cheating, such as mobile phones, are banned from taking the exam for two to four years. Cheating restrictions, however, are not evenly enforced across the country. In 2016 a spokesperson for the Jordan Teachers Association commented: "Education departments in some regions are known to be very rigid about the rules, while others are very lenient. Students are well aware of this and feel how unfair it is, especially for a national standard exam" (Azzeh, 2016). This quotation speaks to the extent to which even seemingly technical higher education policies reflect nuanced negotiations of power in Jordan.

Issues of academic integrity are clearly implicated in broader questions of how young people access university opportunities. Even when they justify or trivialize their actions, and the states seem willing to overlook cheating, C.W. Jones (2015) reminds us that "cheating is damaging to society, eroding norms of honesty, fair play, and reciprocity," and, like other forms of corruption, cheating can undermine a society's sense of trust (p. 7).

Thwarted Ambitions

Hussein Khozai, a Jordanian professor of sociology at al-Balqa Applied University, described the Jordanian exit exam as a "social exam rather than an educational one" (Azzeh, 2013), referring to the larger socio-political significance of schooling and testing in the Arab region. Students' perceived lack of agency over where and what they study in higher education is a major source of frustration in young people's lives and often leads to discontent with the state that is responsible for sorting students.

One of the most striking social effects of centralized admissions is that youth regularly lament a sense of "thwarted ambition" because all but the top performers had very little say over where and what they studied. In centralized admissions systems the primary justification for the state's role in sorting students and tracking them into educational and career paths is workforce planning, based on the premise that the government can align its higher education system to the needs of the economy. Although the guarantee of employment has long since evaporated, Arab states remain active in sorting youth by using exams. As the centralized university admissions are based on exam score, students are frequently sorted into degree programs, and subsequent career paths, for which they have no interest or aptitude.

A common refrain among young people in Syria and Jordan is that students simply cannot pursue their program of choice and that many have no choice over what they study. In 2010, I interviewed a young man from Syria, Nader, who had wanted to study accounting but did not have high enough grades. He said, "There is no taking into consideration what students desire here. Grades alone are what allow you to do what you do." Other interviewees called choice "a luxury" or explained that they "had no future" because they were unable to study their desired major. Hassan, a twenty-one-year-old male studying English translation while also working full-time at an international company, explained: "The problem is that they don't put the right person in the right place. If they gave me opportunity to be a computer programmer, I would be a good programmer because I love it. This is the problem: they put the wrong person in the wrong place." Hassan's comment is illuminating because, instead of admitting that his grades did not qualify him for his top-choice career, he clearly blamed external actors ("they"). Interviews revealed that the experience of having a thwarted educational ambition crossed lines of gender, class, and educational attainment, suggesting that it is a widespread experience for many young people and that barriers to accessing a desired university program are a real and significant source of frustration for them.

Similarly, in Morocco, even with the policy of open admissions, in reality many students are not studying their preferred concentration. A Moroccan professor whom I met in 2013 told me about a study that his team had conducted about how students chose their majors, and the results were surprising. At the time, admissions systems were not automated, which meant that students had to stand in line to submit their application papers, and admission to various departments was first come, first served. In a strange example of perverse incentives, the study found that some students simply submitted application dossiers where lines were shortest. For example, deterred by the three-day line to enrol in law, some students simply enrolled in economics because the line was much shorter.

Families play an important role in shaping young people's life paths. Owing to clear occupational prestige hierarchies, parents pressure students to pursue high-status professions, namely medicine and engineering, due to their social prestige and the honour such professions bring to the families. Young people's individual aptitudes, career aspirations, or interests are frequently disregarded. As a result, many students find themselves in careers for which they are not particularly motivated.

Discontent with admissions systems across the region is exacerbated by perceptions of widespread corruption in the admissions system that privileges those with family connections. Youth from low socio-economic family backgrounds expressed a sense of injustice resulting from the role that political and family connections had in helping students obtain access to university. One interviewee whom I interviewed in Syria remarked: "Imagine – a poor kid has to study forever to get really high grades just to get into a public school. He needs impossibly high marks. But a rich kid has two ways of succeeding. Either he can go to a private university or could find a way into a public university through his family's connections."

At the time of these interviews, Syria's educational reforms were expanding opportunities to study, but it was clear that they were not necessarily decreasing the importance of wealth or connections in education. Young people's sense of injustice undermined the state's rationale for sorting youth: many Syrian young people felt that not only were they being sorted into majors and careers in which they were not interested, but also the sorting process itself was biased towards those who had money and connections. This perception of injustice led them to reject the state's role in sorting youth into educational paths, and contributed to a larger sense that the state lacked the capacity to implement fair policies and, more fundamentally, was not a fair arbiter of future opportunity.

Of course, many young people did have choices: those who performed very well on their exit exam could study almost any subject they desired. Youth who said that the admissions system left them no choice were in reality unhappy with the choices they were offered based on their lower test results. I observed that, rather than blame themselves for lack of preparation, many students blamed the broader system for presenting them with what felt like impossible options: getting exam scores that they were not able or prepared to achieve, or resigning themselves to an undesirable profession. This externalization of blame was evident in nearly all the interviews I conducted in Syria and many that I conducted in Morocco. Youth perceived the state control over sorting students into educational majors, which left youth insecure in the labour market, as the state's inability to fulfil its obligations. This failure contributes to a delegitimization of the larger notion of state-led development, as youth feel subject to extensive state intervention, without enjoying the promised benefits.

Young men seemed more concerned about the link between education and employment than did the women to whom I spoke. In interviews conducted in Syria, young men who attended some form of higher education tended to want not only the credentials of a diploma but also the promise of labour-market security that it traditionally offers, while female respondents valued a wider range of purposes for higher education. Young men who have performed well in school expect to benefit from substantial economic returns and social prestige in the form of secure jobs in medicine or other elite fields. Their concerns with the recent neoliberal reforms focus on the loss of the prestige and economic security that accompany the introduction of new pathways to elite education and employment. Interviews that I conducted in Syria in 2009 and 2010 revealed that lower-income men who had gone on to higher education but had not achieved high marks were the most discontented with the wave of neoliberal reforms. They were tracked into programs that were often unrelated to their interests and did not provide the economic pay-off they expected. Wickham (2002) made a similar argument about Egypt: "For the Egyptian graduates who had been socialized to view themselves as a meritocratic elite, perhaps the greatest source of bitterness was what they perceived as an erosion of the link between merit and reward" (p. 159).

Similarly, in their analysis of why engineers and doctors are over-represented among radical Islamic terrorists, Gambetta and Hertog (2017) explain that "individuals with above-average skills, who have been selected for their university studies on merit, are particularly susceptible to frustration and a sense of injustice when they find their professional future hampered by a lack of opportunities" (p. 35). This finding rings true with my own research on the sources of frustrations among Arab university students and graduates from Morocco to Syria.

Many young people did not have family connections or wealth to help them secure a better future, but they still experienced societal pressure to find gainful employment and provide for their families – without a clear path of how to do so. This burden weighed particularly on men, and many scholars argued that prior to the outbreak of the Arab Spring young, unemployed men were like a tinderbox in the Middle East (Hvistendahl, 2011). My interviews revealed, however, that it is specifically the educated, unemployed men who are most discontent – not simply because they are unemployed, but also because they feel wronged. Contrary to the common assumption in many societies that unemployed men believe they have failed somehow, and internalize their shame, my findings revealed that educated unemployed young men are likely to believe that the entire higher education system, and the state in charge of it, have failed them.

In response to these thwarted ambitions, young people adopt creative strategies to navigate bureaucratic constraints. Drawing on ethnographic interviews at Yarmouk University in Jordan, Adely, Haddad, et al. (2019) identify numerous practices in which young people engage to "try to make the system work for them" (p. 81). For example, young people actively seek to change majors once they are admitted, in order to secure places in more marketable or prestigious programs. In some cases, students switch into a parallel program after being accepted. Another practice young people use is to seek supplementary credentials to make themselves more competitive in the labour market. Students and families also attempt to evade the consequences of exams by using their family connections to secure admission to a particular program or scholarship (Adely, Haddad, et al., 2019). All of these constitute forms of "resourcefulness" that young people use to retain some control over their educational trajectories (Buckner & Hodges, 2016).

"Exceptions" in Jordan

Despite the country's exam-based admissions system, the admissions system in Jordan, unlike other countries in the region, makes no claim to being truly meritocratic. Rather, Jordanian admissions policies involve overtly political calculations (Adely et al., 2019; Reiter, 2002). Demographically, roughly 60 per cent of Jordanians today are of Palestinian origin, and the remainder are considered East Bank or Transjordanian. Admissions policies are part of a larger political balance that has shaped the Jordanian state since the 1970s: in return for the country's tacit acceptance of a huge number of Palestinians, the Jordanian monarchy has granted a series of special privileges to East

Bank Jordanians, who tend to come from rural backgrounds, including gerrymandered voting districts and privileged access to higher education (Burke & al-Waked, 1997).

In higher education there is a historical system of *makruma* (plural, *makarim*) – which translates into "gift" or "generosity." These makarim constitute a targeted affirmative-action program that reserves a portion of places in public universities for Jordanian young people of certain backgrounds and covers the tuition fees for some of them (Cantini, 2012; Emam, 2013). They are called gifts or royal grants from the king, but are also codified in the higher education admissions regulations, and both Cantini (2012) and Reiter (2002) have argued that they are a tool the monarchy uses to consolidate loyalty.

There are makarim designated for families of the security agencies and armed forces, employees of the Ministry of Education, and children of professors, as well as those from disadvantaged groups. While a diverse range of individuals, from Palestinians living in refugee camps to children of professors, benefit, the largest number of makarim is reserved for the children of armed forces members, accounting for about 22 per cent of all seats in university, as of 2015–16 (Adely et al., 2019). Between 2002 and 2012, roughly one-quarter to one-third of all seats were reserved for these special groups of students, although the percentage of makruma recipients at a given institution differs across the country (Malkawi, 2012).

Facing protests in 2011–12, Jordan's Ministry of Higher Education announced changes in its scholarship programs, such that scholarships would be based on financial need rather than geography. Adely, Haddad, et al. (2019) report that in the 2015–16 academic year, 54.7 per cent of admissions occurred through open competition, while the rest were reserved through a quota system, also known as "exceptions" in Arabic. Of total admissions, 21.9 per cent were for children of armed forces members, 10.0 per cent were for students from tribal and under-developed areas of the country, 8.6 per cent were a makruma for children of teachers, 2.0 per cent were for children of university professors, 1.6 per cent were for top-performing students of their district, 1.1 per cent were a makruma for children of refugees, and 0.4 per cent were for children of martyrs and the disabled (p. 85). Both the armed forces and the tribal areas in the south that benefit from makarim overwhelmingly comprise East Bank Jordanians who are more loyal to the monarchy than those of Palestinian origin; unsurprisingly then, makarim has come to be viewed as a form of political patronage (Cantini, 2012; Reiter, 2002).

The makruma system affects who gains access to elite programs. Students admitted from disadvantaged regions are typically the highest-performing students from their regions, but due to differences in the quality or rigour of secondary-school education across the country, the cut-off score for their admission is still much lower than in urban areas. Students in urban Amman with whom I spoke were only too happy to complain about what they perceived as unfair admissions decisions. They recounted stories of a student from an urban area who obtained a 93 per cent mark on the exit exam but was denied admission to a desired program in the competitive system, while a makruma recipient with only a 75 per cent mark might obtain admission to the same program. Adely, Haddad, et al. (2019) report similar disparities: in highly prestigious medical programs, competitive admissions may require a mark of 99 per cent, while an individual accepted through the quota system may require only 85 per cent, which many would argue is still a strong score. Differences in admissions criteria cause tensions, as some students believe that makruma recipients are admitted unfairly. It can also be difficult for makruma recipients to succeed if they are admitted to difficult programs for which they are not well prepared.

Opinions on the makruma system vary. I have spoken to university instructors and professors who have been pressured to pass makruma recipients based on their connections and backgrounds. In 2013, however, I spoke with the president of a public university who was quite supportive of the makruma system, commenting that it was designed as a way for the most-deserving students from poorer and less developed areas to obtain an education, return to their villages, and develop their regions. Similarly, in 2014, a professor of constitutional law at the University of Jordan explained to the media that the quota system worked as a form of positive discrimination, or affirmative action, because it was not reasonable to assume that a tawjihi student in Amman (the capital) and Ma'an (a less-developed region in the south) were really competing on equal terms for admission (al-Natoor, 2014).

Others, however, have argued that quota-based admissions has invoked a "constitutional controversy," as it violates Article IV of the Constitution, which guarantees all citizens equal treatment before the law (al-Natoor, 2014). Indeed, in 2015, suggested reforms to the makruma system became hotly debated, and law-makers expressed "anger and dismay," threating to fire the minister of higher education when there was talk that the Higher Education Council had discussed cancelling the makruma system (Omari, 2015). In response, the minister of higher education stated that makruma exceptions to admissions were there to stay: "Exceptions in university admission criteria will not be cancelled, especially for students who live in remote areas, as the quality of education provided in these regions, and even the infrastructure in some

schools, is lower than in major cities. We have to help these students
and provide them with opportunities" (Malkawi, 2015).

In short, unequal admissions decisions are justified in terms of historical inequities and national development. The effects of this unequal
admissions system are complicated, but one of the most extreme effects
is campus-based violence. The *Jordan Times* reported that from 2011
to 2015 there were more than 296 incidents of violence on Jordanian
university campuses, involving close to 4,000 students, mostly males
and mostly students enrolled in the humanities. From 2010 to 2013,
on-campus fights involved 3,999 students and resulted in 31 severe,
57 moderate, and 155 minor injuries, in addition to property damage
(Malkawi, 2016). The consequences of violence can be severe: students
can be expelled, universities closed, and classes cancelled after gangs of
angry students fight one another, often breaking windows and chairs
or burning tires. For example, in December 2016, the *Jordan Times*
reported that seventeen students were expelled or suspended from the
University of Jordan after a brawl of two hundred students broke out
in November. In another example, in 2013 at Mutah University, located
outside of Karak, hundreds of students were involved in a brawl related
to student council elections: one police car was set on fire, and a twenty-
one-year-old bystander died of a heart attack while trying to flee.

Causes of campus violence are multifaceted; tribal honour, often
relating to female conduct, is considered a primary cause. Fights frequently break out if females from one tribe are accused of dating males
from another tribe. In March 2012 a fight broke out at the University of
Jordan when a male student saw a female relative talking to men from
another tribe and fired several blanks from a firearm. In 2013, while
living in Jordan, I interviewed a number of young Jordanians about
violence on campuses. Mohammed, a young man who had studied at
the University of Jordan, told me, "The reason for 95 per cent of fights
on campuses is girls." He explained that if a girl from one tribe or extended family network (*asheera*) was seen talking to a boy from another
tribe, the boys from her extended tribal family might start a fight with
her male direct relatives because many of the male students felt it was
important to defend their female relative's honour. Although the percentage of students involved in campus violence is small, it is associated with students coming from areas with strong tribal affiliations
where defending honour is viewed as an important aspect of one's
identity. Hussein Khuzaay, a professor of sociology at the University of
Jordan, explained in the *Jordan Times* that part of the blame lay in "the
tribal society that fosters violent and vengeful tendencies" and that
views men as "manly and heroic" when they engage in violent defence

of another tribe member (Al Harahsheh, 2017). Although the culture of defending the honour of distant relatives is changing, and many young educated urban Jordanians are increasingly permissive of male-female interactions between non-relatives, violence remains a major concern on many campuses.

Although gender relations and socially constructed conceptions of respect may be the primary cause of campus violence, makruma admissions policies are also recognized as a contributing factor. Critics state that those who engage in campus violence have been overwhelmingly accepted through the makruma system (Omari, 2015). My own interviewees also seemed to believe that makruma recipients were more likely to engage in fights over female honour for cultural reasons. In addition, makruma recipients accepted into programs that are too difficult for them often skip class and loiter on campuses.

At the institutional level a number of universities, including the Jordan University of Science and Technology and the University of Jordan, have sought to limit campus violence through strict policies. The universities have increased sanctions against violence: students are now expelled for engaging in violence, and, as of 2017, these penalties were finally being implemented to full effect, with seventeen students being expelled from the University of Jordan because of violence. The university has also instituted other reforms such as requiring identification to enter campus, installing security cameras, and training campus security in how to control fights.

In 2013, the Higher Education Commission, Jordan's regulating higher education body, decided that "students expelled as a result of violence [would] not be accepted into any other public or private university" ("Classes halted," 2013). In response to the events in Mutah in 2013, described earlier, the commission held an emergency meeting and took a strong stance, reiterating that those involved in such actions must be expelled and prevented from re-enrolling at other universities in the country. However, the policy was not initially implemented in areas with strong tribal influences. For example, some of the students who had engaged in violence at Mutah University and been expelled were later re-admitted owing to "external pressures" – a euphemism for political pressures from leaders. Misleh Tarawneh, the former dean of student affairs at the university, resigned from his post in protest against the decision to allow these students to return.

The issue has remained in news headlines in Jordan. In 2016, at a meeting with public university presidents, King Abdullah strongly denounced campus violence, and universities discussed the many efforts they had taken to reduce it. In 2018, the Lower House in Jordan passed a law to allow university security guards to have the status of law enforcement officers, thereby giving them greater authority to combat violence. It remains to be seen how admissions policies will be revised; to date, tribal power and connections seem to have undermined existing policies. Ultimately the national government can issue strict policies, but the power to admit, punish, and expel students remains in the hands of local university administrators who must navigate between stated national policies and local communities exerting their own cultural and political pressures.

Privatizing Pathways

Seeking to expand access while leaving exit exams intact, many Arab nations have created programs that allow students to enrol in higher education through alternative access channels. Egypt, Jordan, and Syria all instituted "dual-track" admissions. These programs, typically called parallel programs (*al-mawazi*, Arabic), accept students who did not gain admission to subsidized seats through regular competitive systems, in return for substantially higher fees (Adely et al., 2019). Specific policies differ somewhat by country: in Egypt, high-fee programs take place in different classrooms; in Syria two programs were opened, one called Parallel and one called Open Learning, in which students study on weekends; and in Jordan students are enrolled in identical programs and sit beside their higher-achieving peers. Cantini (2012) reports that the parallel system, which was introduced in Jordan in 2002, was intended to be an evening program, only permitting students to take classes after five o'clock. It was assumed that this internal differentiation would limit protest over the ability of students in the parallel system to gain admission by paying more. However, in as early as 2003, students in the parallel program have been integrated into regular classes. Cantini (2012) reported that during his fieldwork at the University of Jordan in 2003–5, students could be admitted into the parallel system with only 65 per cent of the score needed to gain admission to the competitive seat. Since then, competition for both the funded, competitive seats and the seats in the parallel program has increased significantly.

Parallel programs serve dual purposes: they expand access to students who might not have gained admission otherwise, and generate income for the university. Since the 1990s, the deepening of a neoliberal economic agenda and rising student enrolments across the Arab states have resulted in reduced per-student state funding for higher education. In the 1990s, public universities in Egypt established fee-paying programs that were taught in English (Bollag, 1996). Starting in 2006, the Egyptian government allowed public universities to charge small fees that allowed students with lower exit exam scores to enrol in the faculties of Law, Commerce, and Arts (Fahim & Sami, 2011). In Jordan, the parallel program has been essential to the generation of revenue for public universities. Cantini (2012) reported, based on fieldwork in 2003–5, that students in a parallel program paid roughly seven times the tuition fees paid by students in a competitive seat. Since that time, however, fees in both the competitive and the parallel programs have increased substantially, resulting in a narrower gap. Badran and Badran (2018) found that in Jordan the average fees across subsidized programs in public universities were USD 1,217, compared to USD 3,954 in the parallel programs, or slightly more than three times the subsidized fee.

Parallel programs, where they have been enacted, have had a significant impact on enrolments. Huge numbers of students have been rapidly incorporated into their national higher education systems, including many who would not have been able to attend otherwise. When I lived in Syria in 2009 and 2010, the parallel program accounted for about 50,000 students, compared to the competitive programs in public universities, which constituted 288,000 students, or about 15 per cent of all students. Another third was also enrolled in evening and weekend courses in Open Learning programs (Buckner, 2013).

At the same time, in interviews I conducted in Syria and Jordan with young people, parallel programs generated real concern. Some believed that parallel programs, by allowing new and less qualified entrants into higher education, were weakening the power of a university credential in the labour market. Similarly, scholars have raised concerns about declining quality due to overcrowding (Massadeh, 2012). Others believed that the programs were simply money-making schemes by governments that had forsaken their promises of free higher education (Buckner, 2013). Cantini (2012) reported that those students who gained admission to the competitive seats "more overtly denounce[d] this trend" towards a privatized access channel. More recently, Adely et al. (2019) reported that the fees of the parallel programs in Jordan were scheduled to increase by up to 180 per cent. Students have protested such increases, and students and scholars alike have argued that these programs represent a de facto privatization of higher education that is unaffordable to many (Massadeh, 2012).

Not all countries in the region, however, use standardized exams to sort students into majors, reflecting different relationships between the state and its young citizens. Two other models are used. First, there is the broad access model of the Arab Gulf states, where all national secondary-school graduates can enrol in a higher education program of their choice. In the Arab Gulf states, including the UAE and Qatar, there is very little desire or attempt to weed out all but the best and brightest. Rather, admissions systems provide substantial support to facilitate admission and allow students to select their own concentrations. A second model is found in Lebanon, where access is determined at the institutional level in a predominantly private system, reflecting the fragmented nature of state power. In both models, exams are less consequential than they are elsewhere. In distinct ways, however, the higher education admissions in these countries are linked to their own states' legitimacy, and each state is struggling with reforms to its systems.

Higher Education in the Arab Gulf States

The social contract in the Arab Gulf states is fundamentally different from that in the Levant and North Africa, due to their national wealth from natural resources. The nation-building period of the Arab Gulf states coincided with the discovery of oil and an influx of huge numbers of foreigners, which made the latter simultaneously economically wealthy and an ethnic minority group in their new homeland. The social contract of the Arab Gulf states reflects this unique set of circumstances and is built on the premise of shared wealth and mutual benefit: in return for the granting of authority and political legitimacy to select tribal families, all citizens would benefit from the nation's oil wealth. Fyfe (1989) wrote, "It is not an exaggeration to say that sharing out the oil wealth lies at the heart of the conceptual legitimacy of the Gulf skhaikhs" (p. 11). In the post-independence era, citizens of the Arab Gulf states were guaranteed, and now have come to expect, a wide range of social services including free health care, free education, subsidized housing, subsidized utilities, and preferential employment opportunities.

This conception of a strong state committed to significant provision of social services has shaped higher education admissions. At the most basic level it has created two separate higher education systems: free public systems for national citizens and sprawling, tuition-dependent private systems, primarily for non-nationals.

Within the public system the foundational logic is not meritocracy but capacity building. Admission to higher education in the Gulf states rests on the assumption that all those who are willing and able to attend higher education should be able to attend at no cost. Unlike in North Africa, where free access is permitted only to those who pass a rigorous exit exam, in the Arab Gulf states passing coursework is sufficient for secondary-school graduation. For admission to higher education, students are required to sit for English- and mathematics-proficiency assessments, and those who score above a minimum threshold are granted admission to university. Starting in 2016, the government of the UAE introduced a standardized computer-based test for all students in grade twelve, known as the Emirates Standardized Test (EmSAT), which covers Arabic, English, mathematics, and physics, and scores on this test have become the basis for admissions to public universities.

One of the defining features of higher education in both the UAE and Qatar is that English is the medium of instruction in most programs, a policy choice that signals a commitment to modernization and development through integration into the global economy. This choice of a primarily English-language system has had a profound effect on admission to higher education: students must demonstrate English proficiency. As Arabic is the medium of instruction throughout secondary school, academic English proficiency constitutes a major barrier to access.

Prior to 2004, all students in the UAE went through the Foundation Program of Intensive English, known informally as the Foundation program, which served as an academic bridge by providing intensive English preparation for university. Foundation program teachers would determine when a student was capable of pursuing university, based on in-class work. This program was free to Emiratis, and in the past they could study more or less indefinitely in these programs until they passed. Many students did study for two years or more.

The Foundation program was costly, however; at one point it was estimated to take up one-third of the higher education budget (Pennington, 2017). In 2004 the Ministry of Higher Education began allowing students to take an English-proficiency assessment that would exempt them from the Foundation program and permit direct entry to federal universities. Students who did not receive a high enough score to enter university directly could continue in the Foundation program, later called an Academic Bridge program (ABP). These students and their families then had to pay to sit again for the International English Language Testing System (IELTS) exam to prove proficiency.

In 2004 the minimum standard for direct entry was initially a score of 5.0 on the IELTS, although this has since been increased to 5.5. It is worth noting that a score of 5.0 on IELTS is well below the English-proficiency level required in the vast majority of American, Canadian, British, and Australian universities, and there is legitimate debate over whether it is really a sufficient standard for university study. That said, in 2004 only 3 per cent of Emiratis qualified for direct entry to federal institutions (Salem & Swan, 2014). In 2010 the percentage qualifying had increased to roughly 10 per cent (Moussly, 2010), and by 2014 it was 20 per cent (Pennington, 2017). While the ministry focuses on the fact that more Emiratis are gaining direct entry to university every year due to improvements in the secondary-school curriculum, the reality is that as of 2017 more than 75 per cent of secondary-school graduates in the UAE were not prepared to enrol directly in the English-language higher education programs of public universities.

In 2013, reforms were proposed to eliminate the Foundation program by 2018, citing costs to both the government and families (Salem & Swan, 2014). Starting in the 2019–20 academic year, the existing Foundation program at the Higher Colleges of Technology was phased out, and English-language support was added to General Studies courses. However, ABPs still exist at Zayed University and UAE University, and students are permitted to be "pre-admitted" to university with an EmSAT English score of 1100, compared to the 1250 required for direct entry. According to data from Zayed University, more than a thousand students each year are enrolled in the ABP, and completion rates over the past decade are roughly 75 per cent for women and 50 per cent for men (UAE Open Data Portal, 2021).

The phasing out of the Academic Bridge altogether was pushed back because the ministry recognized that most Emirati students were not ready to enter an English-speaking university program directly out of secondary school. Notably, the country's capacity-building model has never proposed that students pay for the program, and students do not suffer severe consequences for a lack of preparation – reflecting the vision of state-led development in the region, where social services are provided by the government at no cost. More sympathetically, it acknowledges the reality that Emirati students should not have to bear the consequences of fragmented language-education policies that simply do not provide them the option of pursuing higher education in their native language.

Language competency also lies at the heart of shifting admissions policies in Qatar. Between 2003 and 2006 the RAND Corporation came to Qatar to revolutionize and modernize its educational system, including major governance reforms at Qatar University, the large national university. Programs were internationally accredited, and the university began to teach in English. As part of the reforms, they recruited faculty and staff from abroad and supported research by creating new graduate degrees. For students, they raised the level of English proficiency required for admission.

One of my interviewees in Qatar explained that this put many Qatari students and families in the difficult position of not having the English language abilities to pursue university. He explained: "Many Qatari families were like: our kids are citizens of this state, and they cannot meet the admission requirements of the branch campuses, and now they cannot meet language requirements of Qatar University. At the time, there was a group of families who saw no options for their children." In 2011 the reforms were significantly rolled back, and the university resumed teaching in Arabic, leaving many foreign professors unsure of their futures. One interviewee stated very simply that the reversal in policy was a "political decision." Another professor in Qatar said, "It is my understanding that this announcement was made overnight. The president of Qatar University apparently didn't know about the change until he read about it in the newspaper." In both the UAE and Qatar, governments are not trying to limit enrolments to higher education, but language remains a fundamental issue, and admissions policies flip between a desire to raise standards in the name of quality and and a desire to lower them to match students' actual levels of proficiency.

Findlow (2006) has noted that the adoption of English for most subjects has created a "linguistic dualism" that perpetuates a prestige hierarchy. In an ethnographic study in the UAE she argues that Arabic is associated with "cultural authenticity," including religion, traditions, and a focus on the local community. In contrast, English is associated with ideas of modernity, global outlook, business, material status, and secularism (p. 25). These ideas map onto and perpetuate institutional hierarchies. The students she interviewed thought that studying medicine and engineering at a national university had the highest prestige, followed by technological and business programs, which were considered "entrepreneurial,"; education, law, and Islamic law, all of which are taught in Arabic, were thought to be the lowest-prestige programs.

Paying for Access in Lebanon's Privatized System

Lebanon and Palestine are the only two states in the region where students apply for admission directly to universities. As mentioned in the previous chapter, higher education in Lebanon has a large and dynamic private sector: there is one large public university – the LU – and dozens of smaller private universities, including older prestigious institutions such as the American University of Beirut and the University of Saint-Joseph, as well as many other more vocationally oriented institutions founded after the end of the civil war in 1990.

In Lebanon, like other countries in the region, students are sorted into tracks in secondary school based on the results of a primary-school leaving exam, focusing on a science and mathematics stream, an arts and literature stream, or a technical and vocational stream. Unlike other countries in the region, which use Arabic as the language of instruction in public schooling, throughout Lebanon secondary school is taught in either French or English. At the end of secondary school, students in the literary and scientific tracks sit for a final exam known as the Lebanese Baccalaureate (Baccalaureat Libanais). If students pass the Bac, they are permitted to enrol in any university that will accept them. Students in the technical and vocational stream sit for the Technical Baccalaureate and are able to enrol in various post-secondary programs. The final year of secondary school in Lebanon is considered the academic equivalent of the first year of an American or Canadian college or university, and so bachelor's degree programs are only three years long.

Unlike the centralized systems in much of the region, in Lebanon students typically apply to a certain program within a university. Admission is based on passing a subject-matter exam or general language exam. For example, admission to the LU requires both a Lebanese Baccalaureate and passing grades on four faculty-administered tests: Arabic, English and/or French, economics, and mathematics. This means that, while students in Lebanon have much more say than others over where and what they study, their options are still constrained by decisions made in their early years, mainly their secondary-school track and whether they studied in English or French at the secondary level.

Additionally, the options of students in Lebanon are highly constrained by their finances. When I asked one Lebanese university graduate how he chose his university, he stated simply, "Well, first off, I knew my budget." Administrators and professors confirmed that financial considerations are one of the primary factors determining students' access in Lebanon. As the system is highly privatized and few universities offer financial aid or scholarship programs, families' options are constrained by how much they can afford, although some university programs are flexible and allow students to work and study at the same time.

This market-based model, in which admissions decisions are made by institutions rather than a centralized agency, reflects the reality of Lebanon's weak state. It also means that Lebanese youth are less likely to direct blame for thwarted aspirations at the state than are youth in other countries. Reema, a young Lebanese woman who had studied media at the LU and subsequently found employment in teaching Arabic at a private centre, told me that if she could go back in time, she likely would have chosen to study a different subject. Rather than directing anger at the government, she placed most responsibility on the individual student to figure out what degrees were in demand, stating that "the student, here, has to think about what is demanded."

Essentially, in Lebanon, the absence of a strong government means that there is no clear target for anger or frustration: instead, there seems to be large-scale resignation. Lebanon's market-based admissions process reflects the lack of control that the Lebanese state has over the lives of its citizens. The state stakes no claim to the right to sort youth into future paths. What is striking about this absence of control over admissions in Lebanon is that it seems to signify a broken state rather than a strong commitment to market provision. There is certainly widespread frustration at the ineptitude of the state, but this is not targeted towards a specific person or regime. Reema explained: "Of course, people are frustrated at the government – there is no water, there is no electricity, because of the corruption of the state. We say the whole country is corrupt, politically. And yet, there are no protests. Here, people know nothing will change. Nothing will change. If you see, for example, someone unqualified get a job, you say, 'What can we do? This is Lebanon.' There is no solution. Your only solutions are, you can travel or you can shut up. There is no other solution."

This lack of faith carries over into the education system more broadly: the public primary and secondary education system enrols less than three in ten students because many families choose to pay costly tuitions to send their children to private schools instead. The privatized nature of higher education seems to reflect a divided state that cannot serve as a model of reform for other countries in the region.

Higher Education Admissions and State Legitimacy

Mazawi (2005) has argued that higher education in the Arab world is concerned with the "distribution of sociopolitical power" (p. 68). This chapter has detailed how admissions systems are a policy tool for the state to distribute power, and specifically that they have become institutionalized into broader social contracts, making them difficult to reform. In contrast to technical reforms that suggest creating better tests or devolving admissions decisions to university personnel, I argue that a preferable starting point for reforming admissions systems in the Arab world is to understand the deep and powerful constellations of interests and values that uphold the current systems. Each country's admissions system reflects the underlying logic of the state. In countries relying on high-stakes exit exams, the logic is meritocracy. Through its end-of-year exams, the public education system is imbued with the authority to assess students' knowledge and abilities and then sort the students into different life paths. Standardized exit exams largely determine who attends university, what programs they study, how much they pay, and what careers they can eventually enter, and therefore a good performance on tests is a highly legitimate way of securing the state's bounties for oneself and one's family.

Nonetheless, the legitimacy of exams rests on the perceptions that the state's educational bureaucracy is both effective and egalitarian. In reality, the logic of meritocracy is deeply undermined by inequality, privatization, and corruption. Wealthy families maintain access to a disproportionate number of seats in university because of their children's higher-quality secondary education and private tutoring. Within these systems, cheating or relying on connections to secure seats are among the ways in which youth are contesting the putative meritocracy of the state and thereby purchasing "better futures" (Cohen, 2004); this allows them to reclaim a sense of control in the face of the formalized and centralized authority of the state.

In countries where admissions systems are not based exclusively on exit exams, they reflect the role of the state in young people's lives. In Jordan, preferential treatment for East Bank Jordanians and loyal tribes is a form of political patronage. In the Arab Gulf states, the logic of capacity building for national citizens makes it difficult to ever justify *not* investing in supporting students in higher education. In contrast, Lebanon represents a distinct case where privatized admissions permit religious- and class-based sorting, and lack state control.

Despite institutionalized differences in admissions systems, the similarities across the region are noteworthy. First, it is clear that higher education admissions policies are not simply a technical or bureaucratic issue; admission to higher education is highly political and, frequently, politicized. Admissions policies reflect how the state grants, or does not grant, social status to various groups and how young people and their families are navigating these systems to secure opportunities for their future. Additionally, as macroeconomic conditions change, young people are left to navigate increasingly insecure pathways from formal education to the labour market (Shirazi, 2020). This means that the differential resources that young people have with which to navigate increasingly insecure pathways have become even more important. A growing body of research shows that the wealthy and well-connected are most likely to benefit from private tutoring, fee-paying parallel programs, private universities, and opportunities for foreign study. Many of these new privatized options for university also map onto the language of instruction; Hanafi and Arvanitis (2014) explain that in the Arab world, where foreign-language proficiency is used to connote cultural capital, language has become a "selection tool in the higher education system" (p. 728). Given the extent to which higher education admissions systems are woven into Arab societies, a better starting point for reforming admissions systems in the Arab world would be to recognize them as arenas of status competition that serve to maintain a highly unequal status quo.

3

The Question of Quality

The quality of higher education throughout the Middle East and North Africa is characterized by the rhetoric of an all-consuming crisis (Boutieri, 2016; Waterbury, 2020). Technical experts, academics, and policymakers largely agree that higher education, like the primary and secondary schooling before it, suffers from low quality (Badran, Baydoun, & Hillman, 2019). This low quality is blamed for the region's high unemployment rates and weak economic growth (World Bank, 2008b). Concerns over low quality take on heightened significance when framed in terms of the knowledge economy, in which quality is linked to economic growth and development. In response, Arab governments have enacted ambitious reform initiatives to improve quality.

This chapter deconstructs the narrative of low quality that dominates current thinking about higher education development in the region and examines countries' approaches to improving quality. It argues that large-scale quality-assurance reforms are state projects aimed at securing legitimacy from sceptical publics at home and abroad. At the same time, because it can be delegitimizing for Arab states to acknowledge that their public higher education systems are failing, large-scale quality-assurance reforms demand significant political will. For low- and middle-income countries in the region, quality assurance is tied to major government-led reforms and supported financially by the WB, which has the dual benefit of securing finances and signalling state investment in quality. In North Africa, ministries have restructured degrees to mirror those in Europe. Meanwhile, in wealthy Arab Gulf states, quality assurance is not resource generating; rather, foreign consultants and think-tanks seek to align Gulf systems to best practices in the United States and the United Kingdom. Despite their differences throughout the region, the approaches to quality all look to external, foreign, or international models as blueprints for success. This implicit encoding of high quality as "foreign" often sidesteps national policy processes, disregards local perspectives on quality, and ignores the interests of affected stakeholders.

Moreover, despite their efforts, quality-assurance reforms seem to have had a limited impact on teaching and learning in classrooms and in many cases have become subject to politicization. I argue that technical reforms that seek to assure a high quality miss two fundamental points, one socio-political and one educational. First, overly technical approaches ignore the social and political purposes of higher education as a marker of status and a positional good. As the primary state-legitimized product of a university, the degree promises employment and social status. As a result, even seemingly technical issues, such as how to define and measure quality, are embedded within a broader web of a socio-political power over the meaning and power of a university credential and over who should have access to that power.

Second, the technical approach to quality, which implies that the degree of quality can be distilled into measurable and quantifiable indicators, overlooks the fact that teaching and learning are relational: students learn in relation to one another, their professors, the ideas of those who have come before, and also to their selves, past and future. Numeric indicators, including class size and library volumes, are hardly a proxy for the quality of these relationships. My own teaching and fieldwork in the region have continuously impressed upon me the reality that professors in the region are as intelligent, creative, and hard working as professors anywhere in the world. In their nations they are teaching the best and brightest students: hard-working, creative young people who are striving to build better futures for themselves, their families, and their societies amidst major constraints. Perhaps a new approach to improving quality would start with centring the relational aspect of teaching and learning and looking for forms of "everyday excellence" that already exist throughout the region, despite being undermined by the pervasive crisis rhetoric.

The Global Race for High Quality

The so-called quality crisis in Arab higher education must be understood within a global emphasis on educational quality that positions higher education as crucial to economic competitiveness in a global knowledge economy. In the era of globalization, nation states are portrayed as competing with one another for scarce resources, including human resources in the form of skilled labour or "talent" (Brown & Tannock, 2009). Scholars have called this discursive shift, emblematic of neoliberalism, as a shift from the "welfare state" to the "competition state" (Levi-Faur, 2005). The need to improve quality has been mapped onto diverse policy agendas and used to initiate large-scale reforms to educational systems, including curricular reform, program structure, and pedagogical practices.

In 1998, UNESCO convened over 180 countries for the first global conference on higher education, called the World Conference on Higher Education in the Twenty-First Century. Supporting high-quality higher education signals a desire and a willingness to participate in the knowledge economy and to ensure that countries are competitive economically in this new global era (Stromquist, 2002). These commitments made at the world conference were reaffirmed at an annual meeting of the Arab League Educational, Cultural and Scientific Organization in 2001, where governments committed to supporting quality assurance through the creation of new regulatory offices (Arafeh, 2010).

Despite the consensus on the need for high quality, definitions of *quality* are surprisingly rare. UNESCO has defined *quality* as a "multidimensional concept" that must encompass "all functions and activities" of higher education including "teaching and academic programmes, research and scholarship, staffing, students, buildings, facilities, equipment, services to the community and the academic environment" (UNESCO, 1998, p. 26). What this comprehensive definition means in practice for the university, professors, or students is unclear. Moreover, while an underlying assumption is that quality refers to the quality of student learning, in much of the development literature it tends to be measured in ways that are far removed from students' lives, including numerical indicators of student-faculty ratios, faculty publications, and employment outcomes. Yet, it is these same indicators that are used to decry the state of quality in Arab higher education.

The Crisis

For the past three decades the quality of higher education in the Middle East and North Africa region has been decried in local media and international reports. A 2011 report by the Brookings Institution titled *Higher Education in the Arab World* states: "Despite more than a decade of dramatic expansion – in enrolment, female participation, numbers of institutions, and programs – higher education in the Arab world continues to fall far short of the needs of students, employers, and society at large" (Wilkens & Masri, 2011, p. iii). The assumption of failure is pervasive. In their foreword to one of the most comprehensive books on young people's lives in the region, *Generation in*

Waiting, Dr. Anwar Mohammed Gargash, the minister of foreign affairs for the United Arab Emirates, and James Wolfensohn, a former WB president, write that "the quality of education in the region is often low, leaving young people unprepared to compete in the global economy" (Dhillon & Yousef, 2011, p. ix).

This rhetoric is not new. Since the 1980s, Arab academics and officials have worried about declining quality, particularly in the region's middle-income countries, largely due to overcrowding of public universities (Kohstall, 2012). In 2002 the United Nations Development Programme (UNDP) wrote its first regional report on the state of human development in the Arab states, *Arab Human Development Report: Creating Opportunities for Future Generations*. While lauding the substantial expansion in access at all levels of education, the report declared that poor quality was "the Achilles heel of education in the Arab world, a flaw that undermines its quantitative achievements" (UNDP, 2002, p. 54). The report makes a clear link between the low quality of education and the high rates of unemployment in Arab societies: "Problems of quality and relevance have led to a significant mismatch between the labor market and development needs on the one hand and the output of education systems on the other ... The prevalence of unemployment among the educated and the deterioration in real wages for the majority of them exemplify this problem" (p. 54). The report states that there is a "crisis in human development in the Arab region," and in particular there is a "crisis in education" (p. 54), later referred to as "the education crisis" (p. 56). In the 180-page report, the word *crisis* is used five times – three times in the three pages dedicated to education, compared to only once with reference to technology and once with reference to political systems.

Since the release of the first *Arab Human Development Report* in 2002, five additional *AHDRs* have been published, each focusing on a key issue affecting human development: knowledge (2003), freedom (2004), women and gender (2005), security (2009), and, most recently, youth (2016) (UNDP, 2003, 2004, 2005, 2009, 2016). The reports, which have become highly influential and characterize what Sukarieh (2017) calls a "regime" that constitutes a legitimized source of knowledge about the region, have shaped approaches to development among Western donors and governments (p. 72). Over the past two decades the *AHDRs* have consistently emphasized the idea that the region suffers from low-quality higher education (Bayat, 2005). For example, the 2005 *Arab Human Development Report* cites the "lack of knowledge capital as the main long-term problem faced by the Arab world and calls declining quality the most important challenge faced by Arab education" (Gonzalez, Karoly, Constant, Salem, & Goldman, 2008, p. 2).

More recently, the 2016 *AHDR* focuses specifically on the challenges that young people face. Yet, there is surprisingly little new analysis of higher education. In the introductory material the first mention of the word *education* narrowly frames the purpose of education within the context of work, stating that many Arab youth "continue to receive an education which does not reflect the needs of labour markets" (UNDP 2016, p. 5). Similarly, the report's chapter on education, titled "Education and the Transition to Work," implicitly defines the social role of education as its link to employment. Despite bringing new attention to inequalities, the majority of the chapter is actually focused on employment, including job creation, school-to-work transitions, and labour market policies. The authors state that "quality" can be conceptualized as "educational achievement" and be measured by scores on standardized international assessments. Yet the chapter does not discuss what quality looks like in higher education, where there are no standardized international assessments. Instead, it repeats an oft-stated, rarely supported claim that "Arab countries suffer from under-enrolment in scientific disciplines among secondary and tertiary students and a continued reliance on outdated pedagogical techniques such as rote memorization" (p. 74).

The UNDP is not alone in making critiques of quality. In 2013 a report on Arab knowledge economies, published by the Center for Mediterranean Integration at the WB, reiterated the same idea, stating that "the relationship between education and economic growth has remained weak, the divide between education and employment has not been bridged, and the quality of education continues to be disappointing" (CMI, 2013, p. 47). In an interview on how the Arab world should respond to the Arab Spring, WB senior education specialist Adriana Jaramillo stated that universities in the region must "equip young people with the sort of skills relevant to today's labor markets" (World Bank, 2011). In short, there is a clear consensus in the development literature that higher education suffers from low quality and is largely responsible for poor labour market outcomes in the region.

Many scholars have critiqued the premises and arguments made in the various iterations of the *Arab Human Development Report* and related publications that frame youth integration as a social problem (Abu-Lughod, 2009; Adely, 2009; Hasso, 2009; Jad, 2009; Mazawi, 2009; Sukarieh, 2017). Major critiques state that the *AHDRs* essentialize Arab culture as static and inherently patriarchal (Abu-Lughod, 2009; Lavergne, 2004) and that women are portrayed as passive and oppressed (Abu-Lughod, 2009; Adely, 2009; Adely, Haddad, et al, 2019). Hasso (2009) deconstructs how the 2005 *AHDR* operates within a state-led development paradigm (advocated by the UNDP) that seeks to strengthen governments and elites at the expense of broader constituencies, including the marginalized and activists. These scholars' close readings of the *AHDRs* are important contributions to debates on the ways in which powerful agencies advance particular narratives about human development, and they remind us not to accept sweeping generalization uncritically. In the next section I build on the tradition of close reading to unpack the varied lines of argument that frame the discussion of the "quality crisis" in the development literature.

The Technical Approach to Quality

The widespread consensus that higher education in the Arab world suffers from low quality brings together a number of lines of argument that link low student learning to dire economic conditions. It contends first that the offerings and outputs of the higher education system are poor, and second, that due in part to the low-quality output, there is a mismatch between the needs of the labour market and the skills of graduates (Adely, Mitra, Mohamed, & Shaham, 2021; Assaad, Krafft, & Salehi-Isfahani, 2018). Third, it suggests that this mismatch is to be blamed for sluggish economic growth and high rates of unemployment in the region.

On the first point, the technical literature suggests that students are not actually learning very much in university due to poor-quality inputs and a lack of incentives for learning. Commonly criticized are the large class sizes, deteriorating facilities, and overly theoretical or outdated programs of study. Faculties are also roundly criticized for having outdated teaching methods that rely on rote memorization and that do not require students to be creative producers of knowledge or analytical thinkers.

These critiques of large class sizes and deteriorating facilities are not unfounded. Throughout North Africa, universities are like mid-sized cities, with campuses that were built in the middle of the twentieth century for fewer and more elite students. Public universities in Fez and Marrakech enrol upwards of 60,000 students, and Cairo University has over 100,000 students. It is not uncommon to hear stories of students attending lectures with standing room only and an inability to hear professors from the back of the room. This large number of students inflates student-teacher ratios. For example, in interviews that I conducted with faculty members in 2013, I was told that in an English department with 5,000 students in Fez there were only 26 full-time professors, which translates into a student-faculty ratio of 192 students per faculty member.

This does not mean, however, that such large classes are necessarily the norm. In the semester during which I taught at Mohammed V University in Morocco, my two classes held from thirty to forty students, roughly the same number that I taught in a master's program at Columbia University. In the dozens of classes that I observed at universities in the UAE, Lebanon, Morocco, and Jordan, they had roughly twenty to thirty students. Meanwhile, we know that class sizes in introductory classes around the world, including in the United States and Canada, can reach one thousand. Small class sizes alone cannot be equated with a high level of quality, particularly in higher education, where much of the onus for learning is placed on students' independent study. In fact, in the field of higher education, scholars recognize that while neither faculty members nor students enjoy large classes, there are diverse ways of learning, and student learning depends significantly on subject matter and pedagogical style – meaning that large class sizes alone must not be equated with a lack of learning.

Moreover, claims of low quality are rarely substantiated with either evidence or nuance. Figure 3.1 shows the average number of students per faculty member in each world region, using data from the World Development Indicators. To calculate the regional averages, I took the average of country ratios, using the latest year of data available for each country. The ratio in the Middle East and North Africa, with a regional average of 20.9, is higher than in many regions, but not out of line with the global average, and substantially below averages found in sub-Saharan Africa and Southeast Asia.

Blame for low levels of learning is also placed on students' choice of concentrations or fields of study. The major critique is that their concentrations are in the humanities and social sciences, rather than in the scientific and technical fields that are considered imperative for knowledge economies. In its 2008 report the WB explained that one of its measures of quality was the proportion of all university students majoring in science, technology, engineering, and mathematics (STEM); its underlying assumption was that "scientists and engineers are likely to contribute more to economic growth than are social scientists and students of humanity because of the increasing importance of technological innovation and adaptation in the development process" (World Bank, 2008b, p. 20). To support this claim, the authors cite one study from 1991 – seventeen years before their study was published and well before the global spread of the personal computer, internet, and mobile technology. The assumption that the sciences as a concentration are a measure of quality is nonetheless widely accepted in the region. In a study of higher education finance in Jordan, Taher Kanaan, a former

Degrees of Dignity

Figure 3.1. Average Student-Teacher Ratio in Tertiary Education, by Region

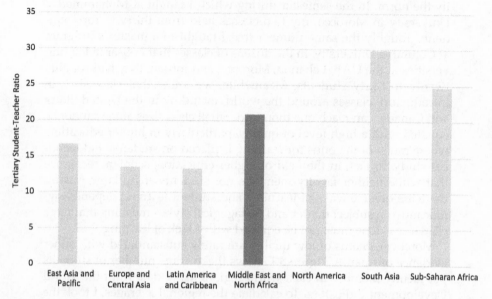

Note: Data accessed through the WB Open Data module for Stata. Indicator SE.TER.
ENRL.TC.ZS (Azevedo, 2011).

minister of higher education in that country, stated: "The proportion
of university students enrolled in science and engineering compared to
humanities and social sciences could be viewed as an index of the quality of human capital at the higher education level" (Kanaan, Salamat, &
Hanania, 2011, p. 40).

In fact, the claim that too many students in the Middle East and
North Africa are majoring in the social sciences and too few are
majoring in science, engineering, and other technical fields is belied
by cross-national evidence. Figure 3.2 shows the regional mean of the
percentage of students majoring in either STEM fields or in the social
sciences, arts, and humanities, using data from the World Development
Indicators on graduates' concentrations. The WDI include data on the
percentage of all tertiary students graduating from various programs,
such as the social sciences, natural sciences, and arts and humanities,
as well as engineering, education, and agriculture. To create this figure,
I grouped arts and humanities graduates with social sciences, journalism, and information into one category and grouped graduates in

Figure 3.2. Higher Education Graduates as a Percentage of the Total, by Field and Region

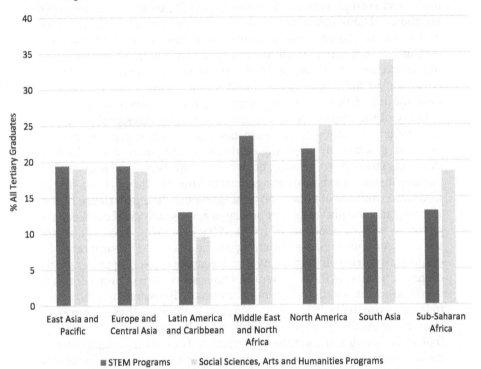

■ STEM Programs   ▨ Social Sciences, Arts and Humanities Programs

Source: Data accessed through the WB Open Data module for Stata. Indicators SE.TER.GRAD.SS.ZS; E.TER.GRAD.SC.ZS; SE.TER.GRAD.EN.ZS; SE.TER.GRAD. HU.ZS (Azevedo, 2011)

natural sciences, mathematics, and statistics with those in engineering, manufacturing, and construction to create a STEM category. These two indicators do not equal 100 per cent because they do not account for all tertiary programs, such as education. To calculate the regional averages, I took an unweighted average of all the country percentages in the region, using the latest year of data available.

The figure shows that countries in the Middle East and North Africa have the highest proportions of students graduating with STEM degrees of any world region, at 23.5 per cent, and which closely mirrors the percentage in North America (21.6).

Moreover, there is very little research to support the idea that Arab economies would benefit from having more STEM graduates. Recent economic research has argued that social sciences and humanities education may be one of the factors driving the growth of creative economies and entrepreneurialism in the United States and other advanced economies (Hanushek & Woessmann, 2015). The link between education and economic growth is not a simple equation – more STEM graduates certainly do not equate to more employed youth or more rapidly growing economies. And yet, much of the technical literature on higher education in the region makes blanket statements about the region's need for more STEM graduates, with very little empirical support.

Many of the greatest criticisms are directed at professors' pedagogy. The didactic pedagogies common throughout the region are decried as out of date and ill-preparing students for the labour market, which demands students to be analytical, critical thinkers. Waterbury (2020) phrases this as "a massive pedagogical failure" (p. 4) and cites a former Jordanian minister of education as singling out "the prevalence of rote learning and the uncritical acceptance of text, which yield obedience to power as well as intolerance" (p. 4). What is striking, however, is that the claims about outdated teaching methods are rarely supported by empirical evidence. In fact, in my many years of observing professors in higher education in the Arab world, I have seen a broad range of teaching styles, from small and intimate seminar discussions to instruction in large lecture halls. What I have not seen is evidence that teaching and learning in Arab classrooms is fundamentally different or worse than that in classrooms around the world, aside from their generally fewer resources. Moreover, it is worth remembering that concerns over faculty pedagogy are common around the world, and academic powerhouses, including China and France, have long relied on rote memorization in universities, without being subject to similar narratives of crisis.

Assessments of the outputs of the education system fare even worse. Outputs are typically measured through performance on international exams at the lower levels of education, and through the global rankings of universities at the level of higher education. A 2009 article by the *Economist* is indicative of the general thinking that Arab universities are falling behind those of other regions, stating: "A listing of the world's top 500 universities, compiled annually by Shanghai Jiao Tong University, includes three South African and six Israeli universities, but not a single Arab one" ("Laggards," 2009). A 2016 Brookings blog post echoes this sentiment, stating: "Only two or three Arab universities are in the list of the top 500 universities in the world (and none are in the top 200)" (Devarajan, 2016). It is worth pointing out that several universities in the Arab world – including King Saud University (Saudi Arabia), King Fahd University of Petroleum and Minerals and Cairo University

(Egypt), and the American University of Beirut (Lebanon) – now rank in the top five hundred. These international rankings are widely criticized in the academic literature on higher education because of their arbitrary indicators such as the number of Nobel Prize winners or the percentage of international students; yet, they often pass as strong evidence in development reports (Marginson & Van der Wende, 2007).

The region's poor quality of higher education is subsequently linked to the high rates of unemployment, which is portrayed as the real crisis because young unemployed youth, particularly men, are viewed as a security threat to many states. The 2002 *AHDR* refers to unemployment as the "scourge of joblessness, which afflicts Arab countries as a group more seriously than any other developing region" (p. iii). Similarly, a 2011 report by the WB points out that "youth unemployment rates in MENA (21 percent in the Middle East and 25 percent in North Africa) are higher than in any other region in the world. Young women and new educated entrants in the labor market are disproportionately unemployed" (Jaramillo & Melonio, 2011, p. 3).

International development organizations suggest that these high rates of unemployment are the result of a "mismatch" between the real needs of the labour market and the outputs of the education system, largely due to misaligned incentives. In its 2008 flagship report on education in the Middle East and North Africa, *The Road Not Traveled*, the WB criticizes the fact that demand for higher education is inflated by employment guarantees in the public sector, while demand for technical education is too low, stating: "The combination of free education at the secondary and higher levels and a policy of guaranteed employment in the public sector has had negative side effects: a demand for higher education that does not correspond to real economic needs" (World Bank, 2008b, p. 14). Michael Rutkowski, sector director for human development in the WB's Middle East and North Africa region, explained that "there are no proper signals sent to higher education establishments in terms of which skills are in demand, and which skills are not in demand," and, as a result, "what we see in the region is that those who graduate from universities cannot find jobs" (World Bank, 2008a). In response, development experts suggest that governments align majors with what is in demand by the economy, and they call for data on employment figures by college major in order to inform students and parents better (Wilkens & Masri, 2011), an irony given that many students have little choice over what they study.

The technical literature summarized here paints a linear if simplistic equation between low quality and misaligned incentives in higher education, and high rates of unemployment and stagnant economic growth in the labour market. This equation is rooted in human capital theory, which views the primary purpose of higher education as skill development for the labour market. Human capital theory assumes that formal education enhances young people's skills, thereby making them more productive workers, and ultimately leads to higher wages and economic growth. The logic is clear: employment is the ultimate outcome of the higher education system, and, as such, high rates of unemployment are a sign of a failing education system – and one in need of reform.

Quality Assurance as Solution

Given the all-consuming crisis rhetoric, governments and higher education institutions across the region have identified the improvement of quality as a policy priority. There is never an easy solution to such systemic "problems," however. Waterbury (2020) has called this a "trilemma," whereby the public policy options available to leaders involve a trade-off between quantity, quality, and costs. It is worth noting that a significant increase in government spending on higher education is rarely mentioned as a reasonable policy option. Instead, the most common approach to improving quality across the region has been the creation of new regulatory bodies – quality assurance agencies – that promise external accountability and oversight. Implicit in this "solution" to the problem of low quality is the assumption that universities, administrators, and faculty members cannot be trusted to maintain a high level of quality on their own. Rather, accountability for improving quality is shifted to independent agencies and councils.

The efforts to improve quality through accountability-enhancing initiatives are supported by the major players in global development. In 2007 the Arab Network for Quality Assurance in Higher Education (ANQAHE) was founded as an independent, non-profit organization to improve the capacity for quality assurance in higher education throughout the region. The network is supported by the Global Initiative for Quality Assurance Capacity and funded by the WB and UNESCO. In a study conducted in 2012 the ANQAHE found that twelve countries in the region had independent quality assurance agencies, while another ten, including Lebanon, Tunisia, Syria, and Qatar, did not have independent agencies. In these countries quality assurance tended to be vested in various departments of the Ministry of Higher Education or its equivalent. Nonetheless, the ANQAHE equates the absence of an independent agency with a lack of seriousness about quality. The report stated that the fact that almost half of the countries in the region did not have an independent quality assurance agency was a "rough indication of the reluctance of some countries to tackle the endemic problem of higher education quality" (ANQAHE, 2012, p. 22). In fact, studies have argued that Lebanon, Tunisia, and Qatar have among the best higher education systems in the region (el-Araby, 2011), suggesting that the link between "high quality" and "quality assurance" is not so simple.

The Role of the World Bank

In the context of the quality crisis, Arab governments have often initiated large-scale reforms to their higher education systems. Educational reform is typically understood as a deliberate, planned effort to improve education and is most often initiated to correct perceived broader social problems (Tyack & Cuban, 1995). Though framed as a singular and time-bound event, "reform" has actually become so pervasive that many argue that it has become the norm in most educational systems. A key insight from decades of global educational reform is that defining and labelling social ills, often resorting to the rhetoric of national crisis, helps to grease the wheels of reform (Sahlberg, 2016). In examining the rhetoric around higher education reform in Morocco and Egypt, Kohstall (2012) finds a similar process in the Arab world. He argues that the all-consuming crisis rhetoric has been used to justify reform, typically in the direction of neoliberal policies, such as raising tuition or expanding privatization. He contends that "the production of a narrative on the crisis of higher education could be considered as the precondition for its reform. In reality, it is an ongoing process that is recycled each time when crucial reform steps are undertaken" (p. 100).

A common approach adopted by middle-income countries has been the convening of higher education leaders and politicians for national conversations about quality enhancement, with the goal of generating a "national consensus" about higher education reform. In 1998, Egypt's higher education minister set up a National Committee for the Enhancement of University and Higher Education. In a similar drive for reform, Morocco's King Hassan II launched the Special Commission for Education and Training in 1999 to debate reform options. The commission was carefully crafted to forge a political consensus, with every political party that was represented in parliament sending at least one member to the commission. Through this process, a national educational reform agenda was developed in 1999, called the National Charter for Education and Training (Charte nationale d'éducation et de formation), and key components of the charter were developed into legislation and passed into law by the Moroccan parliament in 2000.

That said, Kohstall (2012) explains that despite the seeming consensus around reform, it was not clear how reforms would be translated into policy. Moreover, despite the seeming will for reform, in practice the implementation stalled.

I was living in Morocco when King Mohammed VI made an impassioned speech on public education to the nation on 20 August 2013, the sixtieth anniversary of Morocco's "Revolution of the King and the People," in which the French protectorate's authorities deposed the then sultan, Mohammed V, an act that is viewed today as having ultimately strengthening the nationalist independence movement. The king skilfully compared the country's revolution against colonization to today's revolution for human development and social and economic progress. He pointed out that he himself was a graduate of the public-school system and the Law School of Mohammed V University in Rabat, and yet he stated in no uncertain terms that he was "indeed sad to note that the state of education is worse now than it was twenty years ago." He also used the platform as an opportunity to blame the prime minister and the opposition party for their failure to enact reforms ("Full speech," 2013).

When government-initiated reforms stalled in Egypt and Morocco, development agencies played a critical role in helping governments secure the political will to enact reform. Kohstall (2012) explains that "in both cases international development agencies had a crucial impact" (p. 97). There is no reason to think that Arab governments uniformly resisted; in fact, development agencies promised additional resources that could facilitate the passage of desired reform. By aligning reform models to external best practices and expertise, Arab governments were also able to signal their seriousness about reform to sceptical publics.

As a result, quality assurance reforms are typically accompanied by funding and technical expertise from the WB. Large-scale reform in the name of improving quality has occurred in many of the middle-income countries in the region, including Egypt, Jordan, Morocco, and Tunisia. In North Africa, quality assurance for the knowledge economy has occurred in parallel with the restructuring of higher education to mirror the European reforms known as the Bologna Process. The outsized role of development agencies, however, also means that approaches to quality have been dominated by technical approaches and human capital theory. Suggested reforms followed generic models of quality assurance in international development, including the formation of an independent agency to oversee quality assurance processes and the systematic review of educational programs to meet minimum standards. In this model, quality assurance is treated as a primarily technical issue rather than one of resources or politics. In fact, the technical understanding of quality seems to dominate discourses of reform, even when it is accompanied by significant changes in university governance, including reform that transfers power away from institutions or administrators to independent agencies.

Since the late 1990s the WB has funded numerous higher education reform projects that are focused on improving quality throughout the middle-income countries in the region, often resulting in the creation of new quality assurance agencies accompanied by a host of other reforms. Table 3.1 shows the varied higher education projects funded by the WB over the past two decades.

In 1996 Jordan's Council for Higher Education was established to oversee quality assurance and accreditation. At the time, however, the council's work was limited to the accreditation of private universities; it did not regulate quality or have jurisdiction over public universities (Sabri, 2011). In 2000 the WB funded the Jordan Higher Education Development project for roughly USD 35 million, and a subsequent project, Higher Education Reform for the Knowledge Economy, for USD 25 million in 2009. Combined, these projects created new structures to manage levels of quality in higher education. In 2007 Jordan established an independent Higher Education Accreditation Commission, which for the first time set the same guidelines, criteria, and accreditation for both public and private universities. Subsequently, in 2012, the government passed a higher education law that defined clear standards of quality, such as maximum student-faculty ratios, campus size, and resources.

Egypt's reforms were also supported by the WB. The process began with the adoption of a WB credit line and committed to a series of six projects, monitored by a project management unit that included not only Egyptians but also representatives of international donors (Kohstall, 2012). The first of these projects, the Higher Education Enhancement Project, was launched in 2002 with USD $50 million and established the Higher Education Enhancement Project Fund to provide small grants to university faculties so that they could design new programs or reorganize university administration. These grants, while popular with some primarily young and foreign-educated faculty members, benefited science and technical faculties more than the arts and sciences. Moreover, they were "a drop in the ocean" and left the faculties of Commerce, Law, and Literature "largely untouched," despite the fact that they enrolled upwards of 70 per cent of students (Kohstall, 2012, p. 104).

The second WB project was significantly more controversial: it involved establishing the NAQAAE as an independent governmental body to oversee and regulate universities. The proposed law sought

Table 3.1. World Bank Projects in Higher Education

Country	Year	Project title	USD millions
Egypt	1989	Engineering and Technical Education Project	31
	2002	Higher Education Enhancement Project	50
Jordan	2000	Jordan Higher Education Development	35
	2009	Higher Education Reform for the Knowledge Economy	25
Lebanon	1998	Vocational and Technical Education Project	63
Morocco	2010	First Education Development Policy Loan	60
	2012	First Skills and Employment Development Policy Loan	100
	2013	Second Education Development Policy Loan	100
	2014	Second Skills and Employment Development Policy Loan	100
Tunisia	1989	Education and Training Sector Loan	95
	1992	Higher Education Restructuring Project	75
	1998	Higher Education Reform Support	80
	2000	Education Quality Improvement Program	99
	2006	Second Higher Education Reform Support	76
	2016	Tunisia Tertiary Education for Employability Project	70

Source: World Bank (2021)

to externalize authority away from self-governance, while also ignoring the financial and structural inequalities between institutions that explained the differences in quality. The new law stoked the 9th of March, a movement of professors and academics working to defend the autonomy of the university (Farag, 2010; Kohstall, 2012). The 9th of March movement presented an alternative draft law on accreditation that called for wider participation. Eventually the NAQAAE was established by a presidential decree in 2007 and now operates as an independent body that reports directly to the Egyptian president, prime minister, and parliament. Kohstall (2012) argues that the intense political battles over the establishment of the NAQAAE were in part because the reforms were initiated from the outside, largely disregarding the autonomy of the university, and in part because it would disrupt the status quo; Kohstall stated that much of the resistance came from "those defending their privileges" in the current system (p. 105).

The case of Lebanon stands out as an instructive outlier. In Lebanon, quality assurance has proved to be highly political, with politicians being unwilling to commit to a fully independent regulatory body. For almost a decade, experts have been calling for an independent national higher-education quality-assurance body (Hasrouny, 2011). A law was drafted in 2012 to create an autonomous national quality assurance agency for Higher Education. Lebanese higher education experts, including professors and the Lebanese Association for Educational Studies, played a large role in drafting the law and insisted on the full independence of the agency. Politicians at the highest levels of government, however, wanted the agency to be housed within the ministry itself, which reform experts predicted would undermine the legitimacy and independence of the agency. For years the law has remained unsigned, however, exemplifying the stagnation that occurs when the government does not have the political will to enact change.

In April 2019 Lebanon introduced a draft reform that would cut public-sector salaries, including those of professors at LU, the country's largest and only public university. The proposed reforms are part of the government's attempt to secure a loan of USD 11 billion from the IMF for broader economic reforms focused on infrastructure and economic growth; however, they entail significant cuts to public spending. On 6 May 2019, professors at LU began a general strike and protests at Parliament to resist further cuts to the university. As the most affordable institution, the LU plays an important role in the country. Unlike private institutions where tuition is upward of USD 7,000 a year, the LU charges registration fees of USD 500 for Lebanese nationals and USD 1,000 for non-Lebanese, including Syrian refugees. Professors argue that strikes are necessary to protect the quality of higher education in Lebanon. Systematic funding cuts have reduced the university budget to USD 250 million. There is a great irony in the fact that the IMF, sister agency to the WB, is encouraging across-the-board cuts to public-sector institutions, while the WB and other development agencies continue to support investments in higher education for a knowledge economy.

Europeanization in North Africa

The WB played an influential role in supporting quality assurance in North Africa when countries throughout the region decided to undertake major structural reforms to align their higher education systems with those in Europe. In 1999, countries in Europe committed to aligning and harmonizing their higher education credentials to allow for intra-Europe mobility in both education and employment. In France this entailed changing its credentials to a three-year licence (bachelor's degree), a two-year master's degree, and three-year doctorate, known as the *licence-master-doctorat* (LMD) system. In addition, the new degrees are based on the model of credits, with a bachelor's degree requiring 180 credits and a master's degree awarded after another 120 credits. Shortly thereafter, countries throughout North Africa made political commitments to restructure their higher education systems similarly in order to harmonize degrees as part of a broader Euro-Mediterranean higher education area. These reforms institutionalized a new structure of a three-year bachelor's degree and were coupled with other curricular changes, including the introduction of professionally oriented master's degrees and continuous assessment. The shift from a four-year bachelor's degree to a three-year bachelor's degree was a significant change, as it reduced the time required to complete a degree, but it also removed what many saw as a critical fourth year of learning for undergraduate students.

In Tunisia a major higher education reform to align to the Bologna Process began in 2005 and constituted one of the largest reforms since the county's independence. In 2006 the Tunisian government initiated a higher education reform called the Programme de Developpement de l'Enseignement Supérieur et d'Appui à la Qualité (Higher Education and Quality Support Development Program), which was framed as supporting the country's knowledge economy aspirations by improving graduates' learning outcomes. It had an added benefit of aligning Tunisian credentials to the LMD system used in Europe. A new law gave all universities the opportunity to restructure their degree programs in line with the LMD system within three years, and all had done so by 2006 (World Bank, 2015).

The idea of quality assurance, a core component of Europe's LMD reforms, was also introduced and supported by international donors including the WB and the European Union. Between 2006 and 2014 the WB provided a loan of USD 76 million to support Tunisia's reforms through a project called the Second Higher Education Reform Support Project, which followed two prior loans made in the 1990s (World Bank, 2015). The WB project funded the construction of four new higher education institutions, created a funding mechanism known as the Quality Promotion Fund to provide competitive block grants to universities, and, importantly, created a comprehensive quality assurance system for the higher education system. Specifically, WB investments were targeted to "develop a quality assurance and accreditation system" and to "develop financing mechanisms that provide higher education institutions with incentives to improve their quality and performance" (World Bank, 2015, p. 2).

Prior to this, oversight for quality in Tunisia had been managed by the Comité National d'Evaluation (National Committee for Evaluation), which was created in 1995 to carry out internal evaluations of Tunisian higher education institutions. In 2008 a new law was adopted to refine concepts and practices associated with quality, including the creation of a national body for evaluation, quality assurance, and accreditation. The law established an independent quality assurance agency, known as the National Institution for Evaluation, Quality Assurance and Accreditation (IEAQA), that would be responsible for external review and accreditation of both public- and private-sector universities. In practice, implementation was slow. It was not until a 2012 decree that the agency was effectively established, and not until 2015 that it began actual evaluations of Tunisian universities.

The WB has continued to support Tunisia in its higher education reforms. In 2016 it approved an additional USD 70 million for higher education. The press release announcing the new funding stated that the project sought to "address the high levels of unemployment among university graduates in Tunisia" through "ongoing reforms to improve the management of universities and the quality of teaching, and to ensure that students are graduating with the skills demanded by the labor market" (World Bank, 2016).

The case of Morocco has followed a similar path, mirroring Tunisia in both its fast adoption of the LMD system and its slow implementation of independent quality assurance. In Morocco, major higher education reform had been on the agenda since the mid-1990s with the creation of the Special Commission for Education and Training, discussed earlier, and was identified as a key priority under the late King Hassan II. The principle of quality assurance was included as part of the major reform package passed in 2000. Specifically, the Higher Education Organization Act (Law 01-00) required that courses in public and private institutions be accredited and evaluated. In addition, it stated that an official body must be created to assess and regulate the higher education system. Two new national bodies were established: the National Coordination Committee for Higher Education and the Coordinating Committee for Private Higher Education, which were founded in 2003 and 2005, respectively, to license new public and private universities. As part of the same reforms, a fifteen-member National Accreditation and Evaluation Committee was also created to accredit programs, including all new master's degree and doctoral programs. That said, unlike the independent quality assurance agencies that represent best practice supported by development agencies, the three committees were essentially consultative and composed of members who were, for the most part, appointed academics. Their responsibilities were limited largely to delivering opinions on policy matters.

In contrast, the LMD reforms were not officially part of the 2000 reforms. Benchenna (2009) explains that neither the national charter, carefully constructed to appear to be a national political consensus, nor the actual law passed in 2000 includes a "single explicit mention of the LMD architecture" (p. 124). Instead, the LMD system came from outside the country and was adopted even before it was legally decreed. In 2002, at a meeting of France's Council of University Presidents and Morocco's university presidents, the French advocated for the LMD system, and by January 2003, Moroccan university presidents had adopted it during a national educational conference. Less than a year later, in the 2003–4 academic year, universities began introducing the first bachelor's degree programs under the new system. Among Moroccan university stake-holders, the reform was viewed as imposed on them. In their research with Moroccan academics, Ergül, Coşar, and Mous (2017) quote a pro-fessor who explained that the government "brought the reform, put it on the table and said 'take it or leave it'" (p. 162).

It was not until June 2004, however, that the government issued a decree making the LMD system official. Kohstall (2012) stated that Europe's "international model acted like a 'magic wand' for a reform that remained for a long time under debate" (p. 105). While the reforms were justified in the name of improving the quality of learning and the employability of graduates, in reality the reforms were primarily the result of French influence in North Africa (Benchenna, 2009). Kohstall (2012) explained that, "with the LMD reform on the way in Europe, France reactivated its old role as an exporter of ideas and cultural poli-cies towards the Maghreb and francophone Africa" (p. 106).

By 2008, the government was convinced that the broader 2000 reforms had stalled. They initiated the Education Emergency Program (Plan d'Urgence) to help meet the goals of the 2000 charter, which was supported by two large WB loans, in the amounts of USD 60 million for the first Education Development Policy Loan in 2010 and an additional USD 100 million for a second Education Development Policy Loan in 2013. While both focused primarily on improving access to lower secondary schools, two additional loans, the Skills and Employment Development Policy Loans of 2012 and 2014, both directed funding to higher education to address the issue of employability. Much of the funding focused on expanding access to vocational training, and uni-versity funding was tied to performance on key indicators (Jaramillo & Melonio, 2011; Waterbury, 2020).

Building on the 2009–12 reforms, the Ministry of Higher Education initiated an action plan for 2013–16 including a number of projects focused on higher education. This action plan specifically included "the development of a quality assurance system" as a key objective and also called for the implementation of other projects such as the construction of new higher education institutions. The WB specifically supported the creation of an independent quality assurance agency, and a decree was issued in 2014 to formally establish the National Agency for Assessment and Quality Assurance in Higher Education and Scientific Research (ANEAQ). The ANEAQ was founded as part of a pan-African project funded by the European Union, called the Harmonisation of African Higher Education, Quality Assurance and Accreditation (HAQAA) and supported by both the European Union and the African Union.

Across the region the shift from internal to external accountability through the creation of semi-independent quality assurance agencies is clear. Similarly, Kohstall (2012) argues that "'quality assurance' has become the central reference for reform" (p. 95) and that this has been accomplished primarily through the "transfer of international models" (p. 96). There is a clear reliance on external actors and ideas; WB loans have been used to support the adoption of a European degree system. Meanwhile, WB funding has brought about the creation of particular independent agencies, and European Union funding has trained academics in quality assurance. These external influences have played an important role in securing the legitimacy and funding needed to take on large-scale quality-enhancing reforms.

In North Africa, where national governments more or less copied European reforms wholesale with little national debate, the reform process largely sidelined the local policy processes. Members of the local policy community felt that these reforms were imposed from the outside, with little substantive debate by legislators or Parliament (Ghouati, 2009). Academics, rather than being agents of change, were treated as "the passive executors of already-set policy agendas" (Ergül, Coşar, & Mous, 2017, p. 164). The process epitomizes the neocolonial experience: six decades after independence, educational policies in Morocco and Tunisia are still dictated by reforms in France.

A greater irony is that many academics with whom I spoke in Morocco argued that the LMD reforms were actually bad for student learning: they shortened the time to completion of a degree by a full year and, in so doing, watered down the educational content provided by a degree. Reforms made in the name of improving quality resulted in students graduating with a bachelor's degree and entering the labour market with less time to master concepts and develop their skills. Throughout my many years of living in Morocco, one of the constant refrains I heard from academics in the decade after adoption of the LMD reforms was that they had been a disaster for the higher education system – largely because the adoption was associated with students learning *less*, not more. Interestingly, in January 2020, the Moroccan minister of higher education announced unexpectedly that the ministry was reverting course and would be adopting a four-year bachelor's degree in line with the American model (Sawahel, 2020). In making this announcement, he cited ideas of efficiency and quality, stating that the shift would "allow Morocco to open up to international education systems, especially those in Anglophone countries that have demonstrated their efficiency and quality" (Sawahel, 2020).

Relying on External Advice in the Arab Gulf

Rather than relying on WB projects to secure external funding, Qatar and the UAE have taken a different approach: they have brought in external consultants to align their higher education systems to global best practices. Nonetheless, their reforms to improve quality are similar to those in other countries, centred on enhancing "rigour" through independent commissions and on raising admissions standards.

In the early 2000s the UAE established the Commission for Academic Accreditation (CAA) as a fully independent body that licenses the country's many public and private universities and accredits each of their academic programs. The CAA aims to ensure that programs in the UAE meet international standards of accreditation. Its mandate includes licensing private universities, accrediting programs, and supporting institutions in their development of quality assurance mechanisms. As a high-income nation, the UAE is not influenced by the possibility of WB funding but nonetheless relies extensively on foreign consultants, and it has a history of importing the best practices articulated in international higher education development discourses (Ridge, 2014).

More than nearly any other country, Qatar put its faith in external and technical experts to reform its educational system (including Qatar University). In 2001, Qatar's Supreme Education Council commissioned an international think-tank, the RAND Corporation, based in Santa Monica, California, to advise and oversee major reforms to the country's educational system. RAND's advice largely reflected American models of education policy, and in response to Qatar's primary- and secondary-school system underwent reform, including the introduction of independent schools, the publication of school report cards, and the switching of the language of instruction in science courses to English. Although some reforms were welcomed, over the past fifteen years the reforms have become widely criticized on various fronts, with debates ranging from whether the reforms were simply not in place long enough to be effective, to whether Qatar was losing its culture by teaching in English. Others have criticized the reforms as fundamentally ineffective, because Qatar remains low performing on internationally comparative assessments.

In higher education, starting in 2003, the Supreme Education Council also engaged RAND to help with major reforms to Qatar University as part of the same drive to reform education for a knowledge economy. The partnership was initiated by Qatari leadership in response to perceptions of declining quality, including the areas of time to graduation and student engagement, and RAND's formal role was one of supporting university-initiated reforms. As part of its reforms, Qatar University created the Senior Reform Council, composed of senior administrators, professors, and experts from universities in the United States and the United Kingdom. At the university level, reforms focused on the enhancement of administrative operations by improving institutional autonomy and decision-making processes, as well as revitalizing academic offerings, improving faculty quality and performance, improving student achievement, and strengthening the university's sense of community.

One of the strategic decisions made at the time was to uphold high academic standards in the name of quality. In their monograph *The Reform of Qatar University*, Moini, Bikson, Neu, and DeSisto (2009) explain: "Faced with preserving the status quo, in which a university education was available to all nationals, or upholding academic standards, the administration decided that QU would uphold its new standards and aim to serve average and above-average students, while expanding its preparatory Foundation Program" (p. xxiv). One of the overarching goals was to "foster and support student achievement," and, under this objective, key recommendations included strengthening and standardizing admissions requirements, setting minimum standards for retention, and codifying academic regulations. What is striking about these recommendations is that they focus entirely on student preparation and performance, while hardly addressing university-based supports for learning. The reality is that while upholding high academic standards sounds like a perfectly legitimate policy, in practice it means excluding students with weak secondary-school records.

In an interview that I conducted in Qatar in 2019, one researcher described how external reforms were implemented with little local buy-in and created significant resistance: "They revamped Qatar University between 2003 and 2006, and the plan was in place to transform the institution, but there was resistance and complaints. The country's leadership realized that they [the reforms] had disrupted society too much. It was too much for society to absorb, and the main audience for reform is the citizens." He continued: "Although some aspects of QU have become more modern, and students are better than they were in 2002, the plan was to move it to be state of the art overnight"; on that front, he said that "the reforms did not accomplish their goals."

Although it is clear that countries throughout the region have taken different routes, the profiles of reform provided here suggest that governments have turned to the international arena – including the WB, the European Union, and consulting firms based in the United States – to secure the resources and political will needed to institute large-scale reforms in the name of high quality. As a result, quality reforms are often viewed as being imposed from abroad with little local debate, contextualization, or localization. Criticisms are made in the Arab Gulf states of the extent to which the region is reliant on external expertise and global models that lead to reforms that are not desired by local constituencies. In 2013 the Qatar Foundation formally ended its contract with RAND, and the RAND-Qatar Policy Institute closed. A decade after Qatar University reforms were initiated, they are widely viewed as a model for what not to do: external consultants instituted rapid changes, and in their wake many Qataris felt there was no place for their children in higher education. In both the Maghreb and the Arabian Gulf, national populaces contest the idea that embracing the international has been successful in improving the national system. Donn and al-Manthri (2010) argue that the policy frameworks and much of the ministerial discourse adopted by the Gulf Cooperation Council (GCC) countries regarding higher education originate in the former group of eight industrialized nations and are promoted by a "magistry of influence," which relies heavily on foreign expertise (p. 141). They contend that the particular vision of high-quality higher education that circulates among foreign organizations and consultants "is not necessarily one developed in the broader MENA and may not even be appropriate for the region as a whole" (p. 151). It is not surprising then that nearly two decades of reform seem to have had little impact on discourses of declining quality and failing institutions.

The Limits of Quality Assurance

In 2016, I asked Dr. Adnan El Amine, a prominent scholar of Arab higher education and the director of the Lebanese Association for Educational Studies, whether any country in the region had done quality assurance well. He replied: "No, no. They believed, or they claimed, that these agencies would resolve the problem, but you may be sure, these agencies have not resolved the quality issue." Indeed, despite the flurry of reforms, quality assurance policies seem to have had a relatively minor impact on higher education systems in the region. Quality assurance reforms have tended to be additive, leaving broader structural and political constraints unaddressed.

For the most part, quality assurance reforms have typically resulted in the creation of new councils or agencies, which are often added onto and independent of the existing system. Reforms have established minimum standards for entry into private universities, regulated standards such as library facilities, and required individual institutions to undergo an internal quality review or external accreditation. However, they rarely address structural issues and constellations of interests that determine the status quo in higher education systems.

Quality assurance policies and practices seek to align to global best practices while not disrupting the interests of local audiences. As a result, quality assurance has become a platform upon which other political interests are contested, and it serves as a pretext for other reforms. The technical literature imagines and advocates the creation of independent and autonomous quality assurance agencies. And yet in almost no country in the Arab world is the quality assurance agency independent of other state authorities. There is nothing surprising about this lack of independence: Waterbury (2020) recounts long histories of government interference in the operations of Arab universities, including firing rectors, replacing deans, and firing academics, as well as installing secret police on campuses (p. 63). As a result, despite promises of independence, the composition of quality assurance agencies, their mandates, and their power to regulate universities are often politicized. In many cases university administrators and quality assurance commissioners are directly appointed by rulers, making them essentially political appointees rather than academic experts or professionals. One of my interviewees stated that this was yet another "boutique" for the state to play politics.

In Jordan, the director of the Quality Assurance Agency exerts significant control over all universities, akin to what one of my interviewees called "a super minister." One interviewee said that the director of the agency was close to the king and focused on "marginal aspects of quality just to say 'I am controlling you.' It is a formal authority over universities, rather than really improving quality." The concentration of power in a political office has meant that the king retains significant control over issues of university quality in Jordan. In practice, this means that the raising of admissions or graduation standards that would negatively affect loyal constituencies, and the reduction of numbers of university staff to improve efficiency in rural parts of the country where universities are major employers, are all unlikely reforms.

In the UAE, the CAA was considered unique in the region because it was established as a fully independent body and given power to shut down poorly performing universities. Yet my interviewees suggested that the creation of the quality assurance agencies was one way in which the government could enhance employment of Emirati nationals, a policy priority for the country. In 2016 the UAE required all professors to undergo a certification of their university credentials and establish their equivalency in the Emirati system. This policy was framed as an attempt to ensure the integrity of academics' credentials. Many faculty members who had completed their doctorates abroad were highly critical of the policy and insisted that the degree-certification process was a waste of time. One professor, who had completed a doctorate in the United States, explained: "This is a way to create jobs. It is another government office. It is another way to tax the [foreigners] without officially creating a tax. Now we have another governmental department where Emiratis have to work, and it's also a way to tax people, because we [foreign faculty members] have to pay for the degree certification."

In the UAE, a country with a significant expatriate labour force, the role of foreign faculty members was a constant source of tension. In interviews that I conducted with professors in 2016 in the UAE, they said that the Emirati academic labour market, where professors worked on impermanent contracts, undermined the country's stated commitments to quality. One faculty member at a private university in the UAE explained that his university was in the process of seeking American accreditation, which was a time-intensive process; however, faculty members had very little reason to participate in the process: "You know, why would we even worry about this? Students will be here longer than we are. At any point the university administration can cancel your contract, and you are going to have to leave the country."

In middle-income countries one of the most important structural issues is student enrolments. Many universities are required to accept more students than they can accommodate; in other cases, students are funnelled into programs for which they have little interest. For example, despite the official commitment to apply the same quality standards to public and private universities in Jordan, administrators told me that public universities cannot actually meet these standards because they do not control their own admissions. In an interview I conducted with the former vice-president of a public university in Jordan in 2013, he explained that the university administration requests a certain number of students from the centralized Unified Higher Education Admissions Council, but "they don't respect that number. Usually you get double or triple that number. The university requested 3,000, and we ended up taking 8,600 incoming freshmen – 8,600, when we think our capacity is stretched to the limit at 3,000." Similarly, one official at the Higher Education Accreditation Council, who oversaw quality assurance efforts and with whom I spoke, agreed that estimates of capacity were regularly exceeded: the council estimated public universities could absorb 22,000 new students in 2013, but over 40,000 students were placed at their institution by the central authorities. He explained that this constituted a real barrier to meeting quality standards. He stated, "If we wanted to meet international standards of student to faculty ratios, we would need to hire between 1,500 and 1,700 new faculty members."

In Egypt in 2016, I met a professor of English at a public university who explained how their program navigated the grey zone of language, admissions, and quality. As the centralized admissions system allowed students with very poor English to enrol in their program, they had been assigned two hundred incoming English majors, many of whom were neither interested nor proficient in English. In response, the faculty instituted an unofficial and department-specific language-proficiency test that required students to have an intermediate level of English to actually enrol, which cut enrolments in half. "Even though the required level was not high," she said, "the change to the department was remarkable. Professors had more time to devote to students who were enrolled, and were able to hold them to higher standards for reading and literary criticism." As a result, their graduates began to establish a reputation and were recruited to teach in many schools around the city. Despite the improvements in student learning, such a practice actually denied many students a place in the university, and faculty members were accused of favouritism or offered bribes to enrol students who did not qualify, exemplifying the structural realities that shape learning in the Arab world and which can hardly be solved by independent accreditation bodies.

A second important structural issue is employment. Universities are major employers throughout the world, and administrative positions in public universities represent a highly desirable employment for many middle-class families in the Arab world. This may be particularly true in the more rural and less industrialized parts of the region. Employment, like admission, serves as a convenient form of political patronage, which means that public universities tend to have more administrative staff members than are needed (Waterbury, 2020). Moawad al-Kholi, the former president of Menoufia University in Egypt, reflecting on his experience as president, is quoted by Elmeshad (2014): "I have enough staff in the university administration for 10 universities" – which obviously affects the university's budget. Similarly, Waterbury (2020) implies that the reason Mohammed V University in Rabat, Morocco, was divided into two campuses in 1993 was to create more senior-level administrative posts as a form of patronage to loyal constituencies. The result was an unnecessarily divided institution, which was eventually reunited in 2015.

In the absence of state assurances of high quality, many institutions are pursuing alternative and external markers of quality levels, particularly international accreditations that can stand as signifiers in the global era (Farag, 2010). Universities throughout the region already actively pursue these accreditations, including through the regional accreditation bodies of the United States and professional accreditations in business and engineering programs. While there are many benefits to these accreditations, they also imply that the Arab states' university credential does not stand on its own as a symbol of high quality and may continue to erode confidence in the public sector.

Quality and the Linguistic Hierarchy

Discussions of quality map onto long-standing language hierarchies. At the institutional level, programs with more restrictive admissions standards and lower acceptance rates tend to be those that teach in foreign languages. In particular, the sciences and business tend to be taught in French or English, while the humanities and social sciences are taught in Arabic. Throughout North Africa and Lebanon, in public universities, students in the humanities or social sciences, including law and literature, study in Arabic, while those in engineering and sciences study in French or English.

The rank ordering of degree programs in Arab societies, with medicine and engineering at the top and social sciences and humanities at the bottom, discussed in chapter 2, also creates a vicious cycle that perpetuates assumptions of low quality in the social sciences and humanities. As they maintain lower admissions standards, they are often viewed as "catch-all" fields for students who have not been accepted into more prestigious or difficult programs. The social sciences and humanities tend to be taught in Arabic, not English or French, have large classes sizes, and have fewer resources, synonymous with low quality. Perceived as low quality and low prestige, these programs have a difficult time attracting more academically motivated students who might otherwise be interested in the social sciences and humanities. Government policies and social attitudes combine to perpetuate the idea that graduates of social sciences and humanities are less qualified (Cantini, 2012). Reflecting on the power of these discourses, Cantini (2012) cites

Sami Khasawneh (2001) as stating that "there is an essential difference between the students of the humanities and those studying sciences," namely that "the scientific student is interested in learning and willing to promote change even at a societal level, while the humanistic student is less motivated and interested, since the only reason to pursue this career is to have failed the access to the scientific one" (Cantini, 2012, para. 27, citing Khasawneh, 2001).

This self-perpetuating cycle is realized in full when the graduates of low-prestige fields enter the labour market with credentials that some of my interviewees called "meaningless." Indeed, many young people understand the ways in which discourses of low-quality map onto various degrees. A Lebanese man I interviewed in Beirut in 2016 exclaimed: "If you study law at the Lebanese University, you are just giving up. If you study Arabic literature at the Lebanese University, you are also giving up, but at least you get to read interesting stories." This hierarchy of prestige is reinforced by families who encourage students to study subjects that are viewed as competitive and prestigious.

In fact, according to my interviewees, many of the most contentious debates over *quality* reform at Qatar University were actually debates over the role of Arabic as a language of instruction. English is the medium of instruction at the Education City campuses, and Arabic was used originally to teach the social sciences and humanities subjects at Qatar University. This linguistic division implied that Arabic was the language for the masses, while English was the language of the academic elite. When the 2003 reforms changed the language of instruction to English throughout Qatar University, there was the feeling that there was no place for some Qataris who would be better served by studying in Arabic. In 2012, five years after the RAND project had officially ended, the Supreme Education Council announced that the language of instruction in the social sciences would return to Arabic. Today, the colleges of education, arts, and humanities and of law and Islamic Studies all teach in Arabic, while the colleges of science, engineering, and business all teach in English.

The ranking of knowledge along linguistic and curricular lines has a dual effect: it simultaneously undermines the legitimacy of the Arabic language as a language of knowledge and science and frames the humanities and social sciences as less valuable. This linguistic hierarchy has also increased the demand for private primary and secondary schooling that teaches in foreign languages, and it has put particular pressures on low- and middle-income families to learn those languages. In North Africa, Boutieri (2012) carefully deconstructs how language abilities determine students' opportunities. The most prestigious degrees, engineering and medicine, are only available to those who are skilled in French. As a result, even middle- and lower-class families speak to their children in French or send their children to French-medium private schools at young ages.

Reconsidering Higher Education and the Labour Market

In terms of the labour market, technical discourses that view the path from education to employment as linear are overly simplistic. In reality, the region's high rates of unemployment may have very little to do with what, or whether, students are learning in university. Labour markets in the region are characterized by substantial reliance on the public sector, as well as on many family-run businesses and a large informal sector (Assaad, 2014; Kabbani, 2009; Kabbani & Kothari, 2005). They are also heavily segmented along lines of gender and nationality due to policies and social norms, all of which contribute to high rates of unemployment particularly among young people and women (Barsoum, 2016; Kabbani, 2009; Mryyan, 2014; Salahi-Isfahani & Dhillon, 2008. The preference for public-sector employment is common across the region but is particularly acute in the Arab Gulf states, where, with relatively low levels of education, national citizens can obtain well-paying and comfortable positions. Most Arab Gulf states have initiated labour-market-nationalization policies, which require private companies to hire a certain proportion of nationals (Forstenlechner, 2008). Many of the professors with whom I spoke in the UAE felt that these policies likely decreased students' motivations for studying by weakening the link between education and employment.

Moreover, personal or family connections, known as *wasta* in Arabic, are powerful means to finding employment. Scholars have noted that in the Arab world "personal, kinship, and social networks play a particularly important role in accessing employment" (Krafft & Assaad, 2016, p. 3). *Wasta*, however, does not necessarily imply corruption or perverse forms of nepotism; it also represents what sociologists have called "the strength of weak ties" because many young people use personal, kinship, or other social networks to find employment (Granovetter, 1973). When I was living in Lebanon in 2016 and asked about labour market transitions, one young Lebanese woman replied: "Of course there are always those who just study some subject and they know they aren't going to work in it – they are going to get a job through *wasta* or with their family's company. I have a friend who studied at university, but she won't use the degree because her family owns a business. She says,

'I want to study something easy because I already know where I will work.'" From an economic perspective, reliance on family networks undermines the university's human capital production. Assaad, Krafft, and Salehi-Isfahani (2018) examine a range of labour market outcomes for commerce and information technology graduates in Jordan and Egypt and find that family backgrounds matter more than educational factors. In their words, "family background variables drive labour market outcomes" (p. 970). They argue that "students and their families have little reason to seek out the type of higher education that builds productive skills, and HEIs [higher education institutions] ... have little reason to produce them" (pp. 970–1).

That said, it is not clear that the blame should be placed squarely on young people or their universities. In writing about young people's transition to the labour market in the Arab world, Momani (2015) argues: "Although there is no shortage of young, educated Arabs, many remain unemployed or underemployed after graduation, and face many challenges when seeking opportunities to take advantage of their education. These challenges include a corrupt political and social system rife with nepotism and family networks that stunt the ability of talented youth to compete on the basis of meritocracy" (p. 11). This labour-market-centric perspective contrasts starkly with the overwhelming consensus among policy advisers that the problem is primarily the poor quality of the education. In fact, the field would do well to consider what it means for policy that the weak link between education and employment may have more to do with the labour market than the university. Higher education administrators and ministries of higher education are not solely responsible for the current "crisis" of high unemployment, nor can they alone be expected to solve it.

Reconsidering the Credential

Reconceptualizing quality requires moving beyond the current emphasis on rigour. From a technical perspective, the goal of quality assurance is to ensure that students are learning. However, this narrow definition of quality misses the fact that the educational credential – not the knowledge or the skills it purportedly represents – is what most students and families desire above all. While economists view education as related to human capital, sociologists tend to view degrees as a positional good, the value of which is determined by their rarity (Collins, 1979). Meyer, Ramirez, Frank, and Schofer (2007) put it bluntly: "In the modern world, it does one little good to possess the skills of a university graduate if one lacks proper certification from a properly accredited university. Conversely, if an individual does carry the right documentation, his or her actual abilities are often treated as secondary matters" (p. 190). Similarly, when access to employment and economic stability are part of a broad social contract between the state and its citizens, reforms that curtail access to credentials by raising admissions or graduation standards end up denying many citizens what they perceive to be their rights or entitlements. These reforms are understandably contested, regardless of what may be their positive impact on indicators of quality.

In an older era of higher education, when universities were primarily elite serving, the legitimacy of the educational credential was guaranteed by its exclusivity. This model is still held up as a golden age by some – professors in Morocco have told me of their golden days studying for their doctorate in France, where they had close and personal interactions with famous scholars and theorists. In that era the university credential implicitly embodied a deep socialization process and envisaged its holders to be political and social elites. The rapid growth in university enrolments in Arab countries and around the world has democratized this formerly elite institution. In so doing, however, it has also weakened the relative power of the credential (Collins, 1979). The university credential is no longer a mechanism for signalling elite status; instead, it must now signal content mastery and transferable skills.

In the neoliberal era there is concern that the purpose of higher education has been further narrowed to the acquisition of the credential, not to the skills and knowledge it supposedly represents. In an interview I conducted in July 2016, a professor at a public university in the UAE explained that the major problem with her students was a lack of investment in learning: "A lot of our students don't perceive that the steps for getting the degree and the knowledge that you acquire [are] important. They just want to have the paper. If they could buy it, they would buy it." She attributed this to larger labour-market policies, which reward students who have more education with higher salaries. Tying financial incentives to degrees creates perverse incentives for students: "It increased plagiarism. We have a real problem with students buying papers." It is also common to hear of professors being pressured to give higher grades: "The bullying was insurmountable. I mean, they are nice people; they are not bullies. But we would have students in our face, harassing us, screaming, because it's money. It's financial for them." It is hard to see the impact of quality-enhancing reforms when students and families are willing to pay thousands of dollars to purchase an educational credential illegally. Maintaining high quality through close faculty-student relationships is time intensive and difficult; lowering standards is easier for everyone involved. A good level of educational quality benefits society as a whole, and yet the costs of quality assurance are borne by individuals and institutions who have many incentives for accepting less time-intensive forms of learning. Governments, administrators, and entrepreneurs all face pressures to lower admissions standards and accept more students for increased tuition fees. There are often real political incentives for doing so: Waterbury (2020) reminds us that, particularly in authoritarian regimes, higher education systems must "reinforce the legitimacy of the regime and shore up authority of the national leadership" (p. 158). This often entails expanding access to particular constituencies or appointing leaders from among allies, as forms of patronage. They also face pressure to reduce costs, by increasing class sizes or hiring professors on short-term contracts.

The human capital lens, which dominates the literature on higher education, assumes that education plays an important role in preparing young people for employment. In reality, young people attend university for a wide variety of reasons, including prestige, marriage, and personal independence. In fact, the sociological literature reminds us that for many young people university attendance is not primarily an economic calculation but rather is part of an individual's pursuit of status. Young people certainly want a high-quality education, but not if it excludes them. Prior research in the region has found that Egypt's upper-middle-class women view higher education as an intrinsic part of acquiring and maintaining a middle-class identity that involves no real calculation of outcomes (Sieverding, 2009). Different groups view education as a means to attain higher social status and, hence, pursue education out of a desire to avoid shame, maintain privilege, or advance their status group's economic or political interests. Higher education is also viewed as a place to find a future partner for marriage and childbearing. Some have argued that attending higher education benefits women in the "marriage market," which helps to account for females' strong demand for higher education but their low, and declining, labour-force-participation rates (Elbadawy, 2009). In my own experience with young people on university campuses in the region, I also found that, as in North America and Europe, universities are social spaces and present opportunities for students to interact with friends, to flirt, or simply to get out of the house and away from the watchful eyes of parents. In short, young people have multiple motivations for attending higher education that may have very little to do with eventual aspirations for employment.

Redefining Excellence as Both Political and Personal

This chapter argues that it is time to rethink the concept of quality in higher education development. One avenue to redefining quality might start with moving away from focusing on institutional practices or student-level outcomes to reconceptualizing "excellence" as embedded within relations of care. Technical discussions of quality rarely focus on what occurs *within* the classroom and largely ignore the fact that teaching and learning are relational processes: students do not simply memorize knowledge in isolation; they are engaged in discussion and debates with scholars that serve as a form of mentoring and socialization. A relational approach to quality could focus on how students are learning, or pay particular attention to the role that universities are playing in socializing citizens for social and political outcomes. Current approaches to quality ignore the fact that faculty members are political actors, and many are on the front lines of strikes that are demanding better working conditions. This is often considered a detriment to student learning, rather than socialization into political participation. Similarly, an alternative approach to improving quality in the region could begin by recognizing the relational aspect of teaching and learning, focusing on how learning is occurring in community, and recognizing the "everyday excellence" that already exists throughout the region. One of the great casualties of the crisis rhetoric is that there is little incentive or interest in recognizing the intelligence, creativity, and impact of Arab professors and students.

4

Privatizing the Public Good

The rapid growth of private higher education has been called part of a "multidimensional revolution" that is transforming Arab higher education systems (Romani, 2009). Private higher education in the Arab world is not new – many of the oldest and most prestigious universities in the region, including Cairo University, the American University in Cairo, the American University of Beirut, and Université Saint-Joseph, were founded as private religious colleges in the mid-1800s and early 1900s. Yet, in the post-war era, the growth of private higher education in most Arab nations was all but banned, as the government took on primary responsibility for funding and providing higher education. Since the 1980s, however, private higher education has been growing rapidly throughout the Arab world, even in countries that have long histories of predominantly public higher education systems.

By 2008 fourteen Arab nations had officially licensed private universities across the region, and since 2009 Algeria and Libya have followed suit; Algeria's first private university opened 2009. Roughly two-thirds of new universities founded in the region since 1993 are private, and a substantial number are branch campuses of Western universities (Romani, 2009, p. 4). In 2008 the number of private universities in the region stood at 150 and accounted for 41 per cent of all Arab universities (Mahmoud, 2008, p. 15), and in 2010 the percentage of students in private higher education in the Arab world stood at 17.4 (PROPHE, 2021). A decade later, Badran and Badran (2019) reported that across the region there were 300 private universities, which enrolled 30 per cent of all students, suggesting significant growth.

Private higher education is promoted by international development agencies as an efficient and effective policy solution to the challenges of rising demand and costs. At the same time, the regulation of private universities has emerged as site of major policy battles throughout the region, and issues such as admissions standards, composition of university boards, and accreditation have all been contested. Rather than view private higher education as a rational and efficient policy solution, this chapter examines its growth in the region and argues that it is hardly apolitical. That said, the nature of contestation varies significantly across the region. The chapter identifies an overarching pattern: the move to expand private higher education has been relatively slow and contested in North Africa and Syria, while enjoying rapid adoption and substantial growth in Jordan, Lebanon, Palestine, and the Arab Gulf states. I argue that making sense of these differences requires understanding both how state commitments to free public higher education have varied in the region and which constituencies the public system is designed to serve.

In francophone North Africa, as well as Egypt and Syria, higher education has historically operated on the principle of being universal and free. As discussed in chapter 2, access to higher education in these countries is based on ideals of universal merit, and their systems have also long promised free public higher education. Given their long traditions of framing higher education as part of the public good, even modest attempts at introducing tuition, known as cost-sharing in the development discourse, and expanding private higher education have been controversial. Students, administrators, and professors in these countries often described privatization to me as an abdication of the state's responsibility for free, high-quality public education and as a way for wealthy and well-connected elite entrepreneurs to profit from students' desires for education. Given widespread concern over privatization, their governments seek a balance between securing the approval of donors who have promoted private higher education and responding to protestations of their own citizens. In practice, they have tended to embrace private higher education rhetorically, while delaying or undermining its growth and expansion until it becomes widely accepted. Despite slow and contested implementation, however, in many countries private higher education is becoming widely accepted by many middle- and upper-middle-class families, who can afford to pay for professional education that promises better foreign-language instruction and labour market opportunities.

In contrast, other countries in the region have either implicitly or explicitly limited public subsidies to certain groups. The practice of selective subsidies is found in Jordan, Lebanon, and the UAE, countries that conceptualize students as being divided along lines of ethnicity, religion, or citizenship. In each case, public-sector funding serves particular and preferred groups, while private higher education has emerged and expanded to serve those who are not well served in the public sector. Private higher education has flourished but, in doing so, it undermines the state's ability to create a common national identity through its higher education system. In these cases, even when the existence or growth of private higher education is not questioned, its expansion raises educational and political debates. Seemingly technical issues regarding admissions standards or university board composition actually raise fundamental questions concerning the role of the market in providing higher education.

This chapter argues that across the region and despite the differences, private higher education is growing and raising important questions for Arab higher education systems. In formal and informal interviews that I conducted in the region, students and families viewed private higher education as part of a broader pattern of neoliberal educational policies and worried that educational credentials were increasingly "for sale," often to wealthy students (Buckner, 2013; Cantini, 2017; Farag, 2010. Students in public universities worry that their hard-earned credentials may be undermined by the proliferation of similar credentials offered in private universities. At the same time, students in private universities are concerned that they are paying significant sums of money for degrees that are not equivalent to public-sector credentials in a tiered labour market. More fundamentally, the growth of a tuition-dependent and for-profit private sector raises concerns about the state's ability to guarantee future opportunity for its young people if private higher education brings about a narrowing of curricular offerings, widening inequalities, or declining quality in the public sector.

The Growth of Private Higher Education

In the second half of the twentieth century, private higher education was practically non-existent in many parts of the world, and the Middle East and North Africa were no exception (Buckner, 2017). It was even less common in newly independent nations, which were focused on establishing higher education systems that would serve their states in both symbolic and material ways. The idea that higher education could be organized and funded by individuals or investors for profit-making purposes was either inconceivable or rejected. The important task of educating, socializing, and sorting youth into life paths was simply not left to market processes. Rather, the state, which was viewed in many parts of the world as either an arbiter of the public good or as a mediator of group interests, was considered the only legitimate provider of higher education.

Since the late 1980s, however, privatization has spread rapidly worldwide in line with the entrenchment of neoliberalism in education and development. The academic literature on private higher education distinguishes between two phenomena: cost-sharing and private higher education. *Cost-sharing* refers to policies and practices that shift the burden of higher education away from the government and onto institutions, students, and families (Johnstone, 2004). It occurs within public-sector higher education and generally entails both revenue generation and cost-cutting. Revenue generation typically includes increasing tuition fees or starting new fee-paying degree tracks, such as the parallel programs discussed in chapter 2. Cost-cutting implies finding greater efficiencies, such as increasing class sizes and replacing full-time faculty with part-time lecturers. Countries around the world have had to balance increasing demand with rising costs and stagnant public funds, and cost-sharing is a global phenomenon (Johnstone & Marcucci, 2010).

The creation of a privately owned and operated higher education sector is considered one form of cost-sharing because it allows the government to expand enrolments in higher education without expanding the public sector. However, these wholly private institutions differ in important ways from other forms of cost-sharing. Private higher education institutions are "non-state" actors – they are typically tuition dependent and operate in competitive markets for students. In many countries graduates of private universities must undergo additional regulation to have their degrees recognized by the state.

In the academic literature private higher education is thought to grow primarily to meet the needs that are not met in the public sector. The three primary reasons for the spread of private higher education worldwide are identified as "more," "better," and "different" (Levy, 2006b). By far the most common type, *more* means that private higher education has grown to meet demand that is not met in the public sector, due to limited capacity, inadequate resources, or geographic constraints (Kinser et al., 2010). The spread of new demand-absorbing private higher education has been prevalent throughout the Arab world; private universities are founded by a diverse range of providers, including individual proprietors, profit-seeking business interests, charitable organizations, and foundations. The private sector can also expand when it offers a "better" education. *Better* implies a private higher education sector characterized by high quality, endowments of substantial resources, and small classes typical of elite education. This is the model of the Ivy League institutions in the United States and universities such as the American University of Beirut and the American University in Cairo in the Middle East, which educate the elites of their respective countries. Although national public universities remain among the top tier of universities in many countries, the growth of the private sector has also been accompanied by the emergence of new providers, including non-profit or semi-elite private institutions, which are viewed as increasingly competing with public universities, particularly for upper-middle-class students who want more flexibility or choice over their degree (Kinser et al., 2010; Levy, 2018). Private higher education is also thought to expand when it offers something "different" from that of the public sector. This typically takes the form of a specialized curriculum, including those courses with English or other foreign languages as the medium of instruction, or offering religious education.

Private higher education is a truly global phenomenon: in the first decade of the twenty-first century, private-sector enrolments were "the fastest growing segment of higher education" (Altbach, 2005; Levy, 2006b, 2018). In 2018, roughly 32.9 per cent (about one in three) of all students in higher education worldwide were thought to be enrolled in the private sector (Levy, 2018). The Arab world is no different. Throughout the region private education is growing at all levels of schooling, from preschool to university, engendering important national debates over the legitimacy of public education, socio-economic inequalities, and the status of the Arabic language (Akkari, 2010; Benzakour, 2007; Boutieri, 2016).

Apolitical Privatization

International experts and donors have encouraged the expansion of private higher education in the Arab world, ideologically and financially. From an economic perspective, both cost-sharing in the public sector and expanding private providers seem like logical solutions. Higher education is expensive, and governments in the region already devote significant public resources to higher education. Education spending accounts for approximately 10–20 per cent of national spending; in fact, relative to their level of economic development, many Arab countries spend more on higher education than the nations of the OECD do, reflecting a strong national commitment. Development experts contend that public resources will be further burdened by the continued expansion of higher education, compelling national systems to look for alternate sources of funding. Cost-sharing is the preferred solution, and development experts conclude that "it is important that families and students contribute to its cost" (World Bank, 2011).

From an equity perspective, access to higher education is highly unequal and tends to benefit the upper and upper-middle classes, who qualify for higher education at greater rates due in part to the better quality of primary and secondary schooling, which is often acquired in expensive or foreign-language private schools. Comparative education research from around the world shows that free higher education tends to serve as a subsidy for the upper-middle classes, who then invest in private schooling at lower levels to secure admission to higher education. Expanding the percentage of students in a tuition-dependent private sector allows governments to offset the costs of higher education and to reinvest in primary and secondary schooling. This is viewed as particularly important in low-income and lower-middle-income countries, where access to free, high-quality secondary schools is not universal. Given both efficiency and equity concerns, the consensus among many international development experts is that private higher education in the Arab world will, and should, continue to grow.

Some advocates go even further to suggest that private higher education not only is more economically efficient but may also spur improvements in quality. The dominant logic of international development experts and donors, which draws heavily on economic perspectives, argues that because private higher education has to be responsive to the market, it should be more efficient and promote high quality. In contrast, public higher education is viewed as contending with political interests and entrenched bureaucracies, which makes it less responsive to market demand. These frameworks tend to discuss private higher education as a rational and apolitical solution to the region's problems, essentially as an apolitical privatization.

Partially in response to this seeming consensus in global development, private higher education in the Arab world has grown substantially over time. At the same time, within the region the percentage of students in the private sector varies significantly. Table 4.1 shows the percentage of all students in private higher education in 2018, drawing from World Development Indicators data. The table shows that the percentage of all students in the private sector remains at or below 12 per cent in Syria, Morocco, and Tunisia. Meanwhile, the private sector accounts for the majority of all enrolments in Lebanon and the UAE, with other countries ranging between 20 and 30 per cent.

In the sections that follow, I argue that there are two overarching models of private higher education in the Middle East and North Africa: the first, in which private higher education has emerged within

Table 4.1. Enrolment in Private Higher Education (% Total, 2018)

Egypt	19.9
Jordan	27.5
Lebanon	59.1
Morocco	7.3
Qatar	22.7
Syria	3.3
Tunisia	11.5
United Arab Emirates	72.8

Source: WDI (2021)
Note: Includes college and university levels

states that have made official commitments to free public higher education for those eligible; and the second, in which subsidized public higher education has been selective and targeted to certain politically consequential constituencies. Moreover, I argue that, regardless of its size, private higher education remains politically sensitive throughout the Arab world. In North Africa, including Morocco, Tunisia, and Egypt, student groups have actively protested cost-sharing measures of any sort. They argue that cost-sharing in the form of tuition fees undermines legal commitments to free public education. In other countries, including Jordan, Lebanon, and Syria, new private universities have been viewed as a form of crony capitalism, with well-connected allies receiving contracts for new universities. Issues such as admissions standards and board composition have become politicized. More broadly, private higher education is contested throughout the region due to the concerns it raises over increasing inequality, declining quality, and the undermining of faith in the public sector.

The Right to Free Public Higher Education

The public university in much of the post-independence-era Arab world has traditionally been considered a nation-building institution, bringing together students from all corners of the country to forge a new identity as citizen. Differences based on tribal affiliation, religion, region, and mother tongue were downplayed as the new university graduates became the leaders and civil servants of the modern nation state. In line with these approaches, countries such as Algeria, Egypt, Morocco, Tunisia, and Syria have long-standing commitments to provide free public higher education to all secondary graduates, and in addition Algeria, Tunisia, and Syria have legacies of state socialism and have often promised generous subsidies. Yet, despite these commit-ments, in line with global trends, nations throughout the region have expanded private higher education in recent decades (Herrera, 2006; Mazawi, 2005; Reiter, 2002; Rugh, 2002).

In these countries private higher education began in the vocational sector. In the 1980s and 1990s, private, for-profit vocational colleges and institutes proliferated throughout the region, including Egypt, Morocco, and Tunisia, offering two-year certificates or diplomas. They provided advanced training or vocational skills in a variety of subjects such as management, business, and hospitality. They were distinguished from other forms of higher education in that they rarely offered opportunities for further study at university, although many have since become full-fledged universities. In an interview I conducted in 2013, the president of a private university in Casablanca explained that these institutions were "oriented towards business, and cared very little about educa-tion," stating that investors opened private universities "the way one would open a shoe store."

The expansion of private higher education, particularly in the vocational higher education sector, was actively encouraged by the WB and other development agencies. The WB gave Morocco a loan of USD 150 million in 1986 for education sector reform; in addition to explic-itly promoting private schooling at the primary and secondary level, the project encouraged private-sector participation in vocational higher education. A clear goal of the reform was the "increased efforts to mobi-lize private financing in order to reduce budgetary costs" (World Bank, 1986, p. 11) and the "encouragement of private-sector participation" in vocational training and education (World Bank, 1991, iv).

In Tunisia private higher education as a form of vocational training began in the 1980s, also "under pressure from the World Bank," according to a former university president whom I interviewed in 2012. In 1989 the WB gave Tunisia a loan of USD 95 million, in which one of the objectives was to mobilize additional private resources for voca-tional training. In line with this goal, the WB championed "revising leg-islation for private training" to encourage private investment and the reduction of the tax on private providers of training. The project had partially met these objectives by 1997, according to the report (World Bank, 1997, Annex 2).

Since the late 1990s, however, governments have begun to permit private higher education at the university level, which is a generally more controversial move given the prestige and historic nation-build-ing aims of the university. Scepticism over private universities has been widely recognized by Arab scholars. In 1997 Dr. A Halim (1997) wrote:

"Public higher education should not be reduced to being a poor relative of private education, which has been encouraged with great fanfare,
even though it has not even – or at least, not sufficiently – proved itself"
(quoted in Emran, 1997, p. 7).[1] Nonetheless, starting in the 1990s, governments across the region have committed, in official rhetoric, to expanding private universities, often building these commitments into major
reform initiatives and supporting them with various forms of funding.

In Egypt a major overhaul of higher education was passed in 1992
(Law 101), a year after a large WB structural-adjustment policy had introduced privatization of other government sectors. The law permitted
the establishment of new private universities for the first time since
independence, although the first private universities were not licensed
until 1996, when four new institutions were established (Cantini,
2017). Enrolments in private higher education began to grow: in 1999
only four private universities were operating, serving roughly 6,000
students, compared to the twelve public institutions, serving nearly
1.5 million students (Farag, 2000, p. 16). Twelve new private universities were established between 2002 and 2010, bringing the total to
seventeen in 2010 (Álvarez-Galván, 2015). The number of students enrolling in private universities also increased dramatically, from 11,000
in 2000 to 48,000 in 2005, and to 70,000 in 2009 (Fahim & Sami, 2011).
The expansion of private universities in Egypt was highly contested
in the media, in which access to higher education was characterized
no longer as solely a matter of state planning but as operating within
an open market for credentials, governed by individual calculations of
costs and benefits (Cantini, 2017; Galal, 2002; Kohstall, 2012). For example, writing for the major English-language publication *al-Ahram
Weekly*, el-Nahhas (2002) stated that private higher education was "at
odds with the principles of the 1952 Revolution which calls for equal
access to educational opportunities for all citizens."

Since the introduction of private higher education, twenty-four for-
profit private institutions have been authorized in Egypt, most operating around Cairo and Giza and educating middle-class students in
degrees that are oriented to the labour market, such as information
technology, engineering, and medical sciences (Cantini, 2017, p. 136).
Today approximately 20 per cent of all students in higher education
are in the private sector, although the percentage in four-year, bachelor

---

1 "De meme il ne faut pas réduire l'enseignement supérieur public à un parent pauvre
de l'enseignment privé que l'on encourage à grandes fanfare alors qu'il n'a même
pas encore – ou pas suffisamment – fait ses preuves" (A. Halim, in Emran, 1997, p. 7);
translation mine.

degree–granting universities is much smaller. Two surveys of young people in Egypt, in 2009 and again in 2013, found that the percentage of university students in private higher education is less than five (Assaad, Krafft & Salehi-Isfahani, 2018; Buckner, 2013).

In Morocco a new education law was passed in 2000 that permitted the creation of private universities. In interviews I conducted with ministry officials, one director explained that Morocco's official goal was to "keep Moroccans in Morocco," explaining that "right now, Morocco loses a lot of Moroccan students to universities abroad," and there are clear financial incentives to keeping them in the country. However, these incentives seem to conflict with a broader scepticism of private universities. In practice, no regulatory framework was adopted until 2011, which meant that investors had no clear understanding of the policies and laws governing private universities. The delay in developing the framework was widely interpreted among education officials, university presidents, and potential investors as a tactic to prevent the expansion of the private sector. The regulatory framework for private institutions was passed in 2011, and by 2014 five private universities had opened. Private universities are located in a number of the major cities in the country – Rabat, Casablanca, Marrakech, and Agadir. In 2014 there were 34,000 students in private institutions, accounting for roughly 3 per cent of all enrolments. The ministry's stated goal was to increase the number of students in the private sector to 20 per cent. However, as of 2018, only roughly 7 per cent of all students were enrolled in the private sector, and this represents a slight decline since 2014.

Only a year after Morocco's education law had been passed, Tunisia also permitted the creation of new private universities. In July 2001 Tunisia passed a law (Law 2000-73, 25 July 2000), which laid the foundation for the expansion of private higher education (MOHESRT, 2003, p. 48). The law set the minimum standards for admission, requiring that all private university students hold a secondary degree. It also set standards for faculty credentials and student-faculty ratios and allowed graduates to seek ministry equivalence – which in turn would allow graduates of private universities to continue their education or to work in the public sector. In line with this goal, the country's Tenth Development Plan (2002–6) created incentives to encourage the founding of private universities, namely grants that would cover up to 25 per cent of total founding costs and that would rebate "25% of the salaries of full-time Tunisian teachers for a 10-year period" (MOHESRT, 2003, p. 47). Additionally, private institutions were sold parcels of land for one dinar as a symbolic gesture of support (Zghal, 2007). Tunisia's 2003 higher-education-strategy document said that these policies would ultimately support private higher education by enabling "these institutions to attract increasing numbers of both Tunisian and foreign students" (MOHESRT, 2003, p. 48).

Between 2002 and 2014 the number of private higher education institutions in operation grew significantly, from twelve in 2002 to forty-six in 2014 (MOHESRT, 2014). Combined, however, they attracted no more than thirteen thousand students, as private higher education institutes tend to be much smaller than public institutions, sometimes numbering only a few hundred students. The general scepticism of private higher education in Tunisia was summarized by Tunisian professor Riadh Zghal who stated that private higher education had "not managed to take off yet" (Zghal, 2007, p. 58).[2] That said, since then Tunisia has seen slow but steady increases in private sector enrolments, reaching 11.5 per cent in 2018, up from 6.5 per cent in 2003 (WDI, 2021).

Around the same time, Syria also went through similar, fundamental changes in its higher education system. As part of its larger economic transition towards a market-based economy supported financially by the WB, the republic implemented a number of educational reforms in 2001. The reforms transformed the previously free higher education system into a more differentiated system that focused on expanding access and offsetting costs. They included a new law that permitted the founding of private universities. By 2010, fifteen private for-profit higher education institutions were operating in Syria, many of which cost upwards of USD 10,000 a year to attend. It is worth noting, however, that private higher education was only a small player – in 2009, private universities enrolled 24,573 students, constituting roughly 4 per cent of all university students (Buckner & Saba, 2010). After a decade of conflict the Syrian private sector remains very small, at 3.3 per cent in 2018 (WDI, 2021).

In all of these countries, governments officially permitted the establishment of new private universities, often in response to pressures from international development agencies; however, in practice, the expansion of private higher education was slow. My interviewees suggested that, despite a rhetoric of support from the government, private higher education was often intentionally sidelined. In 2012–13, I interviewed a number of professors, former university presidents, and ministry officials in Morocco and Tunisia, and they said that ministry officials were often openly hostile to the private sector.

In both Morocco and Tunisia, private higher education received less support than was promised officially on paper, and administrators

---

2 "Le secteur privé, qui bénéficie d'incitations à l'investissement particulièrement généreuses parmi lesquelles l'acquisition du terrain pour un dinar symbolique, n'a pas encore réussi à décoller"; translation mine.

perceived their Ministry of Higher Education to be somewhat hostile. When I was conducting research in Tunisia in 2012, university administrators stated that many of the incentives for founding private universities were not honoured. The founder of one private university said that, despite promises of faculty-salary rebates, he had not received any money from the government. Another exclaimed that the Law of 2000 was supposed to "guarantee incentives, but these were never honoured." Similarly, private university administrators and ministry officials explained in interviews that while equivalence of diplomas might be legally possible, in reality graduates of private universities could not work in the public sector and would not be accepted for graduate study in public universities because this equivalence was hardly ever granted. Cantini (2017) reports that in Egypt the government failed to give private universities the autonomy they desired and closely regulated the programs they could offer.

Private higher education is contested largely because it is viewed as contradicting governmental commitments to free public higher education. In an interview in 2013 the president of a private university in Morocco explained that, for the government and the Ministry of Higher Education, expanding private higher education was "socially and politically risky" because culturally "private higher education is seen as no good." Another private-university president to whom I spoke in Morocco explained that the ministry "saw itself as the ministry of public higher education only." A strong orientation towards the French model, and its commitment to a free public system, were specifically cited as the reason for the decade-long delay in the implementation of Morocco's privatization reforms and for Tunisia's continuing hesitance to support private higher education. The president of a private institution in Tunisia told me: "Our university system is based on the French system ... and people in the ministry are products of this system. It will take some time. We need political willingness and time; people won't change overnight."

Ridha Ferchiou, the director-general of a private college, L'Institut Tunis-Dauphine, stated in 2010: "We have the impression that they [government officials] want to pit the two sectors against one another, as if they were enemies, while in other places, they are complementary to the point that there is no difference between the two" (Fatnassi, 2010).[3] As

---

3 "On a l'impression qu'on veut opposer les deux structures, comme s'il s'agissait d'ennemis, alors que sous d'autres cieux, ils sont complémentaires, au point qu'on ne ressent aucune différence"; translation mine.

a result, in Tunisia the strategic niche provided by private universities is in accepting the students who have failed in public universities, in serving international students, or in providing highly specialized programs. That said, the percentage of students in private higher education continues to grow as these institutions offer in-demand specializations. In 2018–19 there were twenty-eight private institutions in Tunisia offering engineering degrees, ten offering architectural degrees, and nine offering paramedical degrees (MERIC, 2019b). Additionally, there is some evidence of a competitive dynamic operating between the two sectors. For example, the first public English-language graduate school, the Tunis Business School, was founded in 2010 at the University of Tunis. The institution is considered by many to be the public sector's response to the opening of a private English-language business school, the Mediterranean School of Business, which opened in 2000 and is now considered to be one of the best business schools in Africa.

A second reason for the government scepticism of the private sector that was mentioned in my fieldwork in Tunisia and Syria is that the government is not willing to accept a private sector free from political control. For example, in Tunisia the president of one private university linked opposition to private higher education to the government's desire for political control, stating: "In 2008, Ben Ali limited PHE because he did not want it to be strong.[4] He did not want to lose control." He continued: "The lack of support for PHE goes back to Ben Ali. He saw higher education as a form of values education. With PHE, the state no longer has control."

Today the legal code governing private institutes remains quite restrictive in Tunisia. They are required to be for-profit commercial enterprises, cannot build regional branches, and are required to offer only one subject (akin to a school or faculty); as such, they are still officially registered as single-faculty institutions. In practice, many call themselves a university because they operate multidisciplinary institutions. Additionally, in 2008 the investment required to found a new university was raised to TND 2 million (USD 1 million), a decision made without discussion with investors (Fatnassi, 2010). Private university administrators also criticized the government's delays in approving new study programs. In interviews I conducted with the owners and administrators of private universities, they complained that new private

---

4 Zine el-Abidine Ben Ali was the former president of Tunisia, who served from 1987 until he was ousted in a peaceful revolution on 14 January 2011. His rule was marred by reports of extensive corruption and was considered an authoritarian regime by independent human rights groups.

university programs are only approved if they match a similar program in the public sector, thereby depriving the private sector of opportunities for innovation, and to date, no private institution has permission to offer a doctoral degree (MERIC, 2019b).

Selective Public-Sector Subsidies

In contrast to contested private higher education policies found in North Africa and Syria, private higher education is well established in Jordan, Lebanon, and the UAE. Regardless of what a technical approach might suggest, I argue that high rates of enrolment in the private sector in these three countries do not reflect only logics of economic efficiency. Rather, their private higher education reflects their respective societal divisions. Although private higher education has grown rapidly and easily, it does so because the higher education system does not claim, or aim, to be a nation-building institution for all the people.

Jordan is considered to be a regional model for its success in expanding private higher education. In 1989 the Private Universities Act permitted private universities to operate, and the first private university was officially approved and opened a year later (Burke & al-Waked, 1997). Most private universities in Jordan are "demand-absorbing," founded to educate the overflow of students not accepted into the public sector. However, there are also non-profit institutions founded by endowments from the royal family (e.g., Princess Sumaya University for Technology) and the Catholic diocese of Jerusalem (e.g., American University of Madaba), as well as technical colleges founded by businessmen who want to provide applied training to develop local talent in the hospitality industry (e.g., Ammon Applied University College).

Two factors jointly encouraged the growth of private higher education in Jordan: first, there was significant student demand that the public sector could not absorb; and, second, there was the desire to keep in Jordan the large number of Jordanian students who might otherwise study abroad. In the early 1990s this desire was strong. In 1987 there were 25,084 Jordanians studying abroad from a country of only 3.2 million residents – making Jordan one of the highest sending nations in the world at the time. This high number resulted both in a concern about the large investments families were making that could be used by the country's local economy, and in a desire "to avoid Jordanian students' exposure to the effects of Western culture" (Badr, 1994, p. 14), which had "negative repercussions on [Jordan's] Arab-Islamic culture" (p. 1).

In 2010, private institutions are estimated to have absorbed 35.9 per cent of all higher education students in Jordan, although this number has remained quite stable, ranging between 26 and 30 per cent since 2015 (PROPHE, 20201; WDI, 2021). Students in private universities pay tuition fees that are subtantially higher than the subsidized tuition rates in public universities (World Bank, 2013). For example, Badran and Badran (2019) find that average tuition fees in Jordan in public universities are USD 2,816 (including both subsidized and parallel programs), compared to an average of USD 4,525 across all private universities. Tuition fees are not regulated at private universities, although many are priced competitively with the parallel learning programs in public universities. Due to the affirmative-action policies in public universities, known as the *makarim* (discussed in chapter 2), private universities have grown to serve a niche Palestinian clientele. They also enrol a significant number of international students, as discussed in chapter 5.

In Jordan, privatization is closely linked to the country's broader debates over higher education access for different groups. As discussed in chapter 2, access to higher education has long been part of a larger contract concerned with distributing the benefits of the state to a divided population. Private higher education in Jordan emerged to serve a primarily Palestinian population. The growth of private universities received a substantial boost in the wake of the first Gulf War in 1990, when 300,000 Jordanians of Palestinian origin returned to Jordan from Saudi Arabia, Kuwait, and the UAE. Many of the young returnees had no avenues to access pubic higher education in Jordan because they had not been educated in the Jordanian school system (Bataeineh, 2008; Zughoul, 2000). As a result, "they went to study in the private universities" (Reiter, 2002, p. 143). Similarly, the owners of most private universities in Jordan are of Palestinian origin, and many of the returning faculty members from the Gulf were absorbed into the private university labour market.

The Jordanian private sector initially attracted students who had not been accepted into the public system because admissions policies were politicized to benefit rural and East Bank Jordanian populations. This has led to significant growth in the private higher education sector, particularly among Palestinians. Reiter (2002) states clearly that "the emergence of private universities in Jordan, which has been a matter of public discussion in recent years, is therefore a Palestinian phenomenon, even if no one states this explicitly" (p. 157). Since this time, however, private higher education has diversified and flourished to serve a broader range of Jordanians, including the upper-middle classes who are seeking distinction or opportunities for mobility.

Private higher education is even more entrenched in Lebanon. The establishment of private missionary colleges in the late 1800s predate the founding of Lebanon as a modern nation state, and today forty-five of the country's forty-six higher education institutions are private. The country's only public university, the LU, was founded in 1951, roughly a decade after Lebanon's independence. Although it remains the only public university, its many campuses collectively enrol 40 per cent of all students in higher education. As in other countries in the region, tuition is highly subsidized at the LU, and student tuition and fees are much lower than at private tuition-dependent universities, making it a first choice for many families.

As early as 1961 a framework for founding new private higher education institutes existed in Lebanon (Private Higher Education Act of 26 December 1961). However, the country's devastating civil war which lasted between 1975 and 1990 caused major disruptions to the higher education system, damaging facilities and resulting in significant emigration. After the Lebanese civil war ended, two laws were passed in 1996 to regulate further the creation of new private higher education institutions, and dozens of private universities were founded in its wake. Today, there are roughly fifty private higher institutions in total and they enrol about 60 per cent of all students in higher education.

Most of Lebanon's higher education institutions are affiliated with a religious sect or divided between predominantly Christian or Muslim campuses. During the civil war, sectarian divisions became entrenched; the Lebanese American University established a second Byblos campus to accommodate Christian students and others from the north who were not able to reach the Beirut campus. Over time, the Byblos campus remained predominantly Christian due to its location and history, while the Beirut campus was predominantly Muslim (B.S. Anderson, 2011). Yet, the extent of privatization in the higher education system perpetuates identification with sect and stereotypes, undermining the role of the university in promoting nation-building (B.S. Anderson, 2011).

Moreover, the privatized system is supported by public funds: roughly 75 per cent of government employees receive tuition vouchers for private universities (Waterbury, 2020). The fact that government spending helps its public sector employees enrol in private universities seems to reflect the country's deep sectarianism and a lack of faith in the Lebanese state institutions more broadly.

The Arab Gulf states also tend to have robust private higher education sectors, and expanding private higher education has been an explicit policy goal of these governments (Levy, 2011). Private higher education has grown rapidly in countries throughout the Arab Gulf states, including not only the UAE and Qatar but also Bahrain, Oman, and Kuwait. It is worth noting, however, that most of these private institutions do not compete directly with public institutions for students; they are simply serving different groups of students. This is because, throughout the GCC, higher education has historically been conceptualized as having two distinct sectors, with the public sector catering to citizens and the private sector largely serving non-citizens (Romani, 2009).

In Qatar, citizens make up almost two-thirds of all students in the country's higher education system, and they are disproportionately enrolled in the public system. Official statistics from 2017–18 show that Qataris made up 71 per cent of all students in the public colleges and universities, while comprising only 52 per cent of students in Education City universities and 44 per cent of those in other private colleges and universities (PSA, 2018).

Similarly, in the UAE, the free public, federal universities and Higher Colleges of Technology (HCTs) cater to Emirati citizens, while private higher education has emerged to educate non-citizens, who constitute the majority of residents (Romani, 2009). Data available from the UAE Ministry of Education shows that in the 2018–19 academic year, 93 per cent of all students enrolled in the public federal universities were Emiratis, while only 44 per cent of students in non-federal institutions, which are largely private, were Emirati (MOE, 2020).

The growing and diverse private sector caters to a large non-national student body, which includes both resident non-citizens and an increasing number of foreign student-visa holders. Encouraging the growth of private higher education is part of the country's commitment to developing what it characterizes as homegrown and highly skilled talent for the labour force, which the UAE hopes will reduce its dependence on costly recruitment of those educated abroad. In 2012, the minister of higher education and scientific research stated that both the public and the private sector will "play an essential role" as the UAE transitions to a knowledge economy (Sherif, 2012).

Interestingly, a significant number of Emiratis are also now enrolling in the private sector, complicating the traditional sectoral division. In 2017, statistics show that Emirati nationals made up more than 22,000 of the roughly 60,000 students enrolled in Dubai's branch campuses (KHDA, 2017), representing more than a third of all students and suggesting a growing demand for private higher education among Emirati citizens. Seemingly in response to this growth, the regulation of private higher education has recently become a policy priority. Stricter regulation of the private sector seeks to ensure that students and families trust the higher education system and also supports the government's goals of training a highly skilled labour force locally. Accordingly, a number of emirates have been tightening regulations on private higher education in the name of quality assurance. For example, in 2017, Ras al-Khaimah announced that it would be introducing stricter policies for private universities, and some institutions have been forced to close as a result.

"Selling Degrees"

The overriding perception in the region is that, in contrast to public higher education, which is a public good supported by the state, private higher education is a business. Excess demand for higher education has meant that private higher education is seen as a sound investment for local investors, and in interviews I have conducted in the region, investors gladly admit that they view higher education as a strategic business opportunity. Amal Abou-Setta, an Egyptian academic who previously taught at private Egyptian universities, summarizes some of the critiques in his statements to the media: "I taught in six private universities in Egypt, and I can confirm that ... they are for the most part investment projects that aim for profit at the end of the day, regardless of the quality of the service" (Abou-Setta, 2014). In interviews I held with professors and higher education administrators in Jordan, Morocco, Syria, and Tunisia, most criticized private universities as "selling degrees," with one interviewee calling them "commercial enterprises, not educational institutions." For example, one administrator at a private university in Morocco explained that "there are forty or so private institutes, but only four or five of them are worth considering a university. The rest are just trying to make money."

In some countries, such as Tunisia, private universities are actually required to be for-profit because no legal code exists for a private non-profit university. In other countries, such as Jordan, universities are legally required to be non-profit, but investors can exploit loopholes that allow them to make substantial profits. For example, investors create shell companies that let the land and buildings to the university at high rates. This practice is carried out in plain sight, and government officials are sometimes shareholders.

In addition, in many countries in the region, private university boards and investors are granted significant power or have political connections that exempt them from burdensome regulations. In Lebanon it is widely acknowledged that new private universities are linked to dominant political parties and political elites, who act as patrons and buffer them from regulation that might cut into their profits. The lack of a buffer between private universities and political leaders means that regulating private universities often has a direct impact on the wallets of politicians, making them less interested in closely regulating quality.

Similarly, in Jordan, private entrepreneurs often have a large say in issues of university governance. In a comparative study of university governance in the region, the WB found that investors have large decision-making roles in private universities, while faculty, administration, and students all have much less decision-making power in private universities than they do in public institutions (World Bank, 2013).

In Jordan, debates over how to regulate the private sector have had to negotiate with powerful investors. The local media has publicized the fact that many founders of private universities, who typically serve as university board presidents, do not have a university degree, which has undermined public faith in their quality and led to numerous policy battles over the composition of university boards. In 2001, laws were passed to ensure that private universities maintained minimum levels of academic quality. One law required that all board members hold a bachelor's degree and stated that no investor could serve as the president of a university. Investors vocally protested these new requirements, stating that the government was interfering in their investment properties (al-Farawati, 2001). In 2002 the minister of higher education initiated a dialogue with private universities to discuss the issue of high fees, stating to the press: "We want them to make profit, but we do not want the education process to become merely a profit-making enterprise" (al-Farawati, 2002).

These debates over standards in the private sector have played out over two decades without much resolution. External pressures may induce change, however: in 2019 both Qatar and Kuwait, countries that send a combined 5,000–7,000 students to Jordan for higher education as fee-paying international students, decided to cut dramatically the number of institutions whose degrees they would recognize. Of the twenty-nine universities currently in Jordan, Kuwait will now accredit only five, down from twenty, and Qatar will recognize six, all of which are public except for the Princess Sumaya University for Technology, the country's only private non-profit university. The majority of affected institutions were private, where, Othman (2019) argues, dubious practices have reigned for years. Othman (2019) reports that some universities have lower standards for international students, who pay higher fees, while others allow students to enrol in off-campus master's degrees and graduate in a matter of months.

As public systems are heavily subsidized and have well-established reputations, they remain the first choices in most Arab countries. In contrast, admissions to private higher education institutions are based on market mechanisms – essentially lowering admissions standards when their market position is precarious and raising them when demand outstrips supply. In practice, most private universities have lower admissions standards than public universities do. In Jordan, Tunisia, Egypt, and Syria private universities are all permitted to accept students who have either failed to gain acceptance to public universities or failed out of public universities. As a result, private universities are often considered "an education of last resort" (Ouelhezi, 2009).

Technical debates over admissions standards often become politicized, as governments seek more control over quality and owners eschew regulation that would decrease demand and thereby cut into profits. For example, in 2002 the Egyptian Ministry of Education established a minimum score of 80 per cent on the *thanaweya amma* for students specializing in science at private universities, and a minimum of 65 per cent for those in literature and the humanities ("Crunching the numbers," 2001). These benchmarks are far below admissions requirements in the public sector, where medicine requires scores above 95 per cent and engineering programs typically require 88–92 per cent (Mahmoud, 2008; el-Sebai, 2006).

Similarly, in Jordan, admissions standards are raised or lowered in response to criticisms. In 2003, minimum admissions standards to private universities were lowered to 50 per cent on the national secondary-school exit exam (Carroll, 2003). Then in 2010, in response to concerns about quality, they were raised to 60 per cent but remain lower than the 65 per cent required for acceptance to public universities (Malkawi, 2013). These changing policies reflect the difficulty governments face in balancing investors' desires to make money and popular perceptions of the low quality of private universities.

The growth of a demand-absorbing private sector has contributed to deepening concerns over the quality of higher education. Dr. Adnan El Amine, director of the Lebanese Association for Educational Studies, was pessimistic about the relationship between quality and privatization. He exclaimed that in the wake of permitting new private universities "we have now two types of failures: one is that in private universities there are no real standards regarding the quality of work, and they are working just for getting money ... and, at the same time, the crowded public university is still crowded."

Based on ethnographic fieldwork at October 6 University, a for-profit private university located in a developing district on the outskirts of Cairo, Cantini (2017) writes that many private universities "deal openly with students as customers" despite also needing to establish their reputations and prove their quality to sceptics (p. 262). He argues that private higher education is increasingly viewed as a commodity, with universities "providing services" and students being increasingly treated as "customers" (p. 262). He says that private universities, in contrast to free public universities, which are viewed as "a right," are changing how they interact with students, often emphasizing notions of "care" to attract fee-paying students. If the logic of the public sector is one of rights, the logic of the private sector is one of value, where those who can afford better care or better credentials are able to acquire them. Barsoum (2017) has called this the "allure of easy," whereby in Egypt students who pay substantial fees for their education expect to obtain a degree. In interviews she conducted with graduates of public and private institutions in Cairo, she found that both students and professors understood the unwritten guarantee of "passing." One student, a graduate of a public university, joked that at the private universities "you have to bribe them to fail you" (p. 111). In my own interviews in Tunisia, a professor at a public university echoed this sentiment, exclaiming that the private universities are *voleurs* (thieves) and are full of sub-Saharan Africans "because they guarantee a degree." These well-documented concerns over quality are particularly worrying when they facilitate the entry of wealthy but underqualified young people into high-prestige professions that involve public safety, such as medicine and engineering.

Exacerbating Inequalities

Private higher education is viewed as increasing the importance and role of family wealth in helping young people obtain advantages under the new higher education reforms. Although competitive programs in the public sector remain the most prestigious options in most countries, there are also legitimate concerns that a rapidly growing private sector will magnify inequalities in access and erode the quality of public higher education. Indeed, research in the sociology of education has found that expansion of higher education exacerbates wealth inequalities when the upper classes are able to use their financial and cultural capital to disproportionately gain access to additional spots in higher education.

The fact that private universities are tuition dependent and often charge significant fees raises concerns that a family's financial resources will determine access. Individuals from wealthy backgrounds are able to pay expensive tuitions at private universities to study a desired subject when they have been denied access to the equivalent program at a public university. The wealthy can also pay for private tutors in difficult subjects in university and so are more likely to be accepted into graduate programs.

For example, Syria's reforms, which expanded options for studying in the private sector, were viewed by many young people as exacerbating the role of wealth in determining access to university. In interviews I conducted in Syria in 2009, when private higher education was just emerging, many young people expressed that the role of family wealth in determining access to university was "unfair." One young man, who worked full-time in a small clothing factory to support his family, explained the difficulty faced by those from his background in pursuing advanced degrees: "You need a master's or a doctorate to make money, but you need money to get a master's or doctorate." Another young woman shared his sentiment, stating that "money makes educated people, not the other way around."

The reforms were particularly criticized for helping wealthy youth access high-paying, high-prestige career paths (e.g., medicine and dentistry). For example, although admission to a medical school at the public university requires extremely high marks on the secondary-school exit exam, the new reforms allow academically weaker students to acquire the high status of a medical degree by paying to attend a private medical school. Those in the public system resent this alternative pathway to elite status. Ahmed, a very high-achieving young man enrolled as a medical student at a public university, complained about the flood of new doctors into the profession and the reduced status that his degree now brings. He stated: "The biggest problem in Syria from the perspective of human medicine is the private universities. Private universities require lower grades and still graduate doctors. Medicine takes skills, intelligence, abilities that aren't found in all students. Some students have a little, or a lot, of money and at a private university that makes them a doctor." His concern was not simply about the labour market competition but also about the social status of doctors. Social status used to be doled out by performance on academic exams alone, but for many young people it appears to be for sale to those whose academic achievement is not as high. As an individual who benefited from the former organization of status allocation, this young man resented the new system, which allowed students from particular backgrounds to alter the rules of play.

Egyptians have also been highly critical of private universities; scholars have contended that "a two-tier system is effectively set up under which the wealthy have access to a higher quality education" (el-Nahhas, 2002) or that "less affluent students will not be able to enroll in these institutions, placing them at a disadvantage to the rich" (Fahim & Sami, 2011, p. 60). Gambetta and Hertog (2017) summarize deep criticisms in Egypt that claim that the elites have fled the public system: "The crony capitalists sent their children to expensive private universities such as the American University in Cairo, while public universities were resource starved and left to rot" (p. 37).

In 2012, I examined patterns of access to higher education in Egypt and found that recent higher education policies were contributing to an expansion of the higher education system, allowing a greater proportion of students to attend university. I also found that academic achievement – and the ability of the upper classes to ensure that their children enrolled in the academic secondary school track and achieved higher scores on the exit exam – seemed to be the major source of perpetuating inequalities in access to the public sector. In contrast, privatization was associated with an exacerbation of family wealth and geographical location in determining access. The private sector has grown to serve a niche clientele – wealthy families whose children do not score high enough to enrol in their desired major in the public sector, and particularly those concentrated in Cairo. The ability of wealthy families to enrol in academic secondary schools and then achieve higher scores on the *thanaweya* maintains their advantage in the public sector. This suggests that family wealth plays a large role in students' early lives by ensuring academic success at lower levels of schooling, which allows them to gain admission to the public sector. In contrast, the relationship between family wealth and enrolment in the private sector is the direct result of the ability to pay tuition fees and access campuses. These realities do not go unnoticed or uncontested. In Jordan the student movement *Thab7toona*, which translates into "You have slaughtered us" – a reference to students' discontent over policies that leave them hopeless – has expressed concern that the university may become something that only the wealthy can afford (Cantini, 2012).

Although access to public universities is unequal and biased in favour of urban and wealthy youth, an underlying logic of meritocracy still exists, and females, rural students, and the middle classes are increasingly gaining access to public higher education. In contrast, private universities are governed by the logic of family resources and individual preferences, which has tended to exacerbate inequalities in access.

The Private Sector and the Public Good?

In addition to its impact on inequality, the growth of the private sector raises a number of concerns for both the public sector and the state's ability to support social and economic development. One of these concerns involves curricular offerings: due to market competition the academic offerings of private universities tend to be narrower and more technical than those of public universities, focusing on those programs that are perceived as in demand in the labour market (Levy, 1999). Private universities also tend to limit investments in physical infrastructure, including in programs that require specialized or costly equipment or laboratories. In the long run, this may lead to under-investment or fewer graduates in both the basic sciences and the arts and humanities. Simultaneously, large increases in the number of graduates with applied specializations have raised concerns over how to absorb them into the local labour market.

A second major concern is the possible erosion of public-sector quality. There are reasons to be concerned about private higher education leading to an under-investment in public education. For example, due in part to its expansive private sector, the Lebanese government spends much less on tertiary education per capita than other countries in the region do. Table 1.1 shows that public spending per student in Lebanon is only 19.5 per cent of GDP per capita compared to 25.3 per cent in Jordan, 54.7 per cent in Tunisia, and 82.1 per cent in Morocco. More privatized systems may also result in greater inequalities in access if families are left to fund tuitions on their own.

At the institutional level, private universities can also undermine the quality at public institutions by hiring professors away at higher wages or by skimming the best students. It is common for professors at public universities to combine class sections or skip lectures in order to moonlight at private universities or private language centres, a practice many of them view as justified by their low wages (L. Anderson, 2012). One of the concerns is that students at public universities may be losing the opportunity to build relationships and learn from their country's best and brightest professors.

In fact, it is not impossible that private universities will emerge as a more desirable option than public universities, even in countries where the opposite is true today. If private higher education institutions target the socio-economically elite through appeals to quality or status, they may eventually draw students away from public institutions. This "elite flight" may be particularly likely if privatization is accompanied by under-investment in the public sector. Farag (2010) has warned that this is already occurring in Egypt, where privatization has meant that public universities now "suffer from rapid devaluation" (p. 289). If private higher education institutions continue to charge high tuition to attract the best faculty and provide high-quality resources, it is possible that they could exacerbate inequalities not only in access but also in the quality of education received by students from different backgrounds.

This chapter argues that, despite being a preferred policy solution in the development literature, privatization is hardly apolitical. In many parts of the region, particularly those with long-standing commitments to free public higher education, any form of cost-sharing or privatization is interpreted as threatening state commitments to the provision of free higher education. Yet, despite their detractors, it is also clear that private universities are growing, in part because they meet the demands of students who are not well served in the public sector. Some allow students to study a topic that they could not have studied in a public university, or to study in an English-language environment; others offer students the opportunity to simply study, after having been denied entry to the public system. One of the most important questions moving forward will be how Arab governments regulate the private sector, including issues of quality, profit-making, and scholarships, none of which are apolitical matters.

5
Internationalizing the National University

The gleaming new campus of New York University Abu Dhabi (NYUAD) is located on Saadiyat Island, a natural island off the coast of Abu Dhabi and a cultural and tourist hub for the emirate. Saadiyat's cultural district will include the Zayed National Museum, the Louvre Abu Dhabi, and the Guggenheim Abu Dhabi. The campus's architecture combines the country's Arab and Islamic heritage with the most up-to-date environmental practices; the spacious and green campus includes high-end libraries, facilities, and computer labs. Roughly a decade after its launch, there is no doubt that NYUAD has made an impact: its acceptance rate of 2–4 per cent of applicants makes it as competitive as any American Ivy League university, and it has attracted a diverse faculty of the highest calibre from elite universities around the world.

On the one hand, NYUAD is a clearly Emirati project; it has been funded almost entirely by the Nahyans, the ruling family of Abu Dhabi, which is the largest and wealthiest of the seven emirates in the UAE. Campus construction alone is estimated to have cost a staggering USD 1 billion, and, post-construction, the government of Abu Dhabi continues to provide generous financial aid to qualified students to lure them away from Ivy League universities and other top colleges.

On the other hand, there is very little about NYUAD that speaks to it being a national project. Rather, it feels like a global project that just happens to be located in Abu Dhabi. The sparkling new campus, which integrates cultural and architectural traditions from Abu Dhabi with those of New York City, was designed by Rafael Viñoly Architects, a firm founded by a Uruguayan architect based in New York City. Similarly, its brand is self-consciously "global." NYUAD calls itself "the world's honors college" and seeks to educate "global leaders." Its home university, New York University (NYU), also calls itself "a global university" and insists that NYUAD is not simply a branch of the original campus in Lower Manhattan. Instead, along with its other co-equal campus in Shanghai, the three campuses make up what NYU calls a globally networked university.

NYUAD is only one of many symbols of international higher education in the Arab Gulf states. In Doha, Qatar's capital, the Qatar Foundation hand-picked eleven elite schools and invited them to open branches in a large and state-of-the-art campus known as Education City. After more than ten years, at many of the branch campuses a majority of students are Qatari citizens. Meanwhile, Abu Dhabi's larger and more cosmopolitan rival to the north, Dubai, has created a hub for branch campuses, known as Academic Village. Unlike NYUAD and Qatar's Education City, Dubai's Academic Village targets the roughly 90 per cent of Dubai residents who are non-citizens. It hosts dozens of branch campuses of varying levels of quality to educate a large and diverse non-elite for the labour market.

The founding of NYUAD and other branch campuses and educational hubs in the Arab Gulf states is only one of many types of international engagement in the region. Other forms include the establishment of binational universities, such as the German Jordanian University; generous new scholarship programs that fund Arab students to study abroad; North African universities' participation in European research networks; and the recruitment of foreign students to the region. These initiatives are all ways in which the desire to "be international" is altering Arab higher education systems.

This phenomenon of "going global" is known as internationalization, and it is one of the most fundamental shifts in global higher education (Knight, 2008; Wildavsky, 2012). This chapter explores how and why Arab nations engage in higher education internationalization. It argues that the links between internationalization and preparation for a future knowledge economy are tenuous. Rather, at the individual and institutional level, internationalization is a way to signal legitimacy and distinction. Foreign-language degrees and student or scholarly mobility programs are widely celebrated as "opportunities" that confers status on participating individuals. In the aggregate they constitute a class project of the globally oriented upper-middle class by supporting their aspirations for transnational mobility and status.

At the national level Arab governments link internationalization to discourses of modernization, development, and quality. Throughout the region, internationalization is being used to prove state capacity and to project the image of a government that is simultaneously globally engaged and nationally focused. In the Arab Gulf states, ruling families' support for international branch campuses is part of larger state development and nation branding projects. Given their expense, however, few countries can afford this model. For middle-income countries in the region, including Egypt, Lebanon, Jordan, Morocco, and Tunisia, internationalization offers a way to signal a high level of quality while also securing external resources.

There is no doubt that these projects have positively affected many students, professors, and researchers. But their benefits are not equally distributed. In the Arab Gulf states there are concerns that the substantial government funding put into niche projects and scholarships comes at the expense of public universities and implies that the latter are less prestigious. Critics rightly maintain that branch campuses benefit very few national citizens, at the possible expense of the majorities in national institutions. Throughout the region, opportunities for international engagement map onto long-standing linguistic, geographic, and class divides that benefit those who already possess significant linguistic, economic, social, and cultural capital.

Fundamentally, internationalization reflects a Western orientation that maps onto patterns of colonial influence and benefits Western institutions and businesses. As currently practised, internationalization reinforces the idea that, by adopting Western models of higher education, Arab states will secure external legitimacy associated with high-quality higher education. In so doing, it reproduces global academic hierarchies.

An alternative vision for internationalization in the region would disrupt the assumed linkages between "international," "Western," and "prestige." This might start by recognizing that the Arab world is already deeply internationalized: its youth are multicultural, multilingual, cosmopolitan, and mobile. International engagements are an opportunity to highlight the region's cultural heritage and to share the region's knowledge with a world that is, at best, ignorant, or worse, overtly biased in its perceptions of the Arab world. A second approach would be to strengthen regional collaboration and internationalization – the higher education systems in the region have a lot to offer to those in neighbouring countries, and stronger links between the region's institutions could build opportunities for regional collaboration in tackling similar social issues and promoting knowledge production in Arabic.

The Internationalization Imperative

International academic mobility in higher education is not new. For centuries the renowned institutions of higher learning in the region, including Qarawiyyin in Fez and Al-Azhar in Cairo, attracted Islamic scholars and students from throughout the Middle East, Africa, Europe, and beyond (Farag, 2010). During the colonial era the most promising students travelled to Europe for graduate studies, and after independence international study remained largely dependent on the colonizing power, given the lack of doctorate-granting institutions in the region. This model of international mobility was one of importation, reflecting the power imbalance of the colonial era, yet it also played an important role in developing modern Arab higher education systems.

Over the past two decades, however, greater attention has focused on international engagements in higher education. This internationalization is typically defined as the "integration of international and global dimensions into universities' missions, programs, and operations" (Knight, 2004, p. 11). The "internationalization imperative" affecting higher education around the world is closely linked to knowledge economy discourses, where nations are seen as competing not only for foreign capital but also for labour, characterized as "talent" (Nielsen, 2012). Higher education institutions around the world are being called upon to prepare youth for global labour markets by reforming whom, what, and where they teach. Over the past two decades there has been a veritable revolution in international engagement in higher education, characterized by new actors, models, and types of programming and an increase in the sheer numbers of students and scholars who are studying abroad. In this new global era, a highly internationalized university is now framed as an asset that helps a country be competitive in the global academic and economic marketplace (Wildavsky, 2012).

From this perspective internationalization is both important and desirable. It is framed as one way to improve academic quality, support scientific research, and contribute to mutual understanding, among other positive outcomes. A 2012 report by the OECD claims that integrating internationalization into higher education may "contribute to country-wide growth and innovation" and may "influence key areas of the world and global development" (Hénard, Diamond, & Roseveare, 2012, p. 11). In fact, indicators of internationalization such as an institution's number of international students are used as proxies for quality and are key measures in some global rankings of university quality.

As such, internationalization is part of the larger package of reforms that both universities and countries are expected to pursue in the name of global economic competitiveness. Typical reforms include recruiting foreign students, reforming curricular content to promote international awareness, and teaching foreign languages. In line with these discourses, national governments throughout the Arab region have embraced internationalization in many forms, from offering scholarship programs and recruiting international students to founding branch campuses and binational universities. In the section that follows, I distinguish between "people" mobility, which includes scholarship programs and the recruitment of international students, and "program" or "provider" mobility, which refers to universities and programs moving across borders.

People Mobility

The movement of students across borders is one of the oldest forms of international engagement in higher education and remains one of the primary ways in which students from the world over learn with and from one another. The phenomenon of sending and receiving "international students" is not new, as Arab countries have long histories of student mobility to and from Europe and the Soviet bloc. In the first half of the nineteenth century Muhammad Ali, the Ottoman governor (*Wali*, in Arabic) of Egypt, sent students to learn abroad and invited foreign scholars to Egypt, in the name of modernization and development (Farag, 2010). In the post–Second World War era the purposes and discourses associated with international study have mapped onto geopolitical projects. Farag (2010) reminds us that the mobility of students and scholars between Europe and the Arab world is simultaneously "related to European colonialism and to cosmopolitanism" and the complex relationship between the two (p. 285). Meanwhile, Katsakioris (2016) finds that during the Cold War over fifty thousand Arab students studied in the USSR as part of broader Arab-Soviet co-operation programs. In the next section I discuss many of the well-known scholarship programs supporting student mobility.

Bilateral Scholarship Programs

In the post-colonial era national governments funded a host of bilateral and multilateral scholarly exchange programs in the name of national development, knowledge exchange, and soft power. During the Cold War, scholarship programs were aligned to the geopolitical priorities of the funding nation. Scholarly mobility served as a way to promote the image of the funding nation while also building relationships with future leaders in parts of the world deemed strategic. One of the more prominent programs in the West is the Fulbright Program, which was established in 1946 by J. William Fulbright, a United States senator, as a way to build goodwill and cross-cultural understanding between formerly warring countries and to promote American interests around the world (Lebovic, 2013). Similarly, during the Cold War, Arab students also studied throughout the Soviet bloc, as scholarships for Arab students were incorporated into the USSR's broader geopolitical efforts to gain strategic position in the region through bilateral co-operation in military, industrial, and cultural initiatives (Hannova, 2014). Following Arab nations' independence, Moscow offered state-funded scholarships for Arab students to study throughout the USSR. Katsakioris (2016) shows that the number of Arab students studying in the USSR increased each decade, from 2,000–3,000 in the 1960s, to 4,000–5,000 in the early 1970s, to roughly 10,000 by 1980, and doubling to 20,000 a year by the late 1980s. The largest numbers of students came from Syria, Yemen, Jordan, and Lebanon, with large numbers also coming from Iraq, Algeria, Egypt, Palestine, Sudan, Morocco, and Tunisia.

One historical example of Soviet-era scholarship programs is Czechoslovakia's Operation 90, which provided scholarships for students from "less-developed" countries, including many Arab nations where the Czech government was promoting a sense of international socialist solidarity. Operation 90 was founded in 1956 and offered roughly ninety scholarships a year, with many students coming from Egypt, Syria, and Lebanon. Hannova (2014) reports that Operation 90 prioritized students from prominent families, who had military or political connections and sympathies for socialism, rather than nationalism. In addition, many Arab students from wealthy families paid for their own studies in Czechoslovakia, given its good reputation in the region. In 1960, of 2,000 students studying in Czechoslovakia, 760 were foreign (of whom 400 were Arab) (Hannova, 2014, p. 374). In 1961 the Czech government founded the Seventeenth of November University in Prague specifically to cater to students from Arab and African countries, and included courses on Marxism-Leninism. The university was short-lived, however; the significant investment in scholarships and the education of foreign students was expected to bring about Soviet revolutions in their home countries, but growing disillusionment over high costs with little reward meant that the university shut down in 1974 (Hannova, 2014).

Among Western capitalist countries many scholarship programs that were founded during the Cold War still exist as part of broader cultural diplomacy efforts. For example, the Fulbright Program continues to educate students from around the world. It now funds roughly 8,000 students a year, of whom 4,000 are international students pursuing advanced degrees in the United States. Data on the Fulbright Program indicates that between 2005 and 2015 roughly 1,500 students from the Arab world went to study in the United States through two programs: the Fulbright Foreign Student Program and the Foreign Language Teaching Assistantship. They came from Algeria, Bahrain, Egypt, Jordan, Kuwait, Morocco, Oman, Palestinian Territories, Qatar, Saudi Arabia, Tunisia, and the UAE. Lebanon and Syria are noteworthy exceptions, their exclusion reflecting geopolitical considerations. In part, the Fulbright Program promotes cross-cultural exchanges with the goal of building relationships between citizens of the region and the United States. The application criteria for Jordanians explains that "applicants should be representative and responsible citizens who can contribute to mutual understanding between the people of the United States and Jordan" (JACEE, 2021). The programs are also part of a broader national development project that seeks to bring knowledge and expertise back to the Arab world. Within the region, Egypt, Jordan, and Morocco all have bilateral commissions to support their Fulbright programs, and in each case these commissions are jointly funded by both governments. Bilateral commissions support sending high-calibre students abroad for foreign graduate training as a way to advance their countries' future economic competitiveness. Accordingly, Fulbright grantees enter the United States on a special visa, which requires them to return to their home country for a period of at least two years.

Similar programs, sponsored by the European Commission, have the explicit goal of promoting intercultural exchange and student and staff mobility. Between 2007 and 2013 the European Commission's Erasmus Mundus program sought to "promote European higher education," improve the career prospects of students, and promote exchange programs between Europe and other regions, including the Arab world. Through a set of competitive grants known as Action 2, the Erasmus Mundus program funded partnerships between universities in Europe and those in non–European Union nations, including the North African nations of Algeria, Libya, Morocco, Egypt, and Tunisia. Another program, called the Battuta program, which stands for "Building Academic Ties towards Universities through Training Activities" and was named for the famed Arab scholar Ibn Battuta, funded 285 students at all levels of higher education to study in nineteen partner universities (eight in Europe and eleven in North Africa). Since 2014, when the Erasmus Mundus program became the Erasmus+ program, European nationals have received funding to study in North Africa through the Al Idrisi II program. In its various iterations the Erasmus Mundus program supports the development of higher education in North Africa "in accordance with the foreign policy objectives of the European Union" (EU, 2016). The foreign policy objectives are clear: supporting higher education for economic development in North Africa will result in less migration pressure and stronger trade partners for European countries. These scholarship programs to study in the United States, the United Kingdom, and Europe are part of an older model of international higher education that sought to expand the political influence of funding nations and improve their image abroad.

More recently, a number of Arab Gulf states have launched national scholarship programs for their citizens to study at foreign universities. These programs are framed as meeting the demands of the knowledge economy by building expertise in specific fields. They differ from older models in that they are funded by the Gulf states directly and targeted to their own citizens in the name of skill development, not geopolitical priorities. Table 5.1 provides an overview of national scholarship programs by country, degrees, and subjects funded.

These scholarship programs tend to target specific countries and study programs. For example, Kuwait's scholarship program only permits students to study in the United States. According to the Kuwait Ministry of Higher Education, there are currently over 15,000 Kuwaiti students studying in the United States in thirty-nine approved majors. However, the regulations regarding majors are strict: students can only change majors once and if it will not affect their graduation time. The list of approved majors is specific and dominated by applied sciences. The only disciplinary social sciences on the list are linguistics, psychology, political science, and international relations. The only true humanities subject on the list of approved majors is English, which seems related to strengthening English-language education. Other approved majors include special education and teaching English to speakers of other languages. In terms of the creative arts, approved majors are all applied. While studio art is not approved, architecture, interior design, and graphic design are. Moreover, while the list includes eight different engineering specializations and nine different sub-specializations of business administration, subjects such as history, sociology, anthropology, and philosophy are not approved. Neither is there room for interdisciplinary enquiry or emerging fields such as gender studies, human rights, or global studies.

Student scholarship programs also closely regulate where students can study. Although most programs allow students more options than the Kuwaiti program, which only funds study in the United States, they are often limited to the anglophone world and Europe. Both the UAE and Qatar allow students to pursue degrees in Australia, Canada, the United Kingdom, and other English-speaking countries, as well as in Europe and other Arab nations. The King Abdullah Scholarship Program (KASP) is the only government-funded scholarship program in the Arab

Table 5.1. Overview of Scholarship Programs in Arab Gulf States

Country	Scholarship program	Degrees	Subjects of study	Country of study
Kuwait	Ministry of Higher Education Scholarship	Undergraduate	Architecture, biochemistry, biology, business administration, chemistry, dentistry, nutrition, engineering	USA
UAE	MOHESR Scholarship Program	Language training, bachelor's, master's, PhD programs	Business, computer science, economics, engineering, environment studies, health sciences, information and computer technology, law, management, medicine	USA, UK, Canada, Australia, New Zealand, EU countries, neighbouring Arab countries
Saudi Arabia	King Abdullah Scholarship Program	Undergraduate, master's, PhD programs	Accounting, business, computer sciences, dentistry, digital media, e-commerce, education, engineering, finance, health sciences, hospitality, insurance, law, linguistics, marketing, medicine, natural sciences, nursing, pharmacy, psychology, tourism	Canada, USA, UK, Germany, Italy, Spain, Holland, Australia, New Zealand, France, Japan, Malaysia, China, India, Singapore, South Korea
Qatar	Hamad Bin Khalifa Al Thani Scholarship	Undergraduate, master's, PhD programs		Arab region (including Qatar), Australia, UK, Europe, USA , Canada
	Tamim bin Hamad Scholarship	Undergraduate, master's, PhD programs		Arab region (including Qatar), Australia, UK, Europe, USA, Canada

Gulf that permits students to study in Asian nations. Students in KASP are permitted to study in Japan, Malaysia, China, India, Singapore, and South Korea. That said, in practice, the United States has been the primary destination for Saudi students studying through the program. In addition, in the wake of budget shortfalls, the Saudi government has introduced significant reforms to the KASP to limit overall spending and to use funds more strategically. Starting in 2016, KASP recipients must now study in one of the top fifty academic programs in their field, or at one of the top one hundred universities in the world.

The close regulation of both destinations and degree programs simultaneously reifies Western hegemony in the academic system and implies that certain forms of knowledge are more important or prestigious. The lists of approved programs indicate a rank ordering of knowledges that emphasize technical and applied fields over social science knowledge. This rank ordering of knowledges is reinforced by civil society actors as well. In April 2016, a generous new scholarship program was established to support over 15,000 Arab students from modest backgrounds to study in prestigious universities in the region (Plackett, 2016a). The Abdulla al-Ghurair Foundation for Education, which had an initial budget of USD 1.14 billion over ten years, stated that it would only fund students interested in studying mathematics, science, technology, and engineering. The decision to focus on hard sciences is telling. In an article reported in *Al-Fanar*, Sari Hanafi, the chair of the American University of Beirut's Sociology Department, stated: "We need to encourage top students to do social sciences ... and that means things like scholarships ... How will we solve the problems of ISIS and authoritarian regimes? ... You need real social sciences to properly study this problem and understand it, in order to do anything about it" (Plackett, 2016a). The scholarship program is one of many signals throughout the higher education system that implies that the social sciences and humanities are less valuable and that those who study history, society, the state, and culture are less worthy of support.

International Students

In addition to having scholarship programs that send national students abroad, the region is increasingly educating students from all over the world, predominantly as fee-paying international students. Over the past two decades the total number of international students studying in Arab nations has increased significantly. Figure 5.1 shows the total number of international students in various Arab nations between 2000 and 2018, using data from the World Bank, and Figure 5.2 shows the relative share of international students in systems throughout the region. The figures make it clear that the number of international students has been increasing, and quite dramatically in some countries. Only Lebanon seems to have experienced a decline in its share of international students.

That said, relative proportions vary significantly. Figure 5.2 shows the proportion of all students in each country that are international. It is clear that the three North African countries – Morocco, Tunisia, and Egypt – have proportionally very few international students (~2 per cent). In contrast, in both Jordan and Lebanon, international students make up approximately 10–15 per cent of the higher education system. Meanwhile, the Arab Gulf states enrol a very high proportion of international students, with international students making up almost 40 per cent of the Qatari system and 50 per cent of the Emirati higher education system. The tremendous growth in the number of international students in Qatar and the UAE reflects the countries' investments in expanding the number of private higher education institutions and branch campuses.

Among the middle-income countries Jordan has been a clear "winner" in recruiting international students since 2003, particularly since 2010. Over the past few years the Jordanian minister of higher education met with representatives from Saudi Arabia, Kuwait, Bahrain, India, and Russia to encourage students to attend higher education in Jordan. The number of international students studying in the country has increased in both raw and relative terms, which benefits the country in various ways. They pay substantially higher tuition rates, and their presence also enhances the nation's regional educational reputation by signalling Jordan as a desirable hub for education. Badran and Badran (2018) analyse Ministry of Education data and show that, in Jordan, programs for international students are yielding substantial gains and serve to subsidize the cost of public education. For example, at the University of Jordan, they find that tuition fees from international students enrolled in undergraduate programs average USD 19,782 a year and generate roughly USD 30 million for the university.

Private universities in Tunisia and Morocco have also been successful in attracting increasing numbers of foreign students, albeit from very small initial enrolments, so overall international enrolments remain very small in both countries. Many of the international students in North Africa attend private universities and come from francophone sub-Saharan African nations. In 2012 the president and founder of a private institution in Tunisia told me that roughly 5 per cent of the institution's students were international, primarily from francophone countries in sub-Saharan Africa, including the Congo, Mauritania, and Gabon. He

Figure 5.1. Number of International Students in Higher Education, by Country

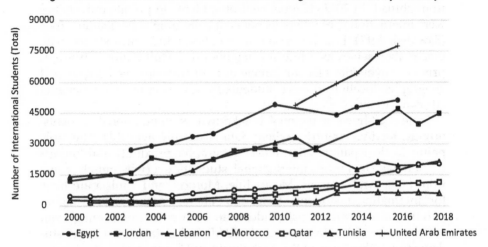

Source: Data accessed through the WB Open Data module for Stata. Indicator UIS.
MS.56.T (Azevedo, 2011)

Figure 5.2. International Students (% Total), by Country and Year

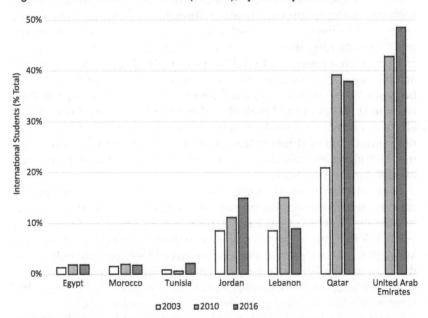

Source: Data accessed through the WB Open Data module for Stata. Indicator UIS.MSEP.56
(Azevedo, 2011)
Note: Data for UAE 2010 comes from 2011 due to missing data in 2010.

said that its goal was to recruit roughly 10–20 per cent of its students from abroad. In 2017, 12.5 per cent of students in private universities were international, of whom 98 per cent were from sub-Saharan Africa (Sawahel, 2017). Like Jordanian universities, which have strategically placed themselves as a hub for neighbouring Gulf nations, Tunisia's private universities take advantage of their francophone heritage and geographic location to serve students from francophone sub-Saharan African nations.

Table 5.2 shows a regional breakdown of international students' origins, for five countries where data is reliably available. The table points to clear patterns that reflect geographic proximity and linguistic heritage. In Jordan international students overwhelmingly come from other Arab nations. Meanwhile, Morocco and Tunisia are hubs for international students from sub-Saharan Africa, with roughly two-thirds of international students in both countries coming from sub-Saharan Africa. In contrast, the UAE and Qatar attract many students from other parts of the Arab world and South Asia.

The technical literature implies that the more international students a university or nation can attract, the better. Attracting international students is touted as a means to generate revenue, develop students' intercultural competencies, and contribute to mutual understanding. In line with this strategic approach to internationalization, the patterns shown here point to the ways in which countries and institutions are strategically positioning themselves as education destinations for students from particular countries. In 2013, I spoke to the director of recruitment at a private university who said that they were proud that their student body was 50 per cent international, and this fact was advertised on their website. It was not until I probed further that she explained that almost all their international students were from one country, Kuwait. Such a high proportion of students from a single country contrasts discourses in which internationalization is equated with learning from high levels of cross-cultural diversity.

Owing to these trends, many believe that international students are concentrated in low-quality private institutions, allowing entrepreneurs to reap the benefits of students' aspirations for social mobility. In my fieldwork in Tunisia I found that many students, who did not actually know much about private universities, would say off-handedly, "Oh, they are for the [sub-Saharan] Africans" and particularly those from wealthy backgrounds who cannot or choose not to study in Europe but want access to what they characterize as "easy credentials."

Similarly, although the high-profile institutions of Knowledge Village and NYUAD are well known and respected, in the UAE the majority of

Table 5.2. Origins of International Students (2017, or latest year available)

Country	Arab states	Sub-Saharan Africa	Central, East, and South Asia
Jordan	83%	1%	9%
Morocco	19%	68%	2%
Qatar	71%	3%	19%
Tunisia	32%	64%	1%
United Arab Emirates	55%	6%	31%

Source: UNESCO Institute for Statistics (2019)
Note: Data on international students' origins is either non-existent or not reliable for Lebanon, Syria, and Egypt.

international students are actually studying in private institutions that are located in free trade zones, which are loosely regulated and primarily tuition dependent and revenue generating. Although the UAE specifically developed its private higher education sector to serve its large number of non-citizens, many of whom were born and raised in the UAE but are not eligible to attend public universities, over the past decade there has been a significant and rapid increase in international students as well (KHDA, 2017). In the Gulf states international students constitute a notable source of both revenue and future labour. Recently the UAE extended the length of international student visas, signalling a desire to develop a homegrown pipeline of highly skilled talent for the labour force and reduce dependence on costly recruitment from those educated abroad.

The two outliers in the region are Morocco and Tunisia. Table 5.3 shows the net mobility rate, which is the total number of inbound students minus the total number of outbound students. A negative net mobility rate indicates there are more students travelling abroad than international students incoming. As the table shows, both Morocco and Tunisia have sent thousands more students to study abroad than they bring to their own institutions. The vast majority of Moroccan and Tunisian students are heading to Europe to study in France, Spain, and the United Kingdom, as well as across the Atlantic Ocean to Canada and the United States. The patterns point to a well-known academic hierarchy: sub-Saharan African students come to North Africa, while North African students head north and west to Europe and beyond to study.

In short, throughout the region the overall number and proportion of international students in higher education systems have been increasing, signalling a high degree of people mobility. While international

Table 5.3. Net International Mobility in Selected Countries

Country	Net mobility (2016)
Egypt	19,679
Jordan	22,431
Lebanon	3,432
Morocco	−30,606
Tunisia	−14,440
Qatar	4,487
United Arab Emirates	65,745

Source: Data accessed through the WB Open Data module for Stata. Indicator UIS. MENF.56 (Azevedo, 2011)

students often bring diverse experiences and backgrounds that can enrich everyone's learning in and out of the classroom, there is no guarantee that internationalization improves learning. The share of foreign students is a poor proxy for the extent of students' cross-cultural interactions or for other forms of ethnic and economic diversity on university campuses. Indeed, the Arab Gulf states are some of the most diverse societies in the world when one considers the number of nationalities and ethnicities working and living there. Although internationalization may imply the mixing of youth from different national backgrounds, it does not necessarily imply exposure to, or empathy with, those of different class backgrounds. Moreover, the growth of internationalization in the Arab world, as in other parts of the world, ignores uncomfortable realities about the state and citizenship: foreign and national students may be more equal in classroom interactions than they ever will be off campus, as social status in Arab societies maps onto citizenship status in subtle and not so subtle ways.

Provider Mobility

Although scholarly mobility is as old as the university, it has only been common in the past few decades for whole institutions to move across borders. The movement of higher education programs and providers across national borders, typically in the form of branch campuses or franchise models, is known in the academic literature as cross-border education. The Arab Gulf is arguably the most active region in the world for cross-border higher education. The region's ability to attract high-profile and prestigious Western universities has been celebrated in the media as evidence of an impressive commitment to developing the human resources needed for a future that is not dependent on natural resources (Swan, 2013). Of an estimated 311 branch campuses in the world, the UAE alone is home to 41, and Qatar, a nation with only roughly 300,000 citizens, has 11 (C-BERT, 2017). By way of comparison, China, a country with a population of over a billion, has 36 branch campuses. Certainly, not all branch campuses are created equal, and the branch campuses in the Arab Gulf states range from the globally elite NYUAD and Sorbonne University Abu Dhabi to much smaller branch campuses, most of which are for-profit and unregulated.

The first prominent educational hub, Education City, was founded with the stated goal of moving Qatar away from its reliance on oil and gas and to transform it into a knowledge-based economy. As expatriates constitute roughly 95 per cent of the labour force, the country's leaders understood that higher education was crucial to developing a local pool of highly-educated Qataris (Donn & al-Manthri, 2010; Hvidt, 2015).

Education City currently hosts eleven universities from around the world, including Virginia Commonwealth University, Weill Cornell Medical College, Carnegie Mellon University, Northwestern University, Georgetown University's School of Foreign Service, Texas A&M University, University College London, and HEC Paris. In addition, the College of the North Atlantic, a community college in Canada, was invited to Qatar to strengthen the vocational education sector. It offers programs in technical fields such as business, engineering, health sciences, and information technology.

Countries choose to host branch campuses for a number of anticipated benefits, including quality and the provision of a specific model of training. Additionally, branch campuses serve as a physical symbol of a country's commitments to global engagement more broadly. They help nations to signal their modernity: "for governments in the GCC, education most certainly has symbolic value in terms of signifying modernity and giving the appearance of the redistribution of wealth through upholding the social contract" (Ridge, 2014, p. 151). Other goals involve some combination of social and economic development, regional and international competitiveness, and prestige.

Nonetheless, branch campuses can be risky ventures for both universities and host countries. Universities may risk their reputations by becoming mired in scandals, watering down the prestige of their academic degree, or by simply failing to attract necessary students and faculty. Indeed, there is no shortage of stories covering scandals and failures of branch campuses. NYUAD has been a focus of criticism by members of its New York–based campus, with workers' rights in the

UAE being one of the primary areas of contestation. As recently as 2018, the university promised to pay thousands of unpaid guest workers from India, Bangladesh, and Pakistan, and concerns over low levels of faculty engagement at the home campus and a lack of academic freedom in branch campuses have dominated media coverage of NYU's Abu Dhabi and Shanghai campuses.

Branch campuses are not without their detractors within Arab societies as well. The governments of Arab Gulf states have paid substantial sums of money to host Western universities. Many Gulf publics are questioning the value of branch campuses and the government's justification for spending so much money on so few citizens. Qatar initially promised Cornell University USD 750 million over its first decade (2001–11) to establish its medical school in Doha. Since then the Qatar Foundation has continued to provide generous support for Education City. In 2014 it spent roughly USD 320 million on Education City, with Cornell University receiving an estimated USD 121.7 million, Georgetown University USD 59.5 million, and Northwestern University USD 45.3 million for their Doha campuses (N. Anderson, 2015).

Education City remains almost entirely funded by the Qatar Foundation, and there is no indication that this will change soon. In an interview I conducted in Qatar, an employee of the Qatar Foundation explained that the current model encourages the idea that Qatar has purchased its elite universities. "It is based on the capitalist system; it suggests that we have a product [knowledge] and you can pay for it." The implication is that Qatar's relationship with branch campuses is one of economic transaction, rather than equal academic partnership.

One of the major critiques of the branch campus system is that it is educating few local students, therefore raising questions about who benefits from these investments. Local students who enrol in the branch campuses have to meet roughly the same admissions criteria as foreign students do. However, initially, local students' academic abilities in English were weak. One interviewee described this as "challenges with academic standards," stating, "At first, English proficiency was a major issue, but they've worked hard to adapt to that and support students." The percentage of local students admitted to branch campuses in their first few years was quite low. In 2010 the inaugural class of NYUAD had 150 total students, and students from the United States represented about a third of these. Eight years later, according to NYU, the undergraduate class admitted in 2019 was 15 per cent Emirati, and the UAE constituted the largest single nationality (NYUAD, 2019). Meanwhile, in Education City many campuses are now majority Qatari. Virginia Commonwealth University, which focuses on the arts, is 80 per cent

Qatari; Texas A&M University is 50 per cent Qatari; and Georgetown School of Foreign Service is 30–40 per cent Qatari.

These changes have occurred in part because primary and secondary education has responded to families' desire for students to attend branch campuses, and in part because specific government initiatives have created pipelines for talented locals to attend them. In practice, this means that local students tend to come from specific feeder schools that prepare them for an elite university education. In Doha these are primarily Qatar Academy and the American School of Doha, which raises concerns that Education City is essentially a bastion for well-educated Qatari elites. Moreover, there is an enduring scepticism over the qualifications of local students. One alumnus of NYUAD with whom I spoke explained: "The number of Emiratis has been increasing. Some people say it's just an agenda, we have to placate the people funding us, and to an extent, I think that's true."

Even as the percentage of local students has increased, branch campuses are still small players in the overall higher education system. Official statistics report that in 2017–18, 18,628 Qatari citizens were enrolled in the public higher education system, which includes Qatar University and two colleges. Meanwhile, in the same year, only 1,313 Qatari citizens were enrolled in the Education City branch campuses (PSA, 2018). Yet, public institutions, which serve the overwhelming majority, are given less financial support and academic autonomy. In an interview I conducted with a higher education researcher in the region, he exclaimed, "You have Education Village, with private and branch campuses, and you have Qatar University. And there is no relationship between them."

Dr. El Amine, a Lebanese expert of higher education, explained his scepticism of the Arab Gulf states' branch campuses: "They are paying them to be there, and *Ahlan wa Sahlan* (Welcome)! – please bring your students, bring your professors." He continued: "But, in terms of students, who are the students studying in these universities? In numbers, they are practically nothing, in the hundreds. How can they change higher education? These are just business for the universities in the [United] States. They are paid for, and you can ask everyone, they are paid by the government of the Emirates to show 'We are good, we have good universities coming from outside.' But in fact, those who are studying there, they are not nationals. The professors are foreigners and the students are foreigners. They are taught in foreign languages." Attitudes like this are not uncommon and reflect the deep scepticism over branch campuses in the Arab Gulf states.

Similar scepticism is exhibited when it comes to the involvement of branch campuses in their societies. The programming of community engagement is framed as one way in which the university can share its expertise with the local community. It typically includes supporting policy dialogue or convening artistic and cultural events. Observers, however, many within Education City itself, have voiced scepticism over how community engagement is actually being conducted. In a personal interview with a former employee at Georgetown's School of Foreign Service–Qatar (SFS–Q), Kayyali (2016) documented the scepticism. The interviewee said: "The not-so-pretty side of things has been community engagement. Random classes have been offered to ministry employees and civil servants because they are just a box for SFS–Q to tick off and say, 'WE ARE ENGAGING.' However, in my opinion, real engagement can only happen when real transfer of knowledge takes place" (Kayyali, 2016, pp. 36–7). In an interview I conducted, an observer suggested that branch campuses had little impact: "In small countries, like the Emirates and Qatar, it's a matter of self-image to say, 'We have good universities.' But the value of it in terms of social change, social value, social knowledge, I assume, is nothing. Epsilon. Very, very small. 0.0001, or something like that."

Similarly, a number of critics have pointed out that many of the academics working in Education City may have been recruited for subject-matter expertise, not necessarily because of an interest in Qatar or Qatari society. This can result in mutual distrust or isolation. Kayyali (2016) cites an interview with an employee of the Qatar Foundation who exclaimed: "There are no structural incentives for their American faculty to integrate and learn about the local Qatari culture. There is distrust, distance and isolation of Education City which is problematic to us" (p. 38). In the UAE I spoke with faculty and students at NYUAD who thought that a similar dynamic was playing out there; they said that they did not really interact with Emirati students, who make up an admittedly small proportion of all students. For example, when I asked one student about his experience with Emirati students at NYUAD, he replied: "In general, we don't interact with them. There are very few students who form an actual bond with Emirati students." One faculty member with whom I spoke said, "I don't have any Emirati students – I don't know them."

Many of those working in and researching branch campuses, however, largely rejected these criticisms as the growing pains associated with any new initiative. One researcher with whom I spoke in Qatar explained: "Yes, there were some challenges at first, but over time these get worked out. The model of co-ed education is working – students work together. There may have to be some accommodation, like a female-only lounge, but these are small changes."

With branch campuses in Doha celebrating their fifteenth year and NYUAD nearing its tenth year, there is no doubt that these ambitious projects have had an impact. In 2019 I spoke with a researcher who had watched Education City change. He explained: "The scene is changing. It has changed dramatically over the past fifteen years." Those working within the Qatar Foundation ecosystem consistently pointed out the impact that Education City had on diversifying the higher education landscape, particularly for females, as some families chose not to send their daughters abroad. A professor who works at one of the campuses in Education City discussed the project's role in addressing female education: "Face it, it's cheaper to send a thousand Qataris abroad than to set up these campuses, but they did it." She explained that part of the narrative about Education City and its founding is that "Qatari women can't go abroad" and are "a segment of the population that isn't being attended to, and so this addresses a local need ... As a project, it's some politics and some social engineering." One young Qatari male with whom I spoke, a graduate of Georgetown's School of Foreign Service, also based his understanding in terms of need, stating, "It's just what was needed."

Neha Vora's (2018) ethnography of teaching and learning at Texas A&M University at Qatar, an American branch campus in Doha, offers a more nuanced view of daily life in branch campuses than is typical in the media. Vora describes how students in her Anthropology 101 course took offence at a core text that portrayed marriage between cousins as exotic, and she reflects on how teaching in Doha helped her understand the extent to which anthropology as a discipline, and American higher education as an enterprise more broadly, continue to rely on orientalist tropes and to centre Western students' perspectives. She suggests that the ethnic, national, and linguistic diversity, close interactions with faculty, and campus resources available to her Doha students create opportunities for learning that are out of reach for students on American campuses. Her book is an ardent call for greater humility among Western scholars who assume that the role of foreign campuses is to "open the minds" of students in the region.

Branch campuses clearly defy oversimplification. They have been highly debated in both the local and the international media and criticized as ostentatious and controversial. At the same time, Arab Gulf states have invested heavily in them and seem to have found a fast track to elite knowledge production and human capital training in the name of improving higher education quality, scientific research, and human development across the region. One reason branch campuses may garner such resistance is that they threaten the traditional hierarchies. The model of the elite branch campus unsettles historic models of internationalization based on sending Arab students to study in the West to obtain academic knowledge and then return to their home countries. Instead, they establish Arab nations as home to elite centres of learning. At the regional level the Arab Gulf states are upending traditional regional hierarchies where older American universities – the American University of Beirut and the American University in Cairo – and national universities such as Cairo University were considered the best institutions and attracted international students from across the region. At the same time, admission into NYUAD is more competitive than admission to its New York campus. It seems that the nouveau elite status of higher education in the nouveau riche Arab Gulf states is most controversial among those who feel that their status is threatened, Western institutions included.

While the elite branch campuses of the Arab Gulf are the most high-profile new universities in the region, other institutions offer distinctive models of what international co-operation could look like. One of the oldest models of foreign co-operation in the Arab world is found in the Middle Atlas Mountains of Morocco where, in 1995, al-Akhawayn University (which means "the two brothers" in Arabic) was established by King Hassan II of Morocco and Crown Prince Abdallah bin Abdel-Aziz of Saudi Arabia as a symbol of mutual respect and partnership. It was founded with the distinctive aim of creating an American-style liberal arts university in North Africa. The university was unlike any other in Morocco – a public, but privately governed, tuition-charging, liberal arts university that has a residential campus and teaches in English, not Arabic or French. Although the university charges tuition, it is officially a public institution and has received government support since its beginnings. Al-Akhawayn has retained an elite character, in part because its tuition fees are high for most Moroccan families and in part because it teaches in English and has competitive admissions, accepting roughly a third of all applicants. Its elite character is also bolstered by the fact that members of the royal family have attended the university. Al-Akhawayn represents a unique model in the region as a symbol of elite liberal arts education that is based on regional co-operation between Saudi Arabia and Morocco and that predates the creation of the Western branch campuses in the Gulf. As a Sunni monarchy whose king enjoys tremendous legitimacy from his long lineage, Morocco has a history of building alliances with Gulf monarchies, which has included funding for infrastructure and social welfare programs. More recently, Morocco's Mohammed V University, a public university, opened a branch campus in Doha.

Another model that has spread throughout the Arab world is the joint or binational university, which has been championed by Germany. In the 2000s the German Academic Exchange Service (DAAD), a semi-governmental organization, helped establish new universities in both Jordan and Egypt based on the German model. The new universities teach German-language courses and promote study in Germany. In 2002 the German University of Cairo was founded by presidential decree as a private university. At the time it was the first German university outside Germany. Following its success, the German Jordanian University (GJU) was founded in 2005 as a new model of public university, in close partnership with the German government and funded for its first four years by DAAD. After two years of studying at the GJU, students can complete their degree program in Germany.

In 2013 I visited the GJU, which is located on the outskirts of Amman but has convenient public bus service from the capital. The contrast between it and the University of Jordan, as a large public university in Amman, is noticeable. Course lectures were officially conducted in English, but students roaming the campus spoke in colloquial Jordanian Arabic, accompanied by code switching between the two around campus. Students wore tight jeans, boots, bright colours, and expensive jewellery and accessories. Very few of the women were veiled, and almost none was wearing the long trench coat common in public universities. I watched mixed-gender groups of girls and boys hanging out together, chatting with one another, as well as girls and boys coupled together who were talking alone – signals of intimacy and mixed-gender interactions that were much less visible at my visits to public universities. It was immediately clear that GJU intentionally attracted a distinctive student body, one that was multilingual, urban, upper-middle class, and Westernized.

The GJU is a high-profile project for the governments of Germany and Jordan. It is a partnership that seeks both to improve the quality of technical education in Jordan and to strengthen links between Germany and Jordan. An employee of DAAD responsible for student recruitment explained to me that the GJU was considered "the crown jewel" of DAAD projects in the Middle East and North Africa region. For Germany, it is a vie for soft power that will expand its influence in the region. Walking the hallways of the university, I could not help but think that it was highly successful. I saw students wearing clothes that bore the German flag, and posters about future options for studying in Germany. For Jordanians, enrolment at the GJU offers a perfect combination of foreign credentials, which are viewed as superior in the local labour market, and a possible pathway to emigrating to Europe.

Internationalization as a National Project

Throughout the region Arab families, universities, and governments have embraced higher education's global mandate. This chapter argues that at the individual and institutional level internationalization signals legitimacy and distinction (Waldow, 2018). As the contrast between the region's middle-income countries and the wealthy Arab Gulf states makes clear, however, internationalization varies across the Arab world. In the region's middle-income countries internationalization tends to be resource generating. Discourses of system strengthening are linked to the idea of individual opportunity by framing internationalization as a way to cultivate opportunities for mobility and migration for a globally oriented middle class. Among upper-middle-class families, foreign-language degree programs and opportunities for student or scholarly mobility are celebrated as a form of expanded opportunity. Their primary benefit is to confer status on participating individuals. In the aggregate they constitute a class project of the globally oriented upper-middle class by supporting their aspirations for transnational mobility and status. Around the world it is those with strong English-language skills, financial resources, and cultural capital that have always been most likely to benefit from internationalization, and the Arab world is no different in this regard.

Internationalization as a class project is useful for Arab governments that are seeking to satisfy the demand of upper-middle-class families, while also signalling to other nations their willingness and ability to participate in a global knowledge economy. For the middle-income nations of the region, internationalization helps garner external resources. Scholarship programs (such as the bilateral Fulbright commissions) and new joint initiatives (such as the GJU) are jointly funded, allowing Arab governments to signal their own investment in their citizens and their ability to garner additional funding from other donors or governments. Contestation over such projects is rare, in part because they serve primarily privileged nationals.

In the Arab Gulf states internationalization tends to be resource intensive and is mapped onto a broader state project of modernization and strategic nationalization of the labour force. In the Arab Gulf internationalization raises basic questions about the role of higher education in nation-building. Romani (2009) argues that "it is highly unlikely that the influx of new higher education venues can proceed without engaging the conflict between nationalism and the necessary *internationalism* of the projects" (p. 5). The importation of international branch campuses in the Arab Gulf states has largely been interpreted, particularly in the West, as "copying" external models and even "importing" the prestige that is associated with elite universities in the United States (Wilkins & Huisman, 2012).

This dominant model of internationalization reifies Western influence and colonial and imperial hierarchies, including a global linguistic hierarchy. For universities, internationalization often entails not only offering foreign-language programs but also teaching in foreign languages, typically English or French. Increasingly, English is characterized as the only truly global language. As a result, "national academic systems enthusiastically welcome English as a contributor to internationalizing, competing, and becoming 'world class'" (Altbach, 2013, p. 2). In the Arab world, language of instruction maps onto status hierarchies between universities. The most elite universities throughout the region teach in English. Other European languages, including French in former French colonies and German in the German universities in Egypt and Jordan, are also promoted as languages of socio-economic power and promise future opportunities for mobility. In contrast, university programs that use Arabic as a language of instruction are characterized as trapping students in local labour markets or limiting them to outdated sources of knowledge.

Beyond language, current approaches to internationalization reinforce the idea that by adopting Western models of higher education, Arab states will secure the external legitimacy associated with high-quality higher education. This Western orientation of many internationalization projects may undermine faith in local capacity and ignore alternative visions of quality. An alternative approach to internationalization in the region would disrupt the assumed linkages between "international," "Western," and "prestige." This might start by recognizing that the Arab world is already deeply internationalized: its youth are already multicultural, multilingual, cosmopolitan, and mobile. International engagements are an opportunity to highlight the region's cultural heritage and to share the region's knowledge with a world that is, at best, ignorant and, at worst, overtly biased in its perceptions of the Arab world. Another approach is to strengthen regional collaboration: stronger links between the region's institutions could build opportunities for regional collaboration to tackle similar social issues and promote knowledge production in Arabic.

6
Between Knowledge and Truth

The worldwide economic shift from industry to information has meant that knowledge is increasingly characterized as the primary driver of national development. Countries around the world are reforming their higher education systems to support research and knowledge production, and universities are increasingly pressured to produce high-quality, relevant, and marketable research. Framed within this global race for knowledge, development experts lament the fact that Arab nations lag far behind in scientific research and have few high-impact scholars or publications in Arabic (Zou'bi, Mohamed-Nour, el-Kharraz, & Hassan, 2015). The technical literature links the region's low levels of scientific research to stagnant economies, arguing that the region needs more scientific, technical, and applied research to support national development.

In the dominant conception, knowledge production is characterized as a largely mechanical affair: time and resources go into the university, and knowledge emerges in the form of publications and patents. Numerous reports highlight the bureaucratic and institutional obstacles to conducting academic research in the region, including a lack of funding and few incentives for professors. They suggest that research productivity can be improved with policies, such as linking faculty members' promotion and pay rises to publications. This focus on productivity has put pressure on Arab academics to publish in internationally indexed journals and often in English (Hanafi, 2011; Hanafi & Arvanitis, 2014). It also creates perverse incentives that lead to the inflation of numbers through low-quality publications or the recruitment of foreign scholars to publish at an institution, resulting in research that may be irrelevant to local communities.

This chapter argues that the technical literature focuses on individual and institutional practices while ignoring the deeper historical and geopolitical factors that shape research production. Drawing on cross-national data, I argue that disparities in research productivity map onto linguistic, economic, and geopolitical power. While state support, institutional resources, and faculty incentives can and do matter, they do not erase the fundamental structural realities that shape the global academic system. Research and patent production are highly concentrated in North America and Europe, supported by the hegemonic status of English (Hanafi & Arvanitis, 2014). Middle-income countries in the Arab world actually have scholarly productivity in line with or above similar nations globally and also have impressively high rates of international co-authorship.

Fundamentally, the focus on productivity ignores the fact that knowledge creation is a creative and social process. It entails collaboration among scholars (Bamyeh, 2015), as well as autonomy, motivation, stability, and a social mandate. Intellectual freedom allows scholars to examine, debate, and critique ideas. In the contemporary Arab world the free pursuit of truth is, more often than not, perceived as a threat to ruling regimes (Waterbury, 2020). Arab states are often unwilling to give researchers the freedom they need, or are unable to give them the stability and the social mandate they need, to be productive (Almansour & Kempner, 2017; George, 2003; Waterbury, 2020).

Recognizing these realities does not discount the need for research on the pressing issues in the Arab world. In fact, it makes it even more important to protect the autonomy, stability, and support for the research that is being done within the region. Supporting research is a long-term process of institution building. More pointedly, supporting research also means supporting faculty members, who are often at the front lines of university-reform initiatives. This chapter concludes with a call for an expansive view of the role of research in development; to view the university's research mission in primarily utilitarian and economic terms is narrow minded. Some of the most pressing questions that the region faces involve the messy social sciences and the so-called fluffy humanities: questions of identity, cultural difference, morality, civic engagement, and subjective well-being.

The University and the Knowledge Society

One of the university's core purposes has always been to preserve, create, and disseminate knowledge. Increasingly, the emphasis on knowledge production is closely tied to discourses about the changing economy, where knowledge is viewed as the driver of innovation, economic growth, and development (Frank & Meyer, 2007). Sociologist

Gili Drori has examined the reasons that the discourse of science is so powerful in the contemporary imagination. She argues that dominant discursive constructions in the field of international development create clear links between science, technology, and development. In this model, investments in basic science lead to technological innovation, which then drives advances in economic development. In her research Drori (1993) finds that the links between science and economic development are not straightforward at all; in fact, she finds that in the least developed countries there is no statistical relationship between investments in science and subsequent technological innovation or economic development. Yet, in global development, scientific research is overwhelmingly viewed as a primary means to progress and development.

Accordingly, investment in research and development has increased steadily over the past few decades. Data shows that in 1996 roughly 1.39 per cent of the world's GDP per capita was devoted to research and development (R&D), which increased to 1.54 per cent in 2006 and 1.73 per cent in 2018 (UIS, 2019). This represents an almost 25 per cent increase in global investment in R&D over the past twenty years. In 2015, as part of the SDGs, the United Nation's global agenda for development, countries committed to supporting scientific research and innovation. SDG 9 states that all countries will "build resilient infrastructure, promote inclusive and sustainable industrialization and foster innovation." This commitment includes a specific target for R&D and calls on countries to increase expenditure in R&D as a proportion of overall GDP. This call has been heeded in the Arab world as well, where numerous Arab governments and regional initiatives have committed to increasing locally relevant research production (Badran, 2018).

The emphasis on science and innovation has had important implications for higher education. Universities produce the majority of new research and development worldwide (Badran, 2018), and in the global era, universities are increasingly orienting themselves towards research excellence (Ramirez, 2010; Ramirez & Tiplic, 2014). At the same time, neoliberal policies have affected public support for research, and discourses of efficiency have focused attention on research outputs. In the post–Second World War era, countries devoted public funding to research and science in the name of national development. In the contemporary neoliberal era, the focus on outcomes and efficiency has contributed to a "contractual" vision of research, where benefits of research are articulated primarily in terms of anticipated benefits to the economy. Geuna (2001) describes "the quest for nationally relevant university research" as resulting from neoliberal policies that seek "accountability and cost reduction" (p. 609). The changes have led to more industry funding and more applied research. Neoliberal practices have also raised concerns over a "research productivity gap" where research production is concentrated increasingly in elite and well-funded institutions and conducted by declining numbers of full-time professors. These discourses have had great currency in the Arab world (Mazawi, 2007), where the region has largely been considered to be failing in knowledge production, and where knowledge economy discourses have been associated with reforming universities and science and innovation systems.

"Far from Innovative"

For at least two decades development publications have argued that the research production of Arab universities is low and lacks innovation. In the early 2000s the United Nations Development Programme published a series of reports on the state of human development in the Arab world, known as the *Arab Human Development Report* (*AHDR*). The first, published in 2002, argued that Arabic scholarship had little impact in international academic circles, with few publications from the Arab world being widely cited (Sakr, 2004). The first *AHDR* found that in 1987 only one paper from each of Egypt, Saudi Arabia, Kuwait, and Algeria was cited more than forty times, while in the United States 10,481 papers were quoted more than forty times, and in Switzerland 523 papers (UNDP, 2002, p. 67). Similarly, the 2003 version, *Building a Knowledge Economy*, focused on knowledge production and dissemination. Over forty scholars, including many Arab scholars based in the region, wrote background papers in English and Arabic for the report (UNDP, 2003). The report was critical of the scholarship in the region: "Despite the increase in the number of published Arabic research papers in specialized global periodicals, Arabic research activity continues to be far from innovative" (p. 70). This discourse, which characterizes the Arab world as having a "knowledge deficit," has been critiqued for placing the blame for low publication rates on Arab scholars and universities, rather than recognizing the myriad factors that affect publication and citation rates (Mazawi, 2007; Sakr, 2004).

Yet, nearly two decades later, discussions of knowledge production in the Arab world continue to frame the region as failing. A 2013 WB publication on higher education governance in the Arab world, *Benchmarking Governance as a Tool for Promoting Change*, states that, lacking a better indicator of student learning, "the number of scientific citations per 100,000 inhabitants is used as a proxy for intellectual contribution to the world body of knowledge" and that, "in this regard, the contribution of MENA countries, as in other developing countries like Malaysia, Chile, and Colombia, is very limited compared to OECD countries (Jaramillo, 2013, p. 12). Statements like this are overly simplistic and overtly biased. The link between academic publications and what the WB has called a country's "intellectual contribution to the world body of knowledge" is anything but straightforward. By simplifying the link between publications and intellectual contribution, publications such as these ignore the variation in structural conditions across world regions.

In the development literature the region's lack of scientific innovation is framed as an impediment to the creation of vibrant knowledge economies. One critique is that, in the Arab world, governments provide most of the funding for research, and there is still little private-sector investment in research and development, which can undermine the economic impact of science and innovation (Badran, 2018). The 2003 *AHDR* notes that the Arab university's low quality "limits the ability of research centers ... to achieve advanced levels of scientific and technological performance" (UNDP, 2003, p. 71). Similarly, a UNESCO report on the state of science in the region states that science and technology policies in the Arab world "have failed to catalyse knowledge production effectively or add value to products and services" and suggests that this is because the incentives and interests of academic researchers are far removed from the needs and priorities of the business community (Zou'bi et al., 2015, p. 435).

The blame for low research production is often placed on higher education, with critiques being made of rote memorization, heavy teaching loads, and a lack of facilities (Dohjoka, Campbell, & Hill, 2017). Development actors also tend to place the burden of research largely on individual faculty members and suggest that research productivity can be improved with better resources and better incentives. This type of discussion implicitly frames knowledge production as a mechanical affair: faculty members' time and resources go into the university, and knowledge emerges in the form of publications and patents. In fact, the professional lives of Arab academics are much more complicated.

Academic Researchers as Knowledge Producers

Academics in the Arab region vary significantly in terms of their academic training, professional goals, and institutional contexts. A study on research productivity commissioned by the International Institute of Education found that only a small percentage of Arab faculty members would be considered "research active," compared to two-thirds of the professors at top universities worldwide (Bhandari & Amine, 2012). This finding is not an anomaly; numerous studies have found that research is a low priority for many academics in the region (Almansour & Kempner, 2017; Amer, 2019; Austin, Chapman, Farah, Wilson, & Ridge, 2014). In addition, Arab academics face several institutional and structural barriers when conducting research, including high teaching loads, weak institutional support for research, a lack of or poorly equipped facilities, limited access to academic journals, and little emphasis on research in promotion decisions (Amer, 2019; Herrera, 2006).

A lack of funding for research is recognized as a major impediment. The 2003 *AHDR* focused on the problems posed by low resources: "The under-funding of higher education impacts negatively on science and technology in particular, because these fields require the provision and renovation of costly special facilities, equipment and materials" (UNDP, 2003, p. 72). A lack of financial support means that the research that is done is on a relatively small scale. Dr. Karim Nasr, Dean of Business Administration at the University of Balamand in Lebanon, explained: "We do some good research, highly relevant and useful, but on an international scale it is minimal. And the reason for this is, we are doing it from a very humble set of resources on a local level. Budgetary allocations to research – if the university does not have a budget for research, it does not happen. There is no other source ... from the government or abroad, it doesn't exist ... not in the sense of a sizable amount that would drive research and make it comparable in terms of the West."

Throughout the low- and middle-income nations in the region, professors' salaries are generally low (Waterbury, 2020). Waterbury (2020) draws on data from *Al-Fanar* that shows that Arab professors are largely missing from the middle class, meaning that in general, outside the Arab Gulf region and possibly Lebanon, "a professor's salary does not provide a comfortable middle-class standard of living" (p. 274). One Egyptian professor writes in a public post titled "Yes, I Am a University Professor" that he only makes EGP 6,000 a month (USD 375). He asks, "How can this be enough for providing the basic needs for our home, wife, children, transportation, clothing, research studies, scientific conferences? ... There's no status for someone, however successful they are in their scientific field, if they're unable to buy clothes for themselves or reach their university in a dignified way" (Badawi, 2019). L. Anderson (2012) similarly laments that the base salary of custodians at the American University in Cairo is higher than the base pay of public university faculty members.

Other studies have found that, given their low salaries, many Arab professors moonlight to make additional money (Almansour &

Kempner, 2017). Waterbury (2020) argues that one of the most pervasive myths of higher education in the Arab world is that of the "full-time professor," when in fact most professors in the region have secondary employment, often due to low salaries. He cites studies that find that anywhere from 20 to 45 per cent of university instructors work outside their home institutions in Morocco (Bourqia, 2011; Cherkaoui, 2011). This often takes the form of teaching on contract at private universities. Regardless, Almansour and Kempner (2017) point out that the choice to take on additional work further reduces their time to conduct research.

A lack of funding for research, combined with low salaries, means that many academics must fund their own research. Unsurprisingly, in a region-wide survey of over 650 researchers across the region conducted by *Al-Fanar*, 84 per cent reported using their own money to conduct research, and 49 per cent of researchers in the lower-middle-income countries of the region stated they would move abroad for improved salaries (Amer, 2019).

Additionally, many academics lack access to the journals or online databases they need to conduct their research. In its survey of researchers *Al-Fanar* found that roughly 50 per cent of all those surveyed did not have reliable access to the internet at their institutions, and 52 per cent did not have free access to academic journals (Amer, 2019). Other surveys with Arab academics have found similar concerns. In a survey with Arab social scientists a large proportion reported that they did not have access to needed sources from their libraries, and many stated that they could not get sources in Arabic from online databases (Hanafi & Arvanitis, 2014). Similarly, after interviewing over seventy faculty members from fourteen countries throughout the region about their views on research, Almansour and Kempner (2017) quote one Tunisian academic who quipped, "Technology did not reach us yet" (p. 228).

In my own research in the region I often spoke to academics who were frustrated by this lack of support and had to be creative in the face of challenges. One professor at Mohammed V University in Morocco told me that although he did have access to well-known databases of academic journal articles, this access was only available on campus, and it was hard for him to find access to up-to-date research. He often asked colleagues at universities in Europe or the United States for access to certain journals, essentially relying on informal networks to obtain knowledge. In the natural and medical sciences other barriers include delays in acquiring supplies, which may be held up in transit or customs; excessive fees on importing necessary equipment; security clearances for recruiting researchers; and a lack of experimental trials in the medical sciences (Amer, 2019).

The lack of resources is only one of the issues that Arab academics face. Professors throughout the region perceive a lack of institutional support for research and the general absence of a research culture, despite being expected to produce research in the name of the knowledge economy. Studies of the working conditions of faculty members in the region have found that high teaching loads and a general prioritization of teaching in promotion decisions disincentivize research (Almansour & Kempner, 2017; Austin et al., 2014). Similarly, Waterbury (2020) cites a survey of Egyptian faculty members in which 86 per cent believed that the legislative and institutional atmosphere was not conducive to research (p. 281). Along these lines, Almansour and Kempner (2017) report that "research is not woven into the fabric of the universities" (p. 228). Specific obstacles include a lack of incentives to conduct research, little administrative support, and the need to navigate excessive bureaucracy when conducting research. An Egyptian professor whom they interviewed stated, "Research is not taken seriously, it's perceived by faculty as a means for promotion, it has no value" (p. 229). The result is a lack of motivation for research. One of their key findings was that "the lack of motivation to conduct research is a serious challenge" for many (p. 224). The result of these obstacles is that most academics in the region portray conducting research as what they call a "self-effort" rather than part of a professional obligation (p. 228). Various studies of the professoriate in the region support the idea that promotion is based primarily on tenure, rather than on research productivity. Boughazala, Ghazouani, and Ben Hafaiedh (2016) write, in the case of Tunisia, notably one of the most research-productive countries in the region, that "faculty members' remuneration is almost totally independent of their effort and their performance" (p. 8). Similarly, Waterbury (2020) quotes a professor from Morocco who states that "two articles in even mediocre journals" will be enough for promotion (p. 279).

A cross-national study of social scientists in the Arab world, conducted by the Arab Council for Social Sciences in 2015, found that university-based research centres were rare in the region. The majority of the 436 social science research centres were based outside of universities. Moreover, those based within universities were concentrated in a few countries, with over half located in only two countries: Algeria and Egypt (57 per cent). Meanwhile, many countries in the region had either zero or one university-based social science research centre (Bamyeh, 2015, p. 19), including Oman (one), Kuwait (one), Syria (one), UAE (two), Qatar (two), Tunisia (none). The council argues that university-based research centres not only offer institutional infrastructure to scholars but also can strengthen the links between teaching and research.

Unsurprisingly, many academics in the Arab world seek to emigrate in search of professional opportunities, and the lack of stability after the Arab Spring has only increased the academic brain drain (Plackett, 2016c). In a region-wide survey of 650 researchers conducted by *Al-Fanar* in 2019, 91 per cent stated that they would like to work elsewhere, and this high proportion cut across age, country, and discipline (Amer, 2019). The highest proportions who wanted to leave were researchers in countries affected by conflict, namely Syria, Yemen, and Libya, where an average of 95 per cent reported wanting to leave. Meanwhile, the survey found that in the Arab Gulf states, despite having better salaries on average, 81 per cent of researchers wanted to emigrate and pointed to a lack of freedom as a primary rationale. Interestingly, although the most sought-after destinations were Europe (68 per cent) and North America (55 per cent), many researchers in the region were also open to emigrating to Arab Gulf states (34 per cent) or other non-Gulf Arab nations (27 per cent). Broadly speaking, the high proportions of researchers who were interested in emigrating points to a high degree of dissatisfaction.

A lack of security and academic freedom affects faculty members' ability to conduct research. In the Gulf states the nature of academic work compounds with an unstable geopolitical environment to undermine a sense of stability. In most GCC nations higher education institutions rely on significant proportions of expatriate faculty members, who, like all workers, are on temporary contracts and can be fired at will. In the UAE they cannot gain tenure and are hired primarily on a contract basis, in contrast to Emirati faculty members who are able to gain a significant degree of job security (Austin et al., 2014, p. 544). In their study Austin et al. (2014) interviewed twenty-nine expatriates working in UAE public universities and found that they viewed their status as essentially temporary workers and expressed the idea that they felt "expendable," which undermined their sense of belonging and commitment to their institutions. There was a pervasive sense of insecurity. One professor explained: "We cannot do anything because somebody may say 'you go,' and then you have to go ... If you [raised a concern] ... you'd get fired. Your contract – no more. After 3 months, you will have to leave" (p. 549). In short, the nature of labour in the Gulf states undermines the creation of a research community because academics' contracts are "temporary, completely dependent on administrative decisions, and susceptible to termination at any time" (p. 550). This lack of job security is closely related to concerns over restricted academic freedom. *Al-Fanar* finds that unlike in the lower- and middle-income countries in the region where salaries are a major concern, one of the primary reasons that faculty members in the GCC want to emigrate is a lack of academic freedom and job security. According to their survey, 62 per cent of researchers in the Gulf would move abroad for more academic freedom, compared to only 26 per cent who sought higher salaries (Amer, 2019).

Ignoring the Structural Realities

One of the most problematic assumptions of development discourses on research is that scholarly outputs are primarily a result of internal investments in productivity rather than a result of structural conditions. In contrast to the development literature, scholars based within the region point to a broader range of issues facing knowledge production, including the fragmentation of academic communities across generations (Bamyeh, 2015). Fundamentally, the global academic system is deeply unequal: high-impact journals are overwhelmingly based in North America and Europe; they primarily publish in English; and they cater to topics that those regions find interesting, ignoring histories of colonization and economic oppression that discount non-Western knowledges (Hanafi & Arvanitis, 2014; Keim, 2008).

Sari Hanafi and Rigas Arvanitis, two of the leading scholars of knowledge production in the Arab world, argue that the "publication system in the social sciences, as in all sciences, is thus a global power structure" (2014, p. 724). Informed by their argument that many factors, including "the political economy of publication," has affected scientific publication in the Arab world, in this section I analyse the structural conditions that shape productivity in the Arab world. Specifically, drawing on data from the WB's World Development Indicators, I analyse data on the number of scholarly publications per 100,000 residents. This indicator is an imperfect measure of actual output – it likely captures publications in the natural sciences better than those in the social sciences and does not take into account applied or policy publications. It also likely better captures scholarship published in English than in Arabic because, according to Waast, Arvanitis, Richard-Waast, and Rossi (2010), "journals that are present in the large bibliographical databases have strong biases against non-English languages and particularly Arabic" (p. 176). Nonetheless, they serve as a one indicator of publications, and governments may be particularly sensitive to these numbers because they are used to measure progress to the SDGs.

Table 6.1 shows the average number of articles published in scientific and technical journals per 100,000 residents between 2004 and 2016 in different world regions. It is clear that there is substantial variation across world regions. The table also shows that scientific publications have in-creased over the past decade around the world, including in the Middle East and North Africa. Scientific publications increased in the Middle East and North Africa from eight per 100,000 people in 2004 to twenty-three in 2016. This is one of the largest growth rates in the world after South Asia and is nearly identical to the growth rate in middle-income countries worldwide. The finding is in line with prior work that has revealed sig-nificant increases in research production in the Arab world over the past thirty years, which suggest that the expansion of higher education and the intensification of knowledge production (enhanced by technology and the internet), as well as the institutionalization of research cultures in the region, may all be factors leading to growth (Siddiqi, Stoppani, Anadon, & Narayanamurti, 2016). In an analysis of publications from North Africa, Waast et al. (2010) found "a rapid increase" in publications by North Africans "from 2,000 in 1985 to over 6,000 new documents per year in 2005" (p. 177). Similarly, Waast and Rossi (2010) found what they call "noteworthy" increases in productivity, particularly in North Africa, stating that "scientific activity gained tremendous momentum during the last twenty years, especially in Maghreb" (p. 343).

That said, despite increases in the Middle East and North Africa region, research production is highly concentrated in two world regions: North America (136 publications per 100,000 in 2016) and Europe and Central Asia (86 publications per 100,000 in 2016). These figures are three to four times larger than the next world region, East Asia, and thirty to fifty times larger than rates in sub-Saharan Africa. Such large disparities in publication rates are not simply a reflection of different levels of funding or any specific public policy concerning research. They reflect long-standing historical trajectories and ongoing dominance of Western and northern academia in the global economic and academic system. The historical dominance of northern univer-sities means that they can continue to recruit the best scholars from around the world, and the dominance of English in the global academic system means that their publications are the most widely published and disseminated worldwide.

Arguably the single largest predictor of scientific publication rates is a country's GDP per capita. Figure 6.1 illustrates the bivariate relation-ship between GDP per capita and a nation's publications per 100,000 residents in 2018 for countries with a GDP per capita under USD 80,000. The grey line on the graph plots the linear relationship among all coun-tries worldwide, excluding those in the Arab Middle East and North Africa, and points to a clear, positive relationship. A simple regression analysis shows that a country's GDP per capita explains 74 per cent of the variation in publication rates cross-nationally. The large and clear

Table 6.1. Scientific and Technical Journal Articles, per 100,000 People

	2004	2008	2012	2016	Growth rate (2004–16)
East Asia and Pacific	15	23	28	33	118%
Europe and Central Asia	58	71	81	86	50%
Latin America and Caribbean	7	11	14	16	124%
Middle East and North Africa[1]	8	13	19	23	188%
All Middle income	6	10	13	16	185%
North America	122	133	140	136	11%
South Asia	2	3	5	7	232%
Sub-Saharan Africa	1	2	2	2	94%

Source: Data accessed through the WB Open Data module for Stata. Indicators IP.JRN. ARTC.SC (Publications) and SP.POP.TOTL (Population) (Azevedo, 2011)
1. The following four countries are included in WB's Middle East and North Africa region but not the book's focus on the Arab Middle East and North Africa: Iran, Israel, Malta, and Djibouti. Using the WB's regional classification of Arab states yields a similarly large growth rate of 1.90 per cent between 2004 and 2016 but a lower overall total (11 per cent in 2016).

association between the wealth of a country and its research productivity suggests clear structural factors at work, factors that are too often ignored in discussions of specific policies and practices that inhibit or incentivize research. Moreover, while it is likely that knowledge production supports innovation and economic development, it is just as likely that national wealth supports the investments necessary for robust higher education, scientific research, and innovation systems.

The figure also shows that the relationship between GDP per capita and publication rates in the Arab Middle East and North Africa states is very different from the global average. The black dots and black line in figure 6.1 show the same relationship for Arab nations in the region. The Pearson's correlation coefficient is only 0.60, and a simple regression analysis shows that GDP per capita only explains 43 per cent of variation in publication rates. It appears that the Arab Middle East is an exception to the global pattern – national wealth is not as strong a factor in determining scientific publications in the region. Many use this fact to critique science, technology, and innovation policies in the region. The weak relationship documented in figure 6.1, however, is largely determined by six resource-wealthy Arab Gulf states and the countries in conflict in the region. When the six GCC nations are excluded from the analysis, publication patterns in the lower- and middle-income countries in the Arab world reflect global trends.

Figure 6.2 shows the relationship between national GDP per capita and publication rates per 100,000 residents for countries with GDP per capita

Figure 6.1. Relationship between GDP per Capita and Scientific Publication Rates (2018)

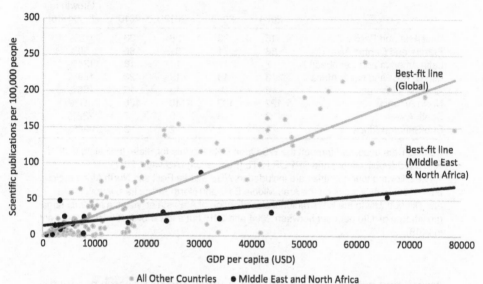

Source: Data accessed through the WB Open Data module for Stata. Indicator IP.JRN.
ARTC.SC (Publications); SP.POP.TOTL (Population), and NY.GDP.PCAP.CD (USD GDP per capita) (Azevedo, 2011).
Note: I classify the countries Iran, Israel, Malta, and Djibouti as outside the Arab Middle East and North Africa, although they are included in the WB's Middle East and North Africa region.

of less than USD 10,000. The black line represents the global average for all countries with a GDP of less than USD 10,000, while the dots represent Arab nations' research productivity in 2018, or the most recent year of data available. The figure shows that research productivity in the region is heterogeneous, yet in general, the middle-income countries of the Arab world appear to be doing well in comparison to peer nations. Some nations, such as Tunisia, have publication rates that are significantly higher than the global trend. Jordan and Lebanon also have above-average productivity levels. Other countries, including Morocco, Egypt, and Algeria have publication rates that are similar or slightly higher than expected for their GDP per capita. In contrast, Yemen, Syria, and Libya are well below the global average for their GDP per capita. It is worth noting that these countries have historically benefited economically from natural resource extraction or have recent histories of conflict, which have likely had a negative impact on their research productivity.

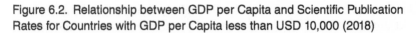

Figure 6.2. Relationship between GDP per Capita and Scientific Publication Rates for Countries with GDP per Capita less than USD 10,000 (2018)

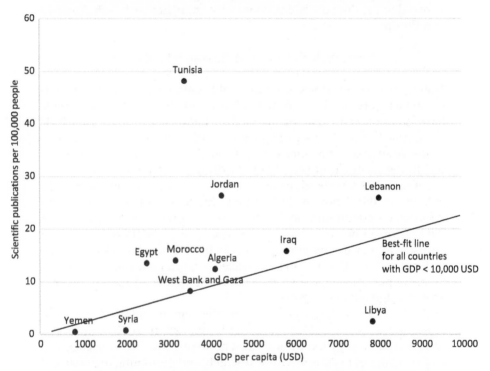

Source: Data accessed through the WB Open Data module for Stata. Indicators IP.JRN. ARTC.SC (Publications); SP.POP.TOTL (Population), and NY.GDP.PCAP.CD (USD GDP per capita) (Azevedo, 2011).

Combined, these figures suggest a broad categorization of countries in the region: first, there are a number of countries with scholarly productivity lower than the global average, including Libya and Yemen, and the countries in the Arabian Gulf. All of these nations rely on resource extraction, and many are experiencing conflict, suggesting that political stability is critical (Almansour, 2016). Second, there are the middle-income countries, which have scholarly productivity rates in line with or above the global averages for countries with similar levels of economic development. Third, there is Tunisia, which stands out in the region and the world, with a productivity rate that is significantly above the global average for middle-income countries. One important takeaway from these findings is that knowledge production in the Arab world is not as dire as it might seem. Rather, it is embedded within a broader geopolitical and economic context where global knowedge production is dominated by countries in North America and Europe.

Investing in Science and Research Production

Noting structural realities is not to say that national policies do not matter. In fact, partially in response to global pressures, Arab governments have committed to making research a national priority. Since 2000 the Council of Ministers of Higher Education and Scientific Research in the Arab World has met regularly to discuss science and technology in the Arab world (Zou'bi et al., 2015). In 2011, UNESCO's Cairo office founded a network of organizations to support emergent technologies in the region, including biotechnology, nanotechnology, and information communications technology. Known as the Network for the Expansion of Convergent Technologies, it connects academia and industry to produce research to support the region's knowledge-based sectors. In 2014, the network organized a regional forum around the theme of galvanizing science education and higher education towards a knowledge-based economy.

Similarly, in 2014, governments of the region endorsed the Arab Strategy for Science, Technology and Innovation in Riyadh, Saudi Arabia. The strategy has three pillars: academic training in science and engineering; supporting scientific research; and promoting regional and international scientific co-operation. It laid out an ambitious set of policies to improve intra-regional co-operation and mobility, including a network of science centres, regional centres of excellence, intra-regional mobility, and partnerships with Arab academics abroad. It also suggests increasing funding for research from the 2014 average of 0.3 per cent of GDP to 3.0 per cent, with 30–40 per cent coming from the private sector. The strategy identifies fourteen priority areas for research: biotechnology, nanotechnology, information technology, water, food, agriculture and fishing, space, energy, desert sciences, the environment, renewable energy, poverty, and disease (Zou'bi et al., 2015). It is notable that this strategy adopts all of the best practices advocated in the literature, including working closely with the private sector, supporting interdisciplinary research, and focusing on the economic value of research. However, the absence of social sciences and humanities in discussions of research in the region is also striking.

Additionally, many Arab governments have devoted significant funding to supporting research, typically justifying this shift in the

Table 6.2. Research and Development Expenditure (% of GDP)

	2000–9	2010–16
Egypt	0.27	0.60
Jordan	0.39	0.72
Morocco	0.59	0.71
Qatar	–	0.49
Tunisia	0.67	0.66
United Arab Emirates	–	0.76

Source: Data accessed through the WB Open Data module for Stata. Indicator GB.XPD. RSDV.GD.ZS (Azevedo, 2011).

name of the knowledge economy. Table 6.2 shows gross domestic spending on research and development for six Arab nations for which there is data. The average spending on R&D increased substantially in Egypt, Jordan, and Morocco after 2010, while percentages in Tunisia remained steady. Before 2000 the percentage in Egypt was roughly 0.20, which increased to 0.27 in the 2000s and has increased to an average of 0.60 since 2010. Since 2010, Jordan, Morocco, and the UAE, have all spent more than 0.70 per cent of their GDP on R&D. These percentages are less than those of upper-middle-income countries globally, which spend an average of 1.57 per cent, but nonetheless speak to significant increases in the last decade.

Many countries in the region have also developed robust scientific communities inside and outside of academia over the past few decades. According to WDI data, in 2016 Morocco had 1,073 full-time researchers per one million residents, and Tunisia has 1,982 – both of which are comparable to or higher than countries recognized for their strong histories of research such as Chile (493 per million) and Argentina (1,259 per million), as well as emerging research giants such as China (1,196 per million) and Thailand (1,208 per million). This is despite the fact that GDP per capita in these countries is two to three times higher than that in Morocco and Tunisia. In fact, with a 2018 GDP per capita of USD 3,439, Tunisia has more full-time researchers per million residents than do some European countries, such as Latvia (1,596 per million), whose 2018 GDP per capita was USD 17,858, and Romania (912 per million), whose GDP per capita was USD 12,400 (WDI, 2021). In short, in line with development models and global commitments, Arab nations have increased investments in scientific research and production, a point that development discourses rarely recognize.

National Science Policy Regimes

Within the Arab region some countries stand out as outliers. Tunisia has a long history of high research productivity that has been recognized inside and outside the region, and Qatar, despite being well below the global average for its per capita wealth, has witnessed a remarkable increase in scientific activity and academic publications over the past decade. Figure 6.3 shows productivity trends in four countries: Qatar and the UAE, both wealthy GCC countries that have below-average research productivity for their GDP per capita, and Jordan and Tunisia, two middle-income countries that have higher-than-average rates of research productivity.

Although all four countries had similar rates at around fifteen scientific publications per 100,000 people in 2004, publication rates in both Tunisia and Qatar had increased to around fifty publications per 100,000 people by 2016. In contrast, in the UAE and Jordan publication rates have stayed stable at around twenty publications per 100,000 residents. These percentages are calculated as a per capita rate and are therefore sensitive to changes in population. Qatar and Tunisia are much smaller than the UAE, and the UAE's population has been growing rapidly. Nonetheless, they point to impressive gains in Qatar and Tunisia, which other scholars have found as well (Siddiqi et al., 2016).

Scholars of the region have observed that Tunisia has been the leader of scholarly publications in North Africa for at least two decades, due in part to the country's long history of prioritizing scientific research. Prior research has also found that Tunisian academics publish significantly more studies and are cited more often than scholars in Morocco and Algeria (Hammouti, 2010). Tunisia has a long history of supporting cross-national research collaborations particularly with francophone Europe. In 2005 the Ben Ali regime launched an initiative to support research collaborations between Tunisia and international institutions (Fryer & Jules, 2013), and over the past two decades Tunisia has been one of the largest recipients of funding by the European Union for collaborative research. In addition, Tunisia had institutionalized a culture of research, with established laboratories and years of public support for research, before the 2011 revolution (Waast & Rossi, 2010). Even after the revolution, it remains among the top funders of scientific research in the Arab world. Tunisia also benefits from institutionalized educational trajectories: it has been one of the best educated countries in the region for some time, with a small and well-educated population and a long tradition of public research universities, ministry support for research, and tight linkages to French academia.

Figure 6.3. Scientific Publication Rates per 100,000 People, 2004–16 (Select Countries)

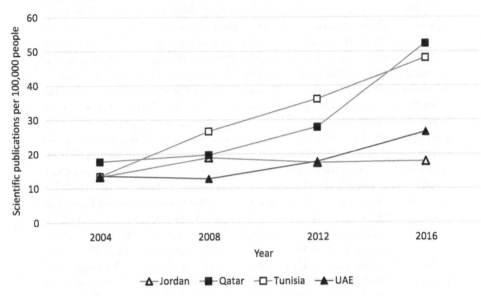

Source: Data accessed through the WB Open Data module for Stata. Indicators IP.JRN. ARTC.SC (Publications); SP.POP.TOTL (Population)

Qatar's approach to supporting research has been more recent and has come from the top. Qatar has fully embraced a knowledge economy discourse that pervades its education, science, and development policies. Since its establishment in 1995 the Qatar Foundation has aggressively pursued its goal of turning Qatar into a knowledge economy. Over the past two decades its initiatives have included creating Education City, with its eleven branch campuses and one Qatari graduate institution; founding three new research institutes; sponsoring dozens of global competitions, summits, and conferences; and spinning off new civil society organizations. In 2019 it advertised itself as having fifty affiliated initiatives. Romani (2009) states that the goal of these initiatives is "to change Arab academe from a site for knowledge reception to one of knowledge production" (p. 4). The Qatar Foundation has begun emphasizing the word *homegrown* in its recent publications, indicating a desire to shift from being a funder and importer of knowledge to being a local producer and exporter of its knowledge. In the next section I discuss the varied ways in which Qatar is supporting a culture of research.

"Publications Have Soared" in Qatar

Despite the clear growth in scientific publication rates shown in figure 6.3, there is much that publication rates do not tell us, such as how Qatar and Tunisia increased their publishing productivity, what types of publications are captured by these statistics, who is conducting research, and on what topics are they focusing. In March 2019 I travelled to Doha to understand how the country had supported research and knowledge production in line with broader development mandates. There was widespread acknowledgment that the country's leadership had explicitly invested in creating an ecosystem and infrastructure to support research. One scholar with whom I spoke put it simply: "There was the feeling that there wasn't enough research." The effort to support research has been led primarily by the Qatar Foundation in line with its broader mission. In 2006 it established the Qatar National Research Fund (QNRF) to provide funding for Qatari researchers "as part of its ongoing commitment to establish Qatar as a knowledge-based economy." The importance of research is clearly articulated on QNRF's website, which states that the Qatar Foundation "views research as essential to national and regional growth, as the means to diversify the nation's economy, enhance educational offerings and develop areas that affect the community, such as health and environment."

Expanding graduate education has also played a role. In 2010 the Hamad Bin Khalifa University was established as a graduate-level Qatari university. Although it is situated in Education City, the same campus complex as the Qatar Foundation's branch campuses, it is considered a homegrown institution. As of 2017–18, the university had over six hundred students, of whom 43 per cent were Qatari (PSA, 2018). Three research centres are affiliated with Hamad Bin Khalifa University, each with a focus on a particular scientific area: the Qatar Biomedical Research Institute, the Qatar Computing Research Institute, and the Qatar Environment and Energy Research Institute. A fourth, focusing on the social sciences, was planned but never opened. These well-funded institutes have developed infrastructure and equipment to support high-calibre research, recruited international researchers, and funded generous two-year post-doctoral fellowships.

In addition, the country's national public university, Qatar University, now offers doctoral programs and has launched post-doctoral fellowship programs that recruit early-career researchers to produce research in Qatar. Initiatives reflect a commitment to building a culture of research through programs such as an annual undergraduate research competition and leadership programs for female researchers. The undergraduate research competition, which began in 2007, provides both funding for undergraduates to undertake research and cash prizes for competition winners. The programs stated goals are to build a culture of research and bring attention and prominence to research as a career option. Many scholars with whom I spoke agreed that these programs have had an impact. One researcher explained: "Ten years ago, you would never hear about research. Now we get surveys on some research topic or another all the time, almost every day. And publications have soared."

Others, however, both inside and outside of Qatar, are sceptical. Some argue that indicators of productivity are easy to manipulate, particularly in a small country such as Qatar, where a few publications can influence per capita numbers. Indeed, UNESCO (2016) reports that international co-authorship in Qatar has soared, from 52 per cent of publications having an international collaborator in 2005 to 92 per cent in 2014, suggesting that international collaboration is indeed a major factor in Qatar's growth. Opinions of these collaborations are nuanced. One researcher in Doha explained: "So there is the criticism that expats are the ones primarily doing the research. It's true, but the critical mass of Qataris is small. There aren't thousands, or even hundreds of researchers, but there are dozens of Qataris who are now active in research." He noted that a culture of research was becoming institutionalized: "the leadership has created the ecosystem for research."

Although the Qatar National Research Fund is narrowly tailored to the needs of Qatar, the benefits of investments in research are rarely limited to one country. In my visit to Qatar I was reminded of the importance of what cross-cultural insights can bring to our collective knowledge. Georgetown University's School of Foreign Service–Qatar has a series of research papers on how an Islamic world-view actually enables, rather than constrains, scientific research. One project found that research on stem cells was actually supported much earlier in certain Islamic countries than in the West: in the United States, stem-cell research generated significant political backlash in the early 2000s from Christians who believed that life began at conception. In an Islamic world-view, however, human life (or ensoulment) is typically thought to occur 120 days after conception. In 2002 the supreme leader of Iran issued a fatwa stating that stem-cell research was a moral good that could help ease human suffering. Qatar has since followed suit with a strong program of stem-cell research (Saniei & Baharvand, 2018). Recognizing research as the social construction of knowledge shines a light on how researchers in Western countries, who have inherited ideals of the Enlightenment and operate within legal systems informed by Christianity, are also historically particular.

The Doha Institute's "Different Approach"

In 2011 Qatari leadership founded the Doha Institute for Graduate Studies as what one of my interviewees called "a different approach" to local knowledge production. The founding vision for the Doha Institute came from Azmi Bishara, a Palestinian Arab intellectual and former member of the Israeli legislature who now lives in Doha in voluntary exile. Funding for the institution is provided by the Qatari royal family. The Doha Institute is unique in Doha and the Arab world: it is an independent graduate-level institute that focuses on the social sciences and humanities. Its programs include public administration, economics, and conflict and humanitarian studies. What sets it apart from institutions in Education City is that, rather than importing English-language programs from North America and Europe, the Doha Institute uses the Arabic language as the primary medium of instruction, publication, and public discourse. English is called a "companion language" for learning and scholarship, and graduates are expected to be bilingual. The promotion of Arabic-language research production is one way in which Qatar is embracing the role of promoting Arabic throughout the Middle East region. Such a role clearly maps onto Qatar's broader geopolitical ambitions of elevating its status in the region, including high-profile projects such as Al Jazeera and Qatar's decision to bid on and host the 2020 FIFA World Cup.

In March 2019 I visited the Doha Institute to understand how it was accomplishing its unique mission. What I found was a small but beautiful campus with gleaming white buildings decorated with geometric patterns that invoke traditional Islamic architecture, and inviting rows of palm trees and fountains. Posters in both Arabic and English advertised talks by professors around the region. An administrator explained that its focus on social sciences also makes it distinctive. One administrator explained: "In the region, there has been a technical and vocational focus. Many people think, Who would study history?"

As with any new educational initiative, however, the reality is complicated and the challenges are clear. Both faculty members and administrators said that a lack of permanence was a key challenge. Almost all the faculty members at the Doha Institute are non-nationals. This is the reality in most higher education institutions in Qatar, as Qataris make up only 10 per cent of the country's population, and only a small number of Qataris have doctorates. Those that do tend to have them in applied and technical fields such as engineering. As a result, the number of Qataris who can be employed by a graduate-level institute in the social sciences is very small. Most faculty members at the Doha Institute have been recruited from well-known universities in the Arab world, including those in Jordan, Lebanon, Tunisia, and Egypt, or as young scholars who have returned from studying in the United States or Europe.

As non-nationals, they must rely on the visa sponsorship system (*kafala*, Arabic), which means that their livelihoods and lives in Qatar are tied to their employment. This system creates a deep-seated sense of instability for faculty members. One non-Qatari explained: "In the GCC, we don't have stability. There's no guarantee of tenure. It hurts our production of knowledge. How can you study what you want to study when your job stability and security is linked to it?" Another stated: "They bring me here, they give me money, but not stability." On the one hand, a lack of security likely contributes to self-censoring. On the other hand, it also affects research productivity in less direct ways. One administrator at the Doha Institute said that without a sense of permanence many faculty members felt as though they were merely passing through, which undermined their motivation for conducting research in Qatar. One professor explained: "The issue starts with security – people don't feel like they really belong here or that they have a future even after ten years. There is no security." Issues of legal status are not fully within the university's control. One professor at the institute said that "even if the university provides stability, your visa might not be renewed by the government, and this is outside the control of the university."

The sense of precariousness was also linked to how the university was governed and seemed to undermine the institution's ability to accomplish its goals. One administrator explained: "The administrators and leaders want to keep their posts, and this affects how the university is run. There is a focus on just making people happy, not doing what you have to do to improve quality."

Beyond day-to-day administration, the structures of the global academic system also impose constraints. Professors and administrators remarked that despite a sincere commitment to using Arabic as a language of teaching and research, it was "hard to focus on Arabic," because "there's no system for publishing in Arabic, no impact factor, no rankings." Indeed, many of the younger faculty members at the Doha Institute have been recruited as recent doctoral graduates from North American and European institutions; they have been trained in English and prioritize publishing in peer-reviewed and internationally recognized journals. One professor explained that for assistant professors who were trying to establish their reputation as scholars in their disciplinary fields, it was crucial that they publish in ranked disciplinary journals, which were almost all in English. Many of these younger faculty members stated that they had little incentive to stay at the Doha Institute or to publish in Arabic if they could move to a university in North America or Europe that could provide a sense of permanence.

Even in the short time I spent at the Doha Institute, I had a sense of the challenges it faces: the Doha Institute represents an alternative model for higher education in a world where success is measured by a single yardstick. One administrator told me: "I'm not certain we will succeed in our mission. I'm not very optimistic. But we have to be patient. We have to say we are here to do something different."

The Hollow Discourse of Productivity

Despite the success of some of these initiatives, the narrow focus on research productivity rings hollow when divorced from broader discussions of who is producing knowledge, and how and why they are doing so. Research is fundamentally a social enterprise, and the political climate and geopolitical context, including neoliberalism and securitization, have undermined the independence of Arab academics. In this section I discuss how neoliberal ideologies and crackdowns on academic freedom have affected research production in the region.

Knowledge economy discourses and neoliberal ideologies have incentivized "outputs" in the form of publications and patents. Increasingly, professors are encouraged to publish in peer-reviewed, internationally ranked journals, with promotions or pay often linked to publishing (Austin et al., 2014; Hanafi, 2011). The global publishing industry is dominated by journals based in Europe and North America that publish in English and give priority to universalizing claims, rather than to localized or contextualized knowledges. Professors in the Arab world must often publish their research in English and frame their questions around topics that are of interest to global or transnational audiences, rather than local or national audiences (Hanafi, 2011; Hanafi & Arvanitis, 2014). In interviews in Qatar, where institutions have fully embraced an output-oriented strategy including annual productivity reviews, and promotions and job stability tied to outputs, professors explained the perverse incentives induced by this approach. One professor stated: "They care about numbers of articles. They don't realize it can take years to do work that is truly impactful."

Sari Hanafi, a professor of sociology at the American University of Beirut, describes the dual experience that Arab academics face. When he publishes in English in peer-reviewed sociological journals, he often garners attention and acclaim from scholars based in North America or Europe who find his work useful to their own theories (Hanafi, 2011).

Meanwhile, few Arab students or scholars have access to those same articles. In contrast, when he publishes in Arabic or writes as a public intellectual in the Arab media, he is often contacted by students and scholars throughout the Arab world and thanked for his contributions. He argues that one of the ramifications of this linguistic divide is that social scientists in the Arab world are financially and professionally incentivized to do research that appeals to readers in North America rather than Arab publics. It often incentivizes a priority on theoretical research, rather than locally relevant or applied knowledge that may inform important policy domains of Arab societies.

This linguistic divide not only has ramifications for what Arab academics publish, where, and in what languages, but also affects the topics they research (Hanafi & Arvanitis, 2014). In a rare study of how the language of publication affects the topic of research, Waast et al. (2010) explore the full holdings of the King Abdul-Aziz Foundation library in Casablanca, Morocco, which, since its founding in 1980, has been committed to gathering all social science publications, in any language, that focus on North Africa. Their bibliometric analysis shows clearly that research topic maps onto language of publication. In examining publications by authors originally from North Africa, they find that the vast majority of publications on philosophy, Islam, history, and education are published in Arabic. In contrast, only 20 per cent of publications on economics and 10 per cent of publications on management are published in Arabic. They argue convincingly that topics deemed important to the "current global research agenda," namely women, the environment, public policy, urban studies, and globalization, are more likely to be published in languages other than Arabic, and presumably French and English, while those related to "cultural life, education and local history" are more likely to be published in Arabic (p. 178).

The determination of what counts as 'interesting' may also be in the eye of the funder. Shana Cohen, drawing on decades of ethnographic work in Morocco, finds that Moroccan academics increasingly spend their time working on policy-relevant research funded by international development agencies. She argues that in the nation-building era, public funding for higher education creates the material conditions necessary for a critical and publicly engaged academia by providing "the material resources and cultural and ideological impetus for critical academic research and analysis" (2014, p. 31). In response to neoliberal austerity, however, many Moroccan academics find that consulting work is the only source of funding for research and turn to it due to a lack of other funding. Cohen acknowledges the benefits of consulting for academics: "The attraction of the remuneration offered by consultant work is legitimate: it offers the possibility of conducting applied research and benefitting from some kind of recognition. It offers as well the revenue for paying off debts and the children's school fees, as enough faculty want to avoid public education. Who can blame them?" (2014, p. 35).

This culture of consulting, however, narrows topics and turns research into concrete deliverable products. Consulting qua research elevates the profile of certain well-known intellectuals, who lend their expertise and credentials to a narrow set of topics outlined by state actors or development agencies, such as the middle class, employment, youth, and education. In so doing, it tends to ignore more theoretical topics, as well as the humanities and critical scholarship. Moreover, academics' participation in the consulting industry creates a set of shared interests between state actors, funding agencies, and intellectuals. After interviewing prominent academics and intellectuals, the French magazine *Tel Quel* reported on the "silence of the intellectuals" in Morocco. The 2009 article argues that inevitably "intellocrats" – a term they use to describe intellectuals who focus their expertise on the administration of policy – "end up legitimising, if not all aspects of government strategy, at least the power of politicians and their stewardship of the country" (cited in Cohen, 2014, p. 36). Cohen asks if the continual assault on the university as a public institution and the increasing ideological linkages between the university and knowledge economy discourses and neoliberal policies has fostered a sense of "opportunism" among Arab academics, "rather than a desire to contribute to non-materialistic collective goals" (2014, p. 40). She worries that the pervasiveness of neoliberal ideologies has cemented a new culture of the high-profile academic, arguing that "the same cohort of academics that engaged with nationalist and Marxist ideas have taken on consulting contracts, in part for the funds, but also for the prestige and status of working within international networks and close to government officials" (p. 41). There is a noteworthy arrogance in the assumption that the West can afford to fund basic research, while research in the Arab world must be applied, relevant, and marketable.

In addition, knowledge production and investment in scientific research in the region are undermined by excessive spending on militarization and geopolitical conflicts (UNESCO, 2015). Research priorities are frequently determined by what the governments perceive to be pressing national security or geopolitical concerns, which in the Arab world include energy, water, and food security (Badran, 2018). However, an over-emphasis on national security and a lack of actual security undermine academic communities. In their analysis of research productivity over twenty years, Waast and Rossi (2010) argue that scientific production "mirrors political turmoil, vagaries of state support and the turnabout of development policies" (p. 344). They point to earlier conflicts, including the Lebanese (1975–90) and Algerian (1991–8) civil wars and the first Gulf War (1990–1), as periods when research productivity stalled in these countries. More recently, the political and economic crises affecting the region in the twenty-first century, including the invasion of Iraq, the Arab Spring, the Syrian civil war, and the rise of the Islamic State of Iraq and Syria (ISIS), have been disastrous to respective academic communities (Almansour & Kempner, 2017; Dillabough et al., 2018) and resulted in significant brain drain.

Academic Freedom

Another political constraint to research productivity in the Arab world is a general lack of academic freedom (UNDP, 2003; Waterbury, 2020). Although the low levels of academic freedom in the region are widely acknowledged, the technical literature that decries low research productivity in the region sidesteps discussions of academic freedom by emphasizing the need for applied and supposedly apolitical science. In this section I argue that the lack of academic freedom in the region is not a coincidence; it is inherent in an institution that is tied closely to broader webs of power in the region, including state and religious authority.

Academic freedom is the ability to pursue independent research and discuss ideas in the classroom with little to no external interference. In the European tradition of higher education, over many centuries universities have secured a buffer from state authority. Professors are typically respected as professionals and given autonomy in their teaching and research. They are primarily accountable to the other professors in their fields, who judge the merits of their work. Even in public universities, when professors are government employees, they are protected from direct state control by the independence of their institutions, faculty associations, and obligations to non-state actors, including students, private businesses, and alumni. Of course, in practice, academic freedom is more of a norm than a right, and has always been susceptible to violation, even in liberal democracies (Altbach, 2007; Waterbury, 2020). Yet, for over a thousand years universities have negotiated the fine line between supporting the governments that authorize and regulate them and critiquing those same governments. This freedom allows professors to pursue their research and participate in public commentary without fear of being punished or silenced. More broadly, academic freedom is viewed as a cornerstone of the scientific process that permits critical debate and exchange of ideas.

It is this Western view of academic freedom that has been enshrined in powerful global organizations. The 1997 UNESCO "Recommendation Concerning the Status of Higher-Education Teaching Personnel" includes a definition of academic freedom that ensures a degree of autonomy for faculty members:

> Higher-education teaching personnel are entitled to the maintaining of academic freedom, that is to say, the right, without constriction by prescribed doctrine, to freedom of teaching and discussion, freedom in carrying out research and disseminating and publishing the results thereof, freedom to express freely their opinion about the institution or system in which they work, freedom from institutional censorship and freedom to participate in professional or representative academic bodies. All higher-education teaching personnel should have the right to fulfill their functions without discrimination of any kind and without fear of repression by the state or any other source. (UNESCO, 1997, para. 26)

Arab scholars have long recognized that this definition of academic freedom hardly applies to the conditions of their work. An academic in the Arab world, Hanada Taha-Thomure (2003) describes growing up in Beirut and teaching primary school in Oman and Bahrain, and she states: "I did not fully experience an educational atmosphere in which professors engaged us on issues, especially if the discussion led to dissent with traditional interpretations of Islam or to criticisms of ruling regimes. Such topics were and still are not open for discussion" (p. 7). Waterbury (2020) reminds us that even while university autonomy and academic freedom are included in Arab universities' founding statements, these guarantees mean little. He quips: "Just as lip service is paid to university autonomy in official documents in the Arab world, academic freedom is similarly enshrined. Nowhere is it respected" (p. 129).

Throughout the region freedoms of all sorts are curtailed in the name of stability and security, and academic freedom is no exception (Grimm, 2018). Sociologists of the state remind us that the schools and university, along with other institutions such as the church, media, and cultural institutions, serve the interests of the broader political system. In place of professional autonomy and peer regulation is external oversight, with both teaching and research being controlled by political authorities (Osman, 2010; Waterbury, 2020). The irony is that in the Arab world, as in many post-colonial settings, the same national universities celebrated as sites of anti-colonial protest that helped to establish their modern nation states are now closely regulated and monitored as sites of potential anti-regime activism.

In Egypt a law dating back to 1936 (Law 20) allows the Ministry of Information to screen all imported books and periodicals. Article 9 states that "in order to maintain public order, it is permissible to prohibit printed matter that is produced abroad from entering Egypt, and this prohibition can come as a special decision from the Committee of Ministers." Similarly, article 10 states: "The Committee of Ministers also has the right to ban the distribution and handling of printed matter of a sexual content as well as that which addresses religions in a way that could destabilize public peace." Combined, these two articles give the government the power to censor curricular content in politics, religion, and sex.

There is also a long history of security presence on campuses in the region, including in Egypt, Jordan, Tunisia, and Syria. Campus police and intelligence personnel, known as the *mukhabarat*, have been pervasive on university campuses, some visibly, others less visibly (George, 2003; Waterbury, 2020). In Egypt during the Mubarak era, plain-clothed police were stationed on university campuses and would call students' personal cell phones to inform them that their actions were being monitored. In Tunisia before the revolution, foreigners needed permission from the Ministry of the Interior to enter campus. Although that law has now been abolished, security guards still make their presence known on campuses. In 2013 I was stopped by security guards at El Manar University outside Tunis for taking a photograph of the campus.

National governments also exert power over universities by controlling appointments (Waterbury, 2020). Despite some initial commitments to autonomy, most public universities in the region lost their independence during the nation-building era. In many countries, including Egypt and Syria, presidents of universities are appointed by political leaders, rather than elected by faculty members, and the tradition of political control remains strong. In Jordan the king must approve appointments of university presidents, and all professors must pass a security check by the state's security police. Jordanian professors told me that they understood these security checks as a form of ideological policing, rather than simply a check of one's criminal record. Brand (1988) has argued that faculty member dismissals were used as "a political weapon" to maintain control of the faculties (p. 208).

Following Egypt's 2011 revolution there was optimism that conditions would improve, and legislation was passed to allow faculty members to elect university leaders directly – an indication of greater autonomy (L. Anderson, 2012). Those advances were quickly reversed, however. Since the military coup in 2013, in which Abdel Fattah al-Sisi ousted Mohamed Morsi, Egypt has experienced rising authoritarianism, and crackdowns on academic freedom have become even more prevalent (Holmes & Aziz, 2019). Professors must obtain approval from security forces to travel abroad for academic reasons such as attending a conference or serving on dissertation committees, and a number of prominent Egyptian academics have been banned from travelling abroad. The Egyptian president regained the power to appoint university presidents and deans. Security forces are allowed on campuses, and university facilities can be designated military installations.

In 2013, Emad El-Din Shahin, a professor of political science at the American University in Cairo, was indicted for conspiring with outside organizations to undermine Egypt's security. In an interview with the newspaper *Al-Fanar*, he explained the surreal absurdity of his situation: "I was abroad giving lectures about – (laughs) – the peaceful resolution of conflict. Someone on Facebook informed me that I was a defendant in a high-profile case. The charges were very vague, like 'grand espionage' – that's what they call it, smuggling arms, forcing the armed forces to move from the eastern front to the western front, etc. There was no evidence against me whatsoever. My lawyer said that if he built a defence strategy, he would be in jail next to me. So I left Egypt" (Bollag, 2016).

In May 2014 Sisi issued a ban on all academics leaving the country without prior governmental approval, which limits the number and types of conferences in which they can participate. Such a blanket ban is in direct violation of article 21 of the Egyptian constitution, which guarantees the independence of academic institutions, and of article 62, which prevents the government from banning freedom of movement. In 2015 one researcher declared the state of academic freedom in Egypt under the Sisi regime as the "lowest point of academic freedom that the country has known" (Linn, 2015). In June 2016 Mozn Hassan, the founder and director of Nazra for Feminist Studies and a women's rights activist, was prevented from leaving Egypt because of her political activism. A similar scene played out when a prominent democracy advocate and professor of political science at Cairo University, Ahmad Hamzawy, was prevented from taking a leave of absence in 2014 and then terminated in 2017.

Research permits can also be denied for arbitrary and vague concerns about security. In recent years professors have been directly targeted by state authorities. In 2016 the German University of Cairo professor Tarek Abol Naga had his contract terminated because the research he was supervising on architecture was deemed "immoral" (el-Galil, 2016). Research support from foreign foundations or agencies raises red flags because the government is suspicious of foreign governments promoting democracy and civil society. Nader (2016) reports in *Al-Monitor* that receiving funds from foreign donors, universities, or institutions is considered espionage in Egypt. In 2016 I was invited to speak at a number of universities in Egypt to discuss higher education admissions. As a foreigner, I had to receive specialized permission from the Department of the Interior to enter the campuses, which took weeks to obtain. The atmosphere was markedly different from my prior visits in 2007 and 2010. In the wake of student protests, all security on university campuses was outsourced to a private company, Falcon Group International, which has close ties to the Sisi regime. Although I received my permit, in many cases foreigners are denied access to campuses, which has had a dramatic impact on international collaborations and cross-border initiatives. An Egyptian colleague explained: "They think every foreigner is a spy. It's all politics. How do you think deans and university presidents make it to where they are? It's all through security. They can't get to where they are without reporting on their colleagues to security."

These crackdowns on academic freedom have been part of a broader trend towards rising authoritarianism in the region, typically justified in terms of national security. Table 6.3 reports on crackdowns on academic personnel between 2010 and 2019 from data collected by the Scholars at Risk (SAR) Academic Monitoring Project. SAR, a civil society organization based in New York, culled media reports to compile data on six different types of threats to academic freedom, from violence to firings to travel restrictions. The table shows a significant number of concerning incidents, particularly in Egypt, where forty-five documented incidents have occurred since 2010, and nine in the UAE, a much smaller country. In 2019 SAR and the Association for Freedom of Thought and Expression in Egypt asked the United Nations' Universal Periodic Review to examine attacks on higher education in Egypt as a human rights issue.

In Morocco, a prominent political activist and professor at Mohammed V University in Rabat, Maati Monjib, went on a hunger strike in 2015 after he was banned from leaving the country to attend a conference in Spain on political transitions. The repression of Monjib is part of a broader trend of crackdowns on political dissent in Morocco in the wake of the country's Arab Spring protests, known as the February 20 Movement. The government accused Monjib of "threatening national security" by organizing a training for journalists (Strangler, 2018).

In the Arab Gulf states, observers have also expressed rising concerns over threats to academic freedom. In 2011, Mohammed al-Ajami, a Qatari citizen, who was a third-year student in literature at Cairo University, was reciting poetry that supported the protests in Tunisia and was surreptitiously videotaped on a mobile phone. In November

Table 6.3. Crackdowns on Academic Personnel, 2010–19

	Killing & violence	Prison	Prosecution	Loss of position	Travel restrictions	Other	Total
Egypt	9	12	7	7	6	0	45
Jordan	1	1	1	0	0	0	3
Lebanon	0	1	1	0	0	0	2
Morocco	0	2	0	1	1	1	5
Tunisia	0	0	1	0	0	1	2
UAE	0	3	2	0	4	0	9

Source: Scholars at Risk Academic Monitoring Project (2019)

2011 he was summoned to Doha, questioned by Qatar's security forces, and subsequently charged with "encouraging an attempt to overthrow the existing regime" and "criticizing the Emir." Initially he was sentenced to life in prison, subsequently commuted to fifteen years (MESA, 2016). In 2016 he was released after a royal pardon.

In 2011 five prominent activists known as the UAE5 were "arrested for crimes including insulting members of the country's ruling families and for posing a threat to state security," according to the *National*, a government-aligned newspaper in the UAE ("Five Emiratis," 2011). One of the arrested academics was Nasser Bin Ghaith, an Emirati human rights activist and economics professor at Sorbonne University Abu Dhabi. The imprisonment of Bin Ghaith has been criticized as undermining the values of freedom of speech in the region. A spokesperson for Scholars at Risk stated that the detention of Bin Ghaith was "a serious and unfortunate blow to the many good efforts of the government and others to develop the Emirates' reputation and position as a centre of knowledge, education and culture, as these can only flourish in places which respect intellectual enquiry, free expression and human rights" (O'Malley, 2011). SAR's advocacy campaign eventually led to the pardoning of Bin Ghaith.

Since the Arab Spring, crackdowns on social scientists in the UAE have deteriorated further. In 2013 the London School of Economics (LSE) called off a conference that had been scheduled at the American University of Sharjah in the UAE on the causes and effects of the Arab Spring, due to "threatened academic freedom" after a senior academic from the school was detained by immigration authorities at the Dubai airport and denied entry to the UAE. In a statement to the BBC a university representative said that "the decision was made in response to restrictions imposed on the intellectual content of the event that threatened academic freedom" (Law, 2013). One of the ironies is that LSE receives significant funding from the UAE; at the time the conference was cancelled in 2013, the LSE had received USD 8.5 million from the Emirates Foundation, which is funded by the UAE government.

Debates over academic freedom at American branch campuses in the Arabian Gulf have also played out in the international media (Koch & Vora, 2019). The UAE has banned several professors from entering the country, and details of these incidents routinely appear in the press. In 2015 Andrew Ross, a professor at New York University who studies migration, was prohibited from boarding a plane to the UAE "for security reasons." Ross explained: "We've been told by our administration that they have agreements with our Abu Dhabi partners about protecting academic freedoms and now it turns out that they really don't have that kind of influence ... They don't really have any say, ultimately, if the state decides to override those protections" (Redden, 2015). In 2018 NYU's College of Journalism suspended its collaboration after two of its journalism professors were denied visas into the UAE. In an opinion piece published in the *New York Times*, one of those professors, Mohamad Bazzi, claimed: "the promise of academic freedom has proved to be largely worthless" (Bazzi, 2017). The Middle East Studies Association's Committee on Academic Freedom made it clear that the UAE's security agenda was at odds with its stated attempt to be a regional knowledge hub, and warned that "it has become obvious that there has been an escalation in insecurity for researchers" (MESA, 2018).

Crackdowns on the pursuit of knowledge are part of the control by a government over the ideological institutions of its country. They also raise a fundamental question concerning the link between higher education and a knowledge economy: can one build a knowledge economy and research culture without respect for fundamental academic freedoms, including the right to critique those in power? The result of these many years of attacks on academic freedom is self-censorship and a focus on technical knowledge rather than on social, cultural, or political knowledge.

In 2016, I spoke with a professor at a public university in the UAE who framed the debate as central to the question of democratization: "What is the right amount of education needed so that Emiratis can replace Westerners at certain jobs at the oil companies, but then, don't really create an independent, free-thinking, critical-thinking society? We have seen in the West that when you create an educated class, they have always turned on the totalitarian government, call it monarchy or whatever you like. Can we find a balance in the Arab world, where we have an inherited ruler, not a democratic government, and create a knowledge society? Because I think that is the ultimate debate: are those things mutually exclusive?" This professor's question applies no less to the Arab world than to many parts of the world where we have witnessed crackdowns on academic freedom, including China, Hungary, and Turkey.

Between Knowledge and Truth

The university has long been a creator and disseminator of knowledge. Around the world, countries are reforming their universities to be engines of economic growth by emphasizing quantitative research outputs in targeted sectors. These reforms have been adopted throughout the Arab world, where knowledge production is emphasized in official documents and policies and linked to countries' participation in the global knowledge economy. On the one hand, there is much to celebrate in the region: in middle-income countries in particular, research productivity rates are above average for countries of similar levels of economic development. These updated and contextualized data should put to rest the idea that the Arab world is truly failing in knowledge production.

On the other hand, the focus on research productivity may actually be harmful. The framing of productivity as an individual or institutional output ignores the structural conditions that shape research production including national wealth, academic freedom, academics' professional identities, universities' organizational cultures, and the hegemony of English globally. The link between research and university rankings also pushes Arab academics to prioritize the global and the abstract, at the expense of the local and the particular. Meanwhile, the focus on applied and useful research in the name of economic development emphasizes the natural sciences and technological development at the expense of the social sciences and the humanities. Some of the most pressing, yet politically contentious, questions the region faces involve the "messy" social sciences and the "fluffy" humanities that are too often dismissed, including questions of identity, inequality, cultural difference, civic engagement, and subjective well-being.

Conclusion
Rethinking Higher Education
and Development

No image of the university was ever more fallacious than that of the ivory tower. No university has ever been or could ever be one. Rather, the university has always been and will always be a terrain of conflict.

Wallerstein, *University in Turmoil*, p. 8

This book examines how globalization is affecting Arab higher education systems. A recurring argument is that development discourses of higher education in the region take a narrow, overly simplistic, and instrumental view. Reforms draw on generic and globally circulating policy prescriptions that emanate from powerful donors and intergovernmental agencies, with little attention being paid to the ways in which such higher education reforms are contested and altered by local actors.

Rather than suggesting better ways to reform, however, this book ends with a call to rethink fundamentally the meanings of higher educational development – a call that is not limited to the Arab world. Such rethinking must begin with an understanding of the university as a social, cultural, and political institution, not an object of intervention. Definitions of development must make space for individuals' social, psychological, and spiritual well-being. It is most likely impossible for the field to do this until it rejects the assumption that Europe and North America are natural models of reform. With humility and empathy we might begin by asking not what the Arab world should be doing better but rather what the rest of the world, including the West, can learn from the Arab world.

Re-politicizing Development

In *Covering Islam*, Edward Said wrote: "The hardest thing to get most academic experts on Islam to admit is that what they say and do as scholars is set in a profoundly and in some ways an offensively political context" (1981, p. xvii). This statement applies no less to scholars of development, comparative education, and higher education. This book argues that discussions of higher education reform and development must recognize the politicized nature of both the university itself and the enterprise of creating knowledge about higher education.

In the literature on educational development, higher education in the Arab world is typically framed as inefficient, ineffective, and irrelevant. Notions of effectiveness and efficiency are used to convey a sense of both the internal and the external irrationality of higher education systems in the region. This book rejects those portrayals; it reminds us that even the most seemingly technical debates over issues such as admission standards, indicators of quality, international students, and academic research actually reflect larger debates over the role of the university in distributing social, political, and economic power.

In higher educational development, recognized experts are engaged in diagnosing the problems of higher education. They suggest best practices such as autonomy and accountability, which then become diffused among transnational policy communities, including the WB, think-tanks, and academia. These professional experts (including myself), who are firmly ensconced in global institutions or Western universities, possess widely accepted scientific credentials that make them authoritative and influential on technical matters of higher education reform, as they draw on "good practices" and international benchmarks. In most discussions of reform, higher education policy is de-politicized in the name of pursuing these best practices on the grounds of their internal or assumed logic.

The de-politicization of a powerful and political institution at its best creates conditions that are ripe for decoupling – misdiagnosis of problems, generic policy solutions that are out of tune with realities on the ground, and stalled implementation. A striking example is the growing focus on university governance, where governance is characterized as management, and best practices include ensuring university autonomy (Jaramillo, 2013). This technical understanding of governance represents an incredible ability to separate governance from government and ignores the fact that decision making involves political and moral considerations. Even worse, globally circulating best practices, such as privatization, may harm young people by exacerbating socio-economic inequalities, failing to prepare them for civic participation, or undermining their trust in their own societies and public institutions.

Over the past decade I have spoken to hundreds of researchers, professors, students, and policymakers across the Arab world. They speak openly of their experiences; without fail, they understand higher education in the Arab world as an institution full of contradiction and compromise. Cantini (2012) reminds us that, in Arab countries, students are acutely aware of the contradictions between the state-sponsored visions of modern citizenship, values, and identities and their lived experiences in universities, and it is in these contexts that "students use their spaces not simply to protest against educational policies but state ones as well" (para. 2). A new approach to higher education development must begin by acknowledging that the embodied wisdom in these lived experiences is at least as valuable as the abstracted technical expertise possessed by credentialled experts.

Fundamentally, higher education development has too narrowly conceptualized the purposes of higher education. The narrow focus in international development on the university's role as a producer of labour and a producer of research ignores its role as a producer of citizens. In the wake of the Arab Spring the role of universities in supporting young people's engagement in civic life is a fundamental question for development. A new approach must begin by centring the university's civic mandates.

Learning From, Not About, the Arab World

This book tells many stories about higher education reform in the Arab world, but they are not unique to the Arab world; they reflect many of the challenges faced by higher education systems around the world, including how to balance access, quality, equity, and financing.

Cheating scandals make front-page news throughout the world. In China and South Korea, where higher education is lauded for its impressive gains, high-stakes admissions exams cause both cheating scandals and high levels of student anxiety and stress about mental health. In 2019 elite universities in the United States were sued by the government over bribery scandals.

Low levels of learning are also a major concern globally. Recent studies of higher education in various national contexts have found low levels of learning, with researchers warning that current organizational cultures and practices "too rarely focus on either improving instruction or demonstrating gains in student learning" (Arum & Roska, 2011, p. 122).

How much students and families should pay for education is also a normative debate and policy problem worldwide. In the United States parents often start saving for college or university from the day their children are born. In the United Kingdom increases in university

tuition have caused street protests. Meanwhile, significant privatization has meant that students and families are treated as "consumers,"
which some argue has a perverse impact on student learning: institutions cater to students' preferences for campus facilities and high marks
regardless of their impact on student learning.

Beyond specific policy domains lie broader questions of the role
of the university's contribution to social and political life, or what is
called the public sphere (Habermas, 1989). Concerns over the role of
the university in promoting the public good are shared by scholars
the world over, including those in liberal democracies. Commenting on American higher education, Henry Giroux (2007) argues for
"reclaiming higher education as a democratic public sphere and
counter institution" that facilitates "a pedagogy of critical engagement" and "civic responsibility" (p. 3). Pressures on universities
have become more intense in the wake of the 2008 global recession
and the rise of anti-global, populist backlashes. Policy austerity has
called for the closing of certain humanities departments and academic presses even at elite institutions. Battles over the limits of
free speech have played out on Canadian and American university
campuses. Populist elections in Hungary have caused the Central
European University to relocate to Austria, and academics have
been directly targeted in Turkey, while chilly political climates are
clamping down on academic freedom in Brazil and China, among
other countries. Although the rise of illiberalism globally may indeed be short lived, we do not know what the future holds. Scholars
of higher education have expressed worry about the precarious state
of public support for higher education in many parts of the world.
Such concerns are ever more pressing in light of the predicted effects
of climate crisis and rapid technological change.

As the global pandemic of COVID-19 spread throughout the world,
we were reminded of how interconnected we are. During these
moments of crisis we also realize that the purpose of higher education
is, as it always has been, more than preparing young people for the
world of work. It gives us an opportunity to imagine new possibilities
for its role in society as a site for imagining alternative futures. Even
when governments are equipped to close down dissent through the
internet and social media, the university has proven that it remains a
singular space for promoting the public good through deliberation, cultural transmission, and solidarity.

In rejecting the presumed inferiority of Arab higher education, this
book began with a new narrative about higher education in the Arab
world: higher education in the Arab world trains creative, diverse,

multilingual, and mobile students to be economically productive and civically engaged amid difficult social and political conditions. In rejecting the natural superiority of Western higher education, the book calls for a new approach to higher educational development. It asks those of us situated in North America, Europe, and other high-income or English-speaking contexts to ask ourselves: What might we learn from the Arab world about the role and resiliency of higher education in an uncertain and unpredictable future?

References

Abdel-Wahid, N. (2009). La Syrie [Syria]. In *Enseignement superieur et marche du travail dans le monde Arab* [Higher education and the labour market in the Arab world] (pp. 191–216). Beirut, Lebanon: Institut Francais du Proche-Orient.

Abou-Setta, A. (2014, June 2). In Egypt, the failure of privatizing education. *Al-Fanar*. https://www.al-fanarmedia.org.

Abu-Lughod, L. (2009). Dialects of women's empowerment: The international circuitry of the Arab Human Development Report 2005. *International Journal of Middle East Studies, 41*(1), 83–103. doi:10.1017/S0020743808090107.

Adely, F. (2009). Educating women for development: The Arab Human Development Report 2005 and the problem with women's choices. *International Journal of Middle East Studies, 41*(1), 105–22. doi:10.1017/S0020743808090144.

Adely, F. (2012). Gendered paradoxes: Educating Jordanian women in nation, faith, and progress. Chicago, IL: University of Chicago Press.

Adely, F., Haddad, A., Husban, A.H. al-, & Khoshman, A. al- (2019). Getting in and getting through: Navigating higher education in Jordan. *Comparative Education Review, 63*(1), 79–97. doi:10.1086/701127.

Adely, F., Mitra, A., Mohamed, M., & Shaham, A. (2021). Poor education, unemployment and the promise of skills: The hegemony of the "skills mismatch" discourse. *International Journal of Educational Development, 82*, 1–9. doi.org/10.1016/j.ijedudev.2021.102381.

Ait Hammou, Brahim. (2012, June 19). Morocco: Cheating and the need to reform the exam system. *Morocco World News*.

Akdere, M., Russ-Eft, D. & Eft, N. (2006). The Islamic worldview of adult learning in the workplace: Surrendering to God. *Advances in Developing Human Resources, 8*(3): 355–63. doi:10.1177/1523422306288428.

Akkari, A. (2010). Privatizing education in the Maghreb: A path for a two-tiered education system. In A.E. Mazawi & R. Sultana (Eds.), *World yearbook of education 2010* (pp. 67–82). London, UK: Routledge.

Alayan, A. (2014, December 3). Why aren't Jordanian children in school? *Al-Fanar*.

Alhebsi, A., Pettaway, L., & Waller, L. (2015). A history of education in the United Arab Emirates and Trucial Shiekdoms. *Global eLearning Journal, 4*(1), 1–6.

Almansour, S. (2016). The crisis of research and global recognition in Arab universities. *Near and Middle Eastern Journal of Research in Education, 2016*(1), 1–13. doi:10.5339/nmejre.2016.1.

Almansour, S., & Kempner, K. (2017). The challenges of delivering public good in Arab universities: Faculty perspectives. *Educational Research for Policy and Practice, 16*(3), 219–34. doi:10.1007/s10671-017-9213-3.

Altbach, P. (2007). Academic freedom in a global context: 21st century challenges. In *The NEA 2007 Almanac of Higher Education* (pp. 49–56). Washington, DC: National Education Association.

Altbach, P. (Ed.). (2013). *The international imperative in higher education.* Rotterdam, Netherlands: Sense.

Altbach, P. & Levy, D.C. (2005). *Private higher education: A global revolution.* Rotterdam, Netherlands: Sense.

Altbach, P. & Peterson, P. (Eds.). (2007). *Higher education in the new century: Global challenges and innovative ideas* (Vol. 10). Rotterdam, Netherlands: Sense.

Álvarez-Galván, J. (2015), A Skills beyond School Review of Egypt. In *OECD Reviews of Vocational Education and Training*. Paris, France: OECD Publishing. doi.org/10.1787/9789264209626-en.

Amer, P. (2019, December 3). Not just money: Arab-region researchers face a complex web of barriers. *Al-Fanar*. Retrieved from https://www.al -fanarmedia.org.

Anderson, B. S. (2005). *Nationalist voices in Jordan: The street and the state.* Austin, TX: University of Texas Press.

Anderson, B.S. (2011). *The American University of Beirut: Arab nationalism and liberal education.* Austin, TX: University of Texas Press.

Anderson, L. (1987). The state in the Middle East and North Africa. *Comparative Politics, 20*(1), 1–18. doi:10.2307/421917.

Anderson, L. (2011). Demystifying the Arab Spring: Parsing the differences between Tunisia, Egypt, and Libya. *Foreign Affairs, 2–7.*

Anderson, L. (2012). Fertile ground: The future of higher education in the Arab World. *Social Research: An International Quarterly, 79*(3), 771–85.

Anderson, N. (2015, December 6). In Qatar's Education City, U.S. colleges are building an academic oasis. *Washington Post.*

ANQAHE (Arab Network for Quality Assurance in Higher Education). (2012). *Second scoping study.* Paris, France: UNESCO.

Arabsheibani, G. (1988). Educational choice and achievement: The case of secondary schools in the Arab Republic of Egypt. *Higher Education, 17*(6), 637–46. doi:10.1007/BF00143779.

Araby, A. el-. (2011). A comparative assessment of higher education financing in six Arab countries. *Prospects, 41*(1), 9–21. doi:10.1007/s11125-011-9185-7.

Arafeh, L. (2010). Quality assurance review in Arab countries. In B. Lamine (Ed.), *Arab Regional Conference on Higher Education* (pp. 442–60). Cairo, Egypt: UNESCO Regional Bureau for Education in the Arab States.

Arbaoui, L. (2012, June 15). Cheating in exams: Author of Facebook leaks to be brought to justice. *Morocco World News.*

Arbaoui, L. (2016, June 7). Bac exams in Morocco: More than 3,000 cases of cheating recorded. *Morocco World News.*

Arum, R., & Roksa, J. (2011). *Academically adrift: Limited learning on college campuses.* Chicago, IL: University of Chicago Press.

Assaad, R. (2014). Making sense of Arab labor markets: The enduring legacy of dualism. *IZA Journal of Labor & Development, 3*(1), 1–25. doi:10.1186 /2193-9020-3-6.

Assaad, R., & Krafft, C. (2015a). The evolution of labor supply and unemployment in the Egyptian economy: 1988–2012. In R. Assaad & C. Krafft (Eds.), *The Egyptian labor market in an era of revolution* (pp. 1–26). Oxford, UK: Oxford University Press.

Assaad, R., & Krafft, C.. (2015b). Is free basic education in Egypt a reality or a myth? *International Journal of Educational Development, 45*(1), 16–30. doi:10.1016/j.ijedudev.2015.09.001.

Assaad, R., Krafft, C., & Salehi-Isfahani, D. (2018). Does the type of higher education affect labor market outcomes? Evidence from Egypt and Jordan. *Higher Education, 75*(6), 945–95. doi:10.1007/s10734-017-0179-0.

Assaad, R., & Roudi-Fahimi, F. (2007). *Youth in the Middle East and North Africa: Demographic opportunity or challenge?* Washington, DC: Population Reference Bureau.

Assaad, R., Salehi-Isfahani, D., & Hendy, R. (2014). *Inequality of opportunity in educational attainment in Middle East and North Africa: Evidence from household surveys.* (Economic Research Forum, Working Paper No. 834). Retrieved from https://erf.org.eg/.

AUB-IFI (American University of Beirut, Issam Fares Institute). (2019). Demands raised by certain groups who participated in the October 2019 uprising. Retrieved from https://www.aub.edu.lb.

Austin, A.E., Chapman, D.W., Farah, S., Wilson, E., & Ridge, N. (2014). Expatriate academic staff in the United Arab Emirates: The nature of their work experiences in higher education institutions. *Higher Education, 68*(4), 541–57. doi:10.1007/s10734-014-9727-z.

Azevedo, J.P. (2011). WBopendata: Stata module to access World Bank databases, Statistical Software Components S457234. Boston, MA: Boston College Department of Economics. Retrieved from http://ideas.repec.org /c/boc/bocode/s457234.html.

Azzeh, L. (2013, January 28). Debate over tawjihi continues without tangible solutions. *Jordan Times*.

Azzeh, L. (2016, January 13). Tougher tawjihi rules necessary, "but constitutional rights must be guaranteed" *Jordan Times*.

Badawi, K. (2019, May 12). "نعم أنا دكتور جامعي" [Yes, I am a university professor]. Al-Falah al-Youm. Retrieved from https://alfallahalyoum.news.

Badr, M. (1994). *Higher education in Jordan: Between government responsibility and the private sector* (Les Cahiers du CERMOC, no. 9). Amman, Jordan: CERMOC.

Badran, A. (2018). Landscape of R&D in the Arab region compared with the rest of the world. In A. Badran, E. Baydoun, & J.R. Hillman. (Eds.). *Universities in Arab countries: An urgent need for change* (pp. 85–104). Cham, Switzerland: Springer.

Badran, A., & Badran, S. (2019). Indicators of institutional and program ranking of universities with reference to the Arab world. In A. Badran, E. Baydoun, & J.R. Hillman (Eds.), *Major challenges facing higher education in the Arab world: Quality assurance and relevance* (pp. 179–210). Cham, Switzerland: Springer.

Badran, A., Baydoun, E., & Hillman, J.R. (Eds.). (2019). *Major challenges facing higher education in the Arab world: Quality assurance and relevance*. Cham, Switzerland: Springer.

Badran, S., & Badran, A. (2018). Who pays what for public & private university education in the Arab region compared with the rest of the world: Context of Jordan. In A. Badran, E. Baydoun, & J.R. Hillman (Eds.), *Universities in Arab Countries: An urgent need for change* (pp. 225–48). Cham, Switzerland: Springer.

Bamyeh, M. (2015). *Forms of presence of the social sciences in the Arab region: Summary of the first report*. Beirut, Lebanon: Arab Council for the Social Sciences.

Barakat, S., & Milton, S. (2015). *Houses of wisdom matter: The responsibility to protect and rebuild higher education in the Arab world*. Doha, Qatar: Brookings Doha Center. Retrieved from https://www.brookings.edu/.

Barsoum, G. (2016). "Job opportunities for the youth": Competing and overlapping discourses on youth unemployment and work informality in Egypt. *Current Sociology, 64*(3), 430–46. doi:10.1177/0011392115593614.

Barsoum, G. (2017). The allure of "easy": Reflections on the learning experience in private higher education institutes in Egypt. *Compare: A Journal of Comparative and International Education, 47*(1), 105–17. doi:10.1080/03057925.2016.1153409.

Bartlett, L., Frederick, M., Gulbrandsen, T., & Murillo, E. (2002). The marketization of education: Public schools for private ends. *Anthropology & Education Quarterly, 33*(1), 5–29. doi:10.1525/aeq.2002.33.1.5.

Bartlett, L., & Vavrus, F. (2014). Transversing the vertical case study: A methodological approach to studies of educational policy as practice. *Anthropology & Education Quarterly, 45*(2), 131–47. doi:10.1111/aeq.12055.

Bashshur, M.A. (1966). Higher education and political development in Syria and Lebanon. *Comparative Education Review, 10*(3), 451–61.

Bashshur, M. (2006). Standards of quality of higher education in Lebanon. In Y.C.M. Bashshur (Ed.), *L'enseignement supérieur dans le monde arabe: Une question de niveau?* [Higher education in the Arab world: A question of level?]. Beirut, Lebanon: Institut Français du Proche Orient. doi:10.1086/445236.

Bataeineh, M.F. (2008). *A historical investigation on the establishment and development of higher education in Jordan* (Doctoral dissertation, Northern Illinois University). Retrieved from ProQuest Dissertations and Theses (250842804).

Bayat, A. (2005). Transforming the Arab world: The Arab Human Development Report and the politics of change. *Development and Change, 36*(6), 1225–37. doi:10.1111/j.0012-155X.2005.00461.x.

Bazzi, M. (2017, September 17). N.Y.U. in Abu Dhabi: A sectarian bargain. *New York Times*.

Benchenna, A. (2009). L'appui de la France à la Réforme de l'Enseignement supérieur (ES) au Maroc: Quelles finalités et quels enjeux? *Journal of Higher Education in Africa / Revue de l'enseignement supérieur en Afrique*,

Benrabah, M. (2013). Language conflict in Algeria: From colonialism to post-independence. Bristol, UK: Multilingual Matters.

Benzakour, F. (2007). Langue française et langues locales en terre marocaine: Rapports de force et reconstructions identitaires. *Hérodote, 3*(126), 45–56. doi:10.3917/her.126.0045.

Bhandari, R., & Amine, A. el-. (2012). *Higher education classification in the Middle East and North Africa: A pilot study*. New York, NY: Institute of International Education. Retrieved from https://www.iie.org/.

Bin Tayyib, M. (2013, February 22). وزارة التربية تكشف غشّاشي البكالوريا والعقوبات المتخذة في حقهم [The Education ministry discovers Bac cheaters and takes measures against them]. *HessPress*.

Bollag, B. (1996, February 9). Egypt's overcrowded universities feel burden of admissions increase. *The Chronicle of Higher Education, 42*(22). Retrieved from https://www.chronicle.com.

Bollag, B. (2016, June 19). A conversation with a scholar who has been sentenced to death. *Al-Fanar*. https://www.al-fanarmedia.org.

Boughazala, M., Ghazouani, S., & Ben Hafaiedh, A. (2016, July). *Aligning incentives for reforming higher education in Tunisia* (Economic Research Forum, Working Paper No. 1031). Retrieved from https://erf.org.eg/.

Bourqia, R. (2011). *Vers une sociologie de l'université Marocaine*. Rabat, Morocco: Conseil Supérieur de l'Education.

Boutieri, C. (2012). In two speeds (A deux vitesses): Linguistic pluralism and educational anxiety in contemporary Morocco. *International Journal of Middle East Studies, 44*(3), 443–64. doi:10.1017/S0020743812000414.

Boutieri, C. (2016). *Learning in Morocco: Language politics and the abandoned educational dream*. Bloomington, IN: Indiana University Press.

Brand, L. (1988). *Palestinians in the Arab World: Institution building and the search for state*. New York, NY: Columbia University Press.

Bray, M. (2006). Private supplementary tutoring: Comparative perspectives on patterns and implications. *Compare: A Journal of Comparative and International Education*, 36(4), 515–30. doi:10.1080/03057920601024974.

Brown, P. (2013). Education, opportunity and the prospects for social mobility. *British Journal of Sociology of Education*, 34(5–6), 678–700. doi:10.1080/01425692.2013.816036.

Brown, P., & Tannock, S. (2009). Education, meritocracy and the global war for talent. *Journal of Education Policy*, 24(4), 377–92. doi:10.1080/02680930802669938.

Buchmann, C., & Hannum, E. (2001). Education and stratification in developing countries: A review of theories and research. *Annual Review of Sociology*, 27(2001), 77–102. doi:10.1146/annurev.soc.27.1.77.

Buckner, E. (2013). The seeds of discontent: Examining youth perceptions of higher education in Syria. *Comparative Education*, 49(4), 440–63. doi:10.1080/03050068.2013.765643.

Buckner, E. (2017). The worldwide growth of private higher education: Cross-national patterns of higher education institution foundings by sector. *Sociology of Education*, 90(4), 296–314.

Buckner, E. (2018). The growth of private higher education in North Africa: A comparative analysis of Morocco and Tunisia. *Studies in Higher Education*, 43(7), 1295–1306. doi:10.1080/03075079.2016.1250075.

Buckner, E., Beges, S., & Khatib, L. (2012). *Social entrepreneurship: Why is it important post Arab Spring?* Center for Democracy, Development and the Rule of Law, Stanford University. Retrieved from https://cddrl.fsi.stanford.edu.

Buckner, E., & Hodges, R. (2016). Cheating or cheated? Surviving secondary exit exams in a neoliberal era. *Compare: A Journal of Comparative and International Education*, 46(4), 603–23.

Buckner, E.S., & Saba, K. (2010). Syria's next generation: Youth un/employment, education, and exclusion. *Education, Business and Society: Contemporary Middle Eastern Issues*, 3(2), 86–98. doi:10.1108/17537981011047934.

Burke, D., & Waked, A. al-. (1997). *On the threshold: Private universities in Jordan*. Boston, MA: Boston College Center for International Higher Education.

Byrne, J.J. (2016). *Mecca of revolution: Algeria, decolonization, and the Third World order*. Oxford, UK: Oxford University Press.

CAA (Commission for Academic Accreditation). (2019). *Core concepts of standards, 2019*. Retrieved from https://www.caa.ae.

Cammack, P., Dunne, M., Hamzwy, A., Lynch, M., Muasher, M., Sayigh, Y., & Yahya, M. (2017). *Arab fractures: Citizens, states, and social contracts*. Washington, DC: Carnegie Endowment for International Peace.

Cantini, D. (2012). Discourses of reforms and questions of citizenship: The university in Jordan. *Revue des Mondes Musulmans et de la Méditerranée* [Online], (131), 147–62. doi:10.4000/remmm.7659.

Cantini, D. (2016). *Youth and education in the Middle East: Shaping identity and politics in Jordan.* New York, NY: I.B. Tauris.

Cantini, D. (2017). *Rethinking private higher education: Ethnographic perspectives.* Leiden, Netherlands: Brill.

Carnoy, M., Froumin, I., Loyalka, P.K., & Tilak, J.B. (2014). The concept of public goods, the state, and higher education finance: A view from the BRICs. *Higher Education, 68*(3), 359–78. doi:10.1007/s10734-014-9717-1.

Carroll, Jl. (2003, September 28). Higher Ed Council lowers acceptance standard for private universities, 50 on tawjihi, 2 years out of high school set as new criteria. *Jordan Times.*

C-BERT (Cross-Border Education Research Team). (2020). *Branch campus listing* [Data originally collected by Kevin Kinser and Jason E. Lane]. Retrieved from http://cbert.org. Albany, NY: Author.

Chaaban, J. (2008). *The costs of youth exclusion in the Middle East.* (Middle East Youth Initiative, Working Paper No. 7). Washington, DC: Brookings Institution.

Chaaban, J. (2009). Youth and development in the Arab Countries: The need for a different approach. *Middle Eastern Studies, 45*(1):33–55. doi:10.1080 /00263200802547644.

Chakir, M. (2008). Youth unemployment blamed for violent demonstrations in Morocco, Tunisia. Retrieved from https://www.arab-reform.net.

Cheating rampant during official exams: Lebanon education minister. (2015, June 17). *The Daily Star* (Lebanon). Retrieved from http://www.dailystar .com.lb.

Cherkaoui, M. (2011). *Crise de l'université: Le nouvel esprit académique et la sécularisation de la production intellectuelle.* Paris, France: Librairie Droz.

Cichocki, J. (2005). *American higher education overseas: Three case studies of cross-national relationships in the Arabian Gulf* (Dissertation, Claremont Graduate University). Retrieved from ProQuest Dissertations and Theses (3179496).

Classes halted indefinitely at Mutah University following clashes. (2013, April 2). *AmmonNews.* Retrieved from http://en.ammonnews.net.

CMI (Center for Mediterranean Integration). (2013). Transforming Arab Economies: Traveling the Knowledge and Innovation Road. Washington, DC: World Bank.

Cohen, S. (2003). Alienation and globalization in Morocco: Addressing the social and political impact of market integration. *Comparative Studies in Society and History, 45*(1), 168–89. doi:10.1017/S0010417503000082.

Cohen, S. (2004). *Searching for a different future: The rise of a global middle class in Morocco.* Durham, NC: Duke University Press.

Cohen, S. (2014). Neoliberalism and academia in Morocco. *British Journal of Middle Eastern Studies, 41*(1), 28–42. doi:10.1080/13530194.2014.878505.

Colclough, C. (1996). Education and the market: Which parts of the neoliberal solution are correct? *World Development, 24*(4), 589–610. doi:10.1016/0305-750X(95)00157-8.

Collins, R. (1979). *The credential society: An historical sociology of education and stratification*. New York, NY: Academic Press.

Colonna, F. (2008). Training the national elites *in colonial Algeria, 1920–1954*. *Historical Social Research / Historische Sozialforschung, 33*(2), 285–95.

Crunching the numbers: Minister of Higher Education Mufid Shehab talks to *al-Ahram Weekly* about making the most of a flawed system. (2001, August 9–15). *Al-Ahram Weekly*.

Cupito, E., & Langsten, R. (2011). Inclusiveness in higher education in Egypt. *Higher Education, 62*(2), 183–97. doi:10.1007/s10734-010-9381-z.

Dale, R. (2005). Globalisation, knowledge economy and comparative education. *Comparative Education, 41*(2), 117–49. doi:10.1080/03050060500150906.

Devarajan, S. (2016, June 27) Future Development: The paradox of higher education in MENA [Web log post]. Retrieved from https://www.brookings.edu/blog/future-development/.

Dhillon, N., Dyer, P., & Yousef, T. (2009). *Generation in waiting: An overview of school to work and family formation transitions*. Washington, DC: Brookings Institution Press.

Dhillon, N., & Yousef, T. (Eds.). (2011). *Generation in waiting: The unfulfilled promise of young people in the Middle East*. Washington, DC: Brookings Institution Press.

Dillabough, J.A., Fimyar, O., McLaughlin, C., Azmeh, Z. al-, Abdullateef, S., & Abedtalas, M. (2018). Conflict, insecurity and the political economies of higher education: The case of Syria post-2011. *International Journal of Comparative Education and Development, 20*(3/4), 176–96. doi:10.1108/IJCED-07-2018-0015.

Dohjoka, N., Campbell, C.A., & Hill, B. (2017). Science diplomacy in Arab Countries: The need for a paradigm shift. *Science & Diplomacy, 6*(1).

Donn, G., & Manthri, Y. al- (2010). *Globalisation and higher education in the Arab Gulf States*. Didcot, UK: Symposium Books.

Dorio, J.N. (2017). Pedagogy of transition: Understanding university student movements in post-2011 Egypt. In R.R. Elmesky, C. Camp Yeakey, & O.C. Marcucci (Eds.), *The power of resistance: Culture, ideology and social reproduction in global contexts* (pp. 339–63). Bingley, U.K.: Emerald Publishing.

Drori, G.S. (1993). The relationship between science, technology and the economy in lesser developed countries. *Social Studies of Science, 23*(1), 201–15. doi:10.1177/030631293023001007.

Drori, G.S. (2000). Science education and economic development: Trends, relationships and research agenda. *Studies in Science Education, 35*(1), 27– 57. doi:10.1080/03057260008560154.

EACEA (Education, Audiovisual and Culture Executive Agency). (2017a). *Overview of the Higher Education System Jordan.* Brussels, Belgium: European Union. Retrieved from https://op.europa.eu/.

EACEA (Education, Audiovisual and Culture Executive Agency). (2017b). *Overview of the Higher Education System, Tunisia.* Brussels, Belgium: European Union. Retrieved from https://op.europa.eu/.

EACEA (Education, Audiovisual and Culture Executive Agency). (2017c). *Overview of the Higher Education System, Syria.* Brussels, Belgium: European Union. Retrieved from https://op.europa.eu/.

EACEA (Education, Audiovisual and Culture Executive Agency). (2017d). *Overview of the Higher Education System, Lebanon.* Retrieved from https:// op.europa.eu/.

Eickelman, D.F. (1978). The art of memory: Islamic education and its social reproduction. *Comparative Studies in Society and History, 20*(4), 485–516. doi:10.1017/S0010417500012536.

Elbadawy, A. (2009). *Three essays on education in Egypt* (Doctoral dissertation, McMaster University, Hamilton, ON). Retrieved from https://macsphere .mcmaster.ca.

Elbadawy, A. (2014). *Education in Egypt: Improvements in attainment, problems with quality and inequality* (Economic Research Forum Working Paper, no. 854). Giza, Egypt: Economic Research Forum. Retrieved from https://erf.org.eg/.

Elmeshad, M. (2014, October 28). A conversation with the new president of Menoufia University. *Al-Fanar.* Retrieved from https://www.al-fanarmedia .org/.

Emam, D. al-. (2013, October 28). Scholarship fund to begin receiving spring semester applications Nov. 10." *Jordan Times.*

Emran, A. (1997). *L'enseignement et la formation universitaire au Maroc: Reflexions psychosociologique sur les réformes ou comment vaincre l'incertitude?* Mohammedia, Morocco: Imprimerie de Fédala.

ENSSUP (Ministère de l'Enseignement Supérieur, de la Recherche Scientifique et de la Formation des cadres) [Morocco]. *Etablissements d'Enseignement Supérieur.* Retrieved from www.enssup.gov.ma/fr.

Ergül, H., Coşar, S., & Mous, F.A. (2017). Transformation, reformation or decline? The university in contemporary Morocco and Turkey. In H. Ergül & S. Coşar (Eds.), *Universities in the neoliberal era* (pp. 145–77). London: Palgrave Macmillan.

Errihani, M. (2008). Language attitudes and language use in Morocco: Effects of attitudes on "Berber language policy" *Journal of North African Studies, 13*(4), 411–28.

EU (European Union). (2016). *Battuta Project: Building academic ties towards universities through training activities.* Retrieved from https://www.battuta.eu.

Fahim, Y., & Sami, N. (2011). Adequacy, efficiency and equity of higher education financing: The case of Egypt. *Prospects, 41*(1), 47–67. doi:10.1007/s11125-011-9182-x.

Fahmy, Z. (2011*). Ordinary Egyptians: Creating the modern nation through popular culture.* Stanford, CA: Stanford University Press.

Farag, I. (2000). Higher education in Egypt: The realpolitik of privatization. *International Higher Education, 18,* 16–17. doi.org/10.6017/ihe.2000.18.6856.

Farag, I. (2010). Going international: The politics of educational reform in Egypt. In A.E. Mazawi & R. Sultana (Eds.), *World yearbook of education 2010* (pp. 285–99). London: Routledge.

Farag, I. (2012). Major trends of educational reform in Egypt. In S. Alayan, A. Rohde, & S. Dhouib (Eds.), *The Politics of education reform in the Middle East: Self and other in textbooks and curricula* (pp. 80–96). New York, NY: Berghahn Books.

Farawati, O. al-. (2001, October 23). Private universities file lawsuit at higher court of justice. *Jordan Times.*

Farawati, O. al-. (2002, January 14). Universities asked to submit 2002 budgets for approval. *Jordan Times.*

Fatnassi, I. (2010, October 25). Enseignement supérieur privé en Tunisie: Rupture du dialogue. *Business News.*

Ferroukhi, J. (2009). L'Algerie. In B. Labaki (Ed.), *Enseignement superieur et marche du travail dans le monde arabe* [Higher education and the labor market in the Arab world]. Beirut, Lebanon: Institut Francais du Proche Orient.

Findlow, S. (2006). Higher education and linguistic dualism in the Arab Gulf. *British Journal of Sociology of Education, 27*(1), 19–36. doi:10.1080/01425690500376754.

Five Emiratis arrested for threatening UAE security. (2011, April 26). The National.

Flah, L. (2012, June 13). Bac math exams leaked on Facebook, 617 cheating cases across the country – Ministry. *Morocco World News.*

Forstenlechner, I. (2008). Workforce nationalization in the UAE: Image versus integration. *Education, Business, and Society: Contemporary Middle Eastern Issues, 1*(2), 82–91. doi:10.1108/17537980810890275.

Fourcade, M. (2006). The construction of a global profession: The transnationalization of economics. *American Journal of Sociology, 112*(1), 145–94. doi:10.1086/502693.

Frank, D.J., & Meyer, J.W. (2007). University expansion and the knowledge society. *Theory and Society, 36*(4), 287–311. doi:10.1007/s11186-007-9035-z.

Fryer, L.G., & Jules, T.D. (2013). Policy spaces and educational development in the Islamic Maghreb region: Higher education in Tunisia. *International Perspectives on Education and Society, 21,* 401–25. doi:10.1108/S1479-3679(2013)0000021017.

Fuller, G.E. (2003). *The youth factor: The new demographics of the Middle East and the implications for US policy* (The Brookings Project on US Policy towards the Islamic World). Washington, DC: Saban Center for Middle East Policy.

Full speech of King Mohammed VI on the 60th anniversary of revolution of king and people. (2013, August 20). *Morocco World News*. Retrieved from https://www.moroccoworldnews.com.

Fyfe, A.A. (1989). *Wealth and power: Political and economic change in the United Arab Emirates* (Doctoral dissertation, Durham University). Retrieved from http://etheses.dur.ac.uk/6505/1/6505_3805.pdf.

Galal, A. (2002). *The paradox of education and unemployment in Egypt* (Report). Cairo: Egyptian Center for Economic Studies.

Galil, T.A. el-. (2016, September 12). Of architecture projects and academic freedom. Retrieved from https://www.al-fanarmedia.org.

Gambetta, D., & Hertog, S. (2017). *Engineers of Jihad: The curious connection between violent extremism and education.* Princeton, NJ: Princeton University Press.

Gardner, D. (2017, October 30). Tunisia: An Arab anomaly, by Safwan M. Masri. *Financial Times*. Retrieved from https://www.ft.com.

George, Alan. (2003). *Syria: Neither bread nor freedom.* London: Zed Books.

Geuna, A. (2001). The changing rationale for European university research funding: Are there negative unintended consequences? *Journal of Economic Issues, 35*(3), 607–32. doi:10.1080/00213624.2001.11506393.

Ghali, H.A. el-. (2010). Higher education and youth unemployment in Lebanon. *Journal of Comparative & International Higher Education, 2*(Spring), 12–13.

Gherib, B. (2011) Les classes moyennes tunisiennes entre mythe et réalité: Éléments pour une mise en perspective historique [The Tunisian middle classes between myth and reality: Elements for an historical perspective]. *L'Année du Maghreb VII* Retrieved from http://anneemaghreb.revues.org/1296.

Ghouati, A. (2009). Réforme LMD au Maghreb: Éléments pour un premier bilan politique et pédagogique. *Journal of Higher Education in Africa, 7*(1–2), 61–78. https://www.jstor.org/stable/24486279.

Giroux, H.A. (2007). Democracy, education, and the politics of critical pedagogy. In P. McLaren & J.L. Kincheloe (Eds.), *Critical pedagogy: Where are we now?* (pp. 1–5). New York: Peter Lang.

Gonzalez, G., Karoly, L., Constant, L., Salem, H., & Goldman, C. (2008). *Facing human capital challenges of the 21st century.* Santa Monica, CA: RAND Corporation.

Granovetter, M.S. (1973). The strength of weak ties. *American Journal of Sociology, 78*, 1360–80. https://www.jstor.org/stable/2776392.

Grimm, J. (2018, November 22). Authoritarian Middle East regimes don't like academics – ask Matthew Hedges. *Open Democracy*. Retrieved from https://www.opendemocracy.net.

GSDP (General Secretariat for Development Planning). (2009). *Qatar National Vision 2030: Advancing Sustainable Development* (Qatar's second human development report). Retrieved from http://hdr.undp.org.

Guazzone, L., & Pioppi, D. (Eds.) (2012). *The Arab state and neo-liberal globalization: The restructuring of state power in the Middle East*. Reading, UK: Ithaca Press.

Habermas J. (1989). The public sphere: An encyclopedia article. In E. Bronner & D. Kellner (Eds.), *Critical theory and society* (pp. 102–7). New York, NY: Routledge.

Hainmueller, J., & Hiscox, M.J. (2006). Learning to love globalization: Education and individual attitudes toward international trade. *International Organization, 60*(2), 469–98. doi:10.1017/S0020818306060140.

Halstead, M. (2004). An Islamic concept of education. *Comparative Education, 40*(4), 517–29. doi:10.1080/0305006042000284510.

Hammouti, B. (2010). Comparative bibliometric study of the scientific production in Maghreb countries (Algeria, Morocco and Tunisia) in 1996–2009 using Scopus. *Journal of Materials & Environmental Science, 1*(2), 70–7.

Hamzawy, A. (2017, March 7). Egypt campus: The students versus the regime. *Al Jazeera News*. Retrieved from https://www.aljazeera.com.

Hanafi, S. (2011). University systems in the Arab East: Publish globally and perish locally vs publish locally and perish globally. *Current Sociology, 59*(3), 291–309. doi:10.1177/0011392111400782.

Hanafi, S., & Arvanitis, R. (2014). The marginalization of the Arab language in social science: Structural constraints and dependency by choice. *Current Sociology, 62*(5), 723–42. doi:10.1177/0011392114531504.

Hanafi, S., & Arvanitis, R. (2016). *Knowledge production in the Arab world: The impossible promise*. New York, NY: Routledge.

Hannova, D. (2014). Arab students inside the Soviet bloc: A case study on Czechoslovakia during the 1950s and 60s. *European Scientific Journal, 10*(10), 371–9. doi.org/10.19044/esj.2014.v10n10p%25p.

Hanushek, E.A., & Woessmann, L. (2015). *The knowledge capital of nations: Education and the economics of growth*. Cambridge, MA: MIT Press.

Harahsheh, O. al-. (2017, September 4). Addressing campus violence remains unfinished business as debate goes on. *Jordan Times*. Retrieved from https://www.jordantimes.com/.

Harik, I.F. (1992). Privatization and development in Tunisia. In I. Harik & D. Sullivan (Eds.), *Privatization and liberalization in the Middle East* (pp. 210–32). Bloomington, IN: Indiana Univesity Press.

Hartmann, S. (2008). *The informal market of education in Egypt: Private tutoring and its implications* (Johannes Gutenberg University Department of Anthropology and African Studies Working Paper No. 88). Mainz, Germany: Institut für Ethnologie und Afrikastudien, Johannes Gutenberg-Universität. Retrieved from https://d-nb.info/.

Hartmann, S. (2013). Education "home delivery" in Egypt: Private tutoring and social stratification. In M. Bray, A.E. Mazawi, & R.G. Sultana (Eds.), *Private tutoring across the Mediterranean: Power dynamics and implications for learning and equity* (pp. 57–75). Rotterdam: Sense.

Harvey, D. (2007). *A brief history of neoliberalism*. New York, NY: Oxford University Press.

Hasrouny, A. (2011, January 23). Lebanon: Higher education at risk without reform. *University World News*. Retrieved from https://www.universityworldnews.com.

Hasso, F.S. (2009). Empowering governmentalities rather than women: The Arab Human Development Report 2005 and western development logics. *International journal of Middle East Studies, 41*(1), 63–82. doi:10.1017/S0020743808090120.

Hatina, M. (2003). Historical legacy and the challenge of modernity in the Middle East: The case of al-Azhar in Egypt. *The Muslim World, 93*(1), 51–68. doi:10.1111/1478-1913.00014.

Hénard, F., Diamond, L., & Roseveare, D. (2012). *Approaches to internationalisation and their implications for strategic management and institutional practice*. Paris, France: OECD.

Hendrixson, A. (2003). *The youth bulge: Defining the next generation of young men as a threat to the future* (DifferenTakes 19, Winter 2003). Hampshire, NH: Population and Development Program at Hampshire College. Retrieved from https://compass.fivecolleges.edu.

Herb, M. (1999). *All in the family: Absolutism, revolution, and democracy in Middle Eastern monarchies*. Albany, NY: State University of Albany Press.

Herrera, L. (2006). Higher education in the Arab World. In J.J.F. Forest & P.G. Altbach (Eds.), *International Handbook of Higher Education* (pp. 409–15). Dordrecht, Netherlands: Springer.

Herrera, L. (2008). *Education and empire: Rights-based reform in the Arab world*. (Presented at the third conference of the Mediterranean Society of Comparative Education "Intercultural Dialogue through Education"). Retrieved from https://repub.eur.nl.

Holmes, A.A., & Aziz, S. (2019, January 24). Egypt's Lost Academic Freedom. *Sada*. Washington, DC: Carnegie Endowment for International Peace. Retrieved from https://carnegieendowment.org/.

Howard-Merriam, K. (1979). Women, education, and the professions in Egypt. *Comparative Education Review, 23*(2), 256–70. doi:10.1086/446037.

Hvidt, M. (2015). The state and the knowledge economy in the Gulf: Structural and motivational challenges. *The Muslim World, 105*(1), 24–45. doi:10.1111/muwo.12078.

Hvistendahl, M. (2011). Young and restless can be a volatile mix. *Science, 333*(6042), 552–4.

Immerstein, S. & Shaikhly, S. al-. (2016, April 4). Education in Syria. *World Education News & Reviews*. Retrieved from https://wenr.wes.org/.

Investigation into tawjihi cheating allegations finds no wrongdoing. (2012, August 15). *Jordan Times*. Retrieved from http://jordantimes.com/.

JACEE (Jordanian-American Commission for Educational Exchange). (n.d.) Jordanian Fulbright Foreign Student Scholarship (Master's Degree)" Retrieved from https://www.fulbright-jordan.org/.

Jackson, M., & Buckner, E. (2016). Opportunity without Equity: Educational inequality and constitutional protections in Egypt. *Sociological Science, 3*, 730–56. doi:10.15195/v3.a31.

Jad, I. (2009). Comments from an author: Engaging the Arab Human Development Report 2005 on Women. *International Journal of Middle East Studies, 41*(1), 61–2. doi:10.1017/S0020743808090119.

Jaramillo, A. (2013). *Benchmarking governance as a tool for promoting change* (World Bank Policy Research Working Paper 81050). Washington, DC: World Bank.

Jaramillo, A., & Melonio, T. (2011). *Breaking even or breaking through: Reaching financial sustainability while providing high quality standards in higher education in the Middle East and North Africa*. Washington, DC: World Bank.

Johnstone, Bruce. (2004). The economics and politics of cost sharing in higher education: Comparative perspectives. *Economics of Education Review, 23*(4): 403–10. doi:10.1016/j.econedurev.2003.09.004.

Johnstone, D.B., & Marcucci, P.N. (2010). *Financing higher education worldwide: Who pays? Who should pay?*. Baltimore, MD: Johns Hopkins University Press.

Jones, C.W. (2012). *Building cititzens for the Arab knowledge economy* (Working Paper No. 02). Ras al-Khaimah, UAE: Al Qasimi Foundation.

Jones, C.W. (2015). *To cheat or not to cheat: Evidence on ethical decision-making from a study of Arab youth* (Working Paper No. 11). Ras al-Khaimah, UAE: Al Qasimi Foundation.

Jones, M.T. (1981). Allocation of students in North African universities. *Higher Education, 10*(3), 315–34. doi:10.1007/BF00139564.

Kabbani, N. (2009). Why young Syrians prefer public sector jobs (Middle East Youth Initiative Policy Outlook No. 2). Washington, DC: Brookings Institution.

Kabbani, N., & Kamel, N.. (2007). *Youth exclusion in Syria: Social, economic & institutional dimensions* (Middle East Youth Initiative Working Paper No. 4). Washington, DC: Brookings Institution.

Kabbani, N., & Kothari, E. (2005). *Youth employment in the MENA region: A situational assessment* (SP Discussion Paper, No. 0538). Washington, DC: World Bank.

Kabbani, N., & Salloum, S. (2011). Implications of financing higher education for access and equity: The case of Syria. *Prospects, 41*(1), 97–113. doi:10.1007/s11125-011-9178-6.

Kanaan, T., Salamat, M.N. al-, & Hanania, M.D. (2011). Political economy of cost-sharing in higher education: The case of Jordan. *Prospects, 41*(1): 23–45. doi:10.1007/s11125-011-9179-5.

Katsakioris, C. (2016). Les étudiants de pays arabes formés en union soviétique pendant la Guerre froide (1956–1991). *Revue européenne des migrations internationales, 32*(2), 13–38. doi:10.4000/remi.7758.

Kayyali, L. (2016). *Branch campus and national development: The case of Georgetown University in Qatar* (Unpublished thesis). Teachers' College, Columbia University, New York.

Keim, W. (2008). Social sciences internationally: The problem of marginalisation and its consequences for the discipline of sociology. *African Sociological Review/Revue Africaine de Sociologie, 12*(2), 22–48. doi:10.4314/asr.v12i2.49833.

Khan, N.-A.I. (2011). *Egyptian-Indian nationalist collaboration and the British Empire.* New York, NY: Palgrave Macmillan.

Khan, Z.R., & Balasubramanian, S. (2012). Students go click, flick and cheat… E-cheating, technologies and more. *Journal of Academic and Business Ethics, 6,* 1–26.

KHDA (Knowledge and Human Development Authority). (2017). *Higher Education in Dubai.* Retrieved from https://www.khda.gov.ae.

Khodr, H. (2011). The dynamics of international education in Qatar: Exploring the policy drivers behind the development of Education City. *Journal of Emerging Trends in Educational Research and Policy Studies, 2*(6), 514–25.

Kinser, K., Levy, D.C., Casillas, J.C.S., Bernasconi, A., Slantcheva Durst, S., Otieno, W., Lane, J., Praphamontripong, P., Zumeta, W., & LaSota, R. (2010). *The global growth of private higher education.* ASHE Higher Education Report Series. San Francisco: Wiley.

Kirk, D., & Napier, D. (2009). The transformation of higher education in the United Arab Emirates: Issues, implications, and intercultural dimensions. In J. Zajda, H. Daun, & L. Saha (Eds.), *Nation-building, identity and citizenship education: Cross-cultural perspectives* (pp. 131–42). Dordrecht, Netherlands: Springer.

Knight, J. (2004). Internationalization remodeled: Definition, approaches, and rationales. *Journal of Studies in International Education, 8*(1), 5–31. doi:10.1177/1028315303260832.

Knight, J. (2008). *Higher education in turmoil: The changing world of internationalisation.* Rotterdam, Netherlands: Sense.

Koch, N., & Vora, N. (2019). Laboratories of liberalism: American higher education in the Arabian Peninsula and the discursive production of authoritarianism. *Minerva,* 1–16.

Kohstall, F. (2012). Free transfer, limited mobility: A decade of higher education reform in Egypt and Morocco. *Revue des mondes musulmans et de la Méditerranée,* (131), 91–109.

Kohstall, F. (2015). From reform to resistance: Universities and student
    mobilisation in Egypt and Morocco before and after the Arab uprisings.
    British Journal of Middle Eastern Studies, 42(1), 59–73.

Krafft, C., & Alawode, H. (2018). Inequality of opportunity in higher
    education in the Middle East and North Africa. *International Journal of
    Educational Development, 62*, 234–44. doi:10.1016/j.ijedudev.2018.05.005.

Krafft, C., & Assaad, R. (2016). Inequality of opportunity in the labor market
    for higher education graduates in Egypt and Jordan. In I. Diwan & A. Galal
    (Eds.), *The Middle East Economies in Times of Transition* (pp. 159–85). London:
    Palgrave Macmillan.

Laggards trying to catch up. (2009, October 26). *The Economist.*

Lane, J.E. (2011). Importing private higher education: International branch
    campuses. *Journal of Comparative Policy Analysis: Research and Practice, 13*(4),
    367–81.

Lavergne, M. (2004). The 2003 Arab human development report: A critical
    approach. *Arab Studies Quarterly, 26*(2): 21–35.

Law, B. (2013, February 22). LSE Middle East conference abruptly cancelled.
    BBC. Retrieved from https://www.bbc.com.

Lebovic, S. (2013). From war junk to educational exchange: The World War II
    origins of the Fulbright Program and the foundations of American cultural
    globalism, 1945–1950. *Diplomatic History, 37*(2), 280–312. doi:10.1093/dh/dht002.

Levi-Faur, D. (2005). The global diffusion of regulatory capitalism. *The
    Annals of the American Academy of Political and Social Science, 598*(1), 12–32.
    doi:10.1177/0002716204272612.

Levy, D.C. (1999). When private higher education does not bring organizational
    diversity, In P. Altbach (Ed.), *Private Prometheus: Private higher education and
    development in the 21st century* (pp.15–44). Westport, CT: Greenwood Press.

Levy, D.C. (2006a). How private higher education's growth challenges the new
    institutionalism, In H.-D. Meyer & B. Rowan (Eds.), *The New Institutionalism
    in Education* (pp. 143–62). Albany: State University of New York Press.

Levy, D.C. (2006b). The unanticipated explosion: Private higher education's
    global surge. *Comparative Education Review, 50*(2): 217–40. doi:10.1086/500694.

Levy, D.C. (2011). Public policy for private higher education: A global analysis.
    Journal of Comparative Policy Analysis: Research and Practice, 13(4): 383–96. doi:
    10.1080/13876988.2011.583107.

Levy, D.C. (2018). Global private higher education: An empirical profile of its
    size and geographical shape. *Higher Education, 76*(4), 701–15. doi:10.1007
    /s10734-018-0233-6.

Linn, E.C. (2015, August 31). Egypt's besieged universities. *Foreign Policy.*
    Retrieved from https://foreignpolicy.com.

Lulat, Y.G.-M. (2005). *A history of African higher education from antiquity to the
    present: A critical synthesis.* Westport, CT: Praeger.

Mahmoud, A. (2008). Challenges facing the privatization of higher education in the Arab world, In A. al-Hawaj, E. Wajeeh, & E.H. Twizell (Eds.), *Higher education in the twenty-first century*. Boca Raton, FL: Taylor & Francis.

Makdisi, G. (1981). *The rise of colleges: Institutions of learning in Islam and the west*. New York, NY: Columbia University Press.

Malkawi, K. (2012, August 23). Over 51,000 applicants compete for 36,000 seats in public universities, acceptances to be announced early next month. *Jordan Times*.

Malkawi, K. (2013, January 19). Five-year higher education strategy failed – Maani. *Jordan Times*.

Malkawi, K. (2014, August 7). Low Tawjihi pass rate suggests fewer applications to private universities. *Jordan Times*.

Malkawi, K. (2015, May 2). Higher Education Ministry to revise sector laws, promote technical specialties. *Jordan Times*.

Malkawi, K. (2016, May 23). Maan university suspends 11 students involved in brawl. *Jordan Times*.

Marginson, S., & Van der Wende, M. (2007). To rank or to be ranked: The impact of global rankings in higher education. *Journal of Studies in International Education, 11*(3–4), 306–29. doi:10.1177/1028315307303544.

Massadeh, N. (2012). Policies governing admission to Jordanian public universities. *Higher Education Policy, 25*(4), 535–50. doi:10.1057/hep.2011.28.

Mazawi, A.E. (2005). Contrasting perspectives on higher education governance in the Arab states. In J. Smart (Ed.), *Higher Education: Handbook of Theory and Research* (pp. 133–89). Dordrecht, Netherlands: Springer.

Mazawi, A.E. (2007). "Knowledge society" or work as "spectacle"? Education for work and the prospects of social transformation in Arab societies. In L. Farrell & T. Fenwick (Eds.), *World Yearbook of Education 2007* (pp. 269–85). New York, NY: Routledge.

Mazawi, A.E. (2009). Naming the imaginary: "Building an Arab knowledge society" and the contested terrain of educational reforms for development. In O. Abi-Mershed (Ed.), *Trajectories of education in the Arab world: Legacies and challenges* (pp. 201–25). London: Routledge.

McDougall, J. (2011). Dream of exile, promise of home: Language, education, and Arabism in Algeria. *International Journal of Middle East Studies, 43*(2), 251–70.

McNeely, C.L. (1995). Prescribing national education policies: The role of international organizations. *Comparative Education Review, 39*(4), 483–507. doi:10.1086/447342.

MDPS (Ministry of Development Planning and Statistics). (2017). *Education in Qatar Statistical Profile 2016*. Doha, Qatar: Author.

MDPS (Ministry of Development Planning and Statistics). (2018). Qatar Second National Development Strategy 2018–2022. Doha, Qatar: Author.

Meehy, A. el-.(2015). *Higher education policies and welfare regimes in Egypt and Tunisia* (Higher Education in the Arab World, Working Paper). Retrieved from https://www.researchgate.net.

MEHE (Ministry of Education and Higher Education) [Lebanon]. (2021). "مؤسسات التعليم العالي في لبنان" [Higher education institutions in Lebanon]. Retrieved from http://www.higher-edu.gov.lb/.

MERIC (Mediterranean Network of National Information Centres on the Recognition of Qualifications). (2019a). *The higher education system in Lebanon, National Report.* Retrieved from http://www.meric-net.eu.

MERIC (Mediterranean Network of National Information Centres on the Recognition of Qualifications). (2019b). *The higher education system of Tunisia, National Report.* Retrieved from http://www.meric-net.eu.

MERIC (Mediterranean Network of National Information Centres on the Recognition of Qualifications). (2019c). *Moroccan Education System, National Report.* Retrieved from http://www.meric-net.eu.

MESA (Middle East Studies Association). (2016, January 15). Poet Mohammed el-Ajami imprisoned for reciting poems critical of Qatar's government. Retrieved from https://mesana.org.

MESA (Middle East Studies Association). (2018, November 15). MESA board statement on deteriorating security conditions for researchers in the UAE. Retrieved from https://mesana.org.

MESRS (Ministère de l'Enseignement Supérieur et de la Recherche Scientifique) [Tunisia]. (2019). *Liste des établissements privés d'enseignement supérieur pour l'année universitaire 2019–2020.* Retrieved from http://www.mes.tn.

Meyer, J.W., Boli, J., Thomas, G.M., & Ramirez, F.O. (1997). World society and the nation-state. *American Journal of Sociology, 103*(1), 144–81. doi:10.1086/231174.

Meyer, J.W., Ramirez, F.O., Frank, D.J., & Schofer, E. (2007). Higher education as an institution. In P. Gumport (Ed.), *Sociology of higher education: Contributions and their contexts* (pp. 187–221). Baltimore, MD: Johns Hopkins University Press.

MOE (Ministry of Education) [United Arab Emirates]. (2020). Number of Enrollments in Higher Education. *Open Data.* Abu Dhabi: Author. Retrieved from https://www.moe.gov.ae/.

MOEHE (Ministry of Education and Higher Education). (2019). *Higher education institutions and academic programs recognized by MOEHE in the state of Qatar (2018–2019).* Retrieved from http://www.edu.gov.qa.

Mohamed, R., Skinner, M., & Trines, S. (2019). Education in Egypt. *World Education News and Reviews.* Retrieved from https://wenr.wes.org.

MOHESRT (Ministry of Higher Education and Scientific Research and Technology). (2003). *Knowledge, an ambition for the future strategy for higher education, scientific research and technology in Tunisia 2010.* Tunis, Tunisia: Author.

MOHESRT (Ministry of Higher Education and Scientific Research and Technology). (2014). *Basic Statistics*. Tunis, Tunisia: Author.

Moini, J.S., Bikson, T.K., Neu, C.R., & DeSisto, L. (2009). *The reform of Qatar University* [Monograph]. Santa Monica, CA: RAND Corporation.

Momani, B. (2015). *Arab dawn: Arab youth and the demographic dividend they will bring*. Toronto, ON: University of Toronto Press.

Momani, M. al-. (2011). The Arab "youth quake": Implications on democratization and stability. *Middle East Law and Governance*, 3(1–2), 159–70.

Monitoring quality in the Arab world – Syria. (2019). *Al-Fanar*. Retrieved from https://www.al-fanarmedia.org.

Moussly, R. (2010, October 3). Majority not prepared for university. *Gulf News*. Retrieved from: https://gulfnews.com/.

MPMAR (Ministry of Planning, Monitoring and Administrative Reform), Government of Egypt. (2016). *Sustainable Development Strategy (SDS)*: Egypt Vision 2030. Retrieved from https://www.arabdevelopmentportal.com.

Mryyan, N. (2014). Demographics, labor force participation, and unemployment in Jordan. In R. Assaad (Ed.), *The Jordanian labour market in the new millennium* (pp. 39–63). Oxford, UK: Oxford University Press.

Mundy, K., Green, A., Lingard, B., & Verger, A. (Eds.). (2016). *Handbook of global education policy*. Chichester, UK: John Wiley & Sons.

Murphy, E. (2013). Under the emperor's neoliberal clothes! Why the international financial institutions got it wrong in Tunisia. In N. Gana (Ed.), *The making of the Tunisian revolution* (pp. 35–57). Edinburgh, Scotland: Edinburgh University Press.

Nader, A. (2016, September 6). Research: No man's land in Egypt. *Al-Monitor*.

Nagi, S., & Nagi, O. (2011). Stratification and mobility in contemporary Egypt. *Population Review*, 50, 1–20. doi:10.1353/prv.2011.0000.

Nahas, C. (2011). Financing and political economy of higher education: The case of Lebanon. *Prospects*, 41(1), 69–95. doi:10.1007/s11125-011-9183-9.

Nahhas, M. el-. (2002, May 9–15). Looking over private universities shoulders. *Al-Ahram Weekly Online*, no. 585. Retrieved from http://weekly.ahram.org.eg.

Nasr, S.H. (1987). *Traditional Islam in the modern world*. London: KPI Limited.

Natoor, A. A. al-. (2014, October 20). طلبة المكارم يشكلون 47% من القبول الموحد. AmmanNet.net.

Nielsen, G.B. (2012). Higher education gone global: Introduction to the special issue. *Learning and Teaching*, 5(3), 1–21. doi:10.3167/latiss.2012.050301.

NYUAD (New York University Abu Dhabi). (2019). *NYUAD at a glance – Fast facts*. Retrieved from https://nyuad.nyu.edu.

O'Malley, B. (2011, April 24). Dubai: Scholar's detention erodes UAE's reputation. *University World News*.

Omari, R. (2015, August 12). Lawmakers protest "assumed" cancellation of exceptions in university admission. *Jordan Times*.

Osman, T. (2010). *Egypt on the brink: From Nasser to Mubarak*. New Have, CT: Yale University Press.

Othman, H. (2019, July 23). Kuwait and Qatar slash the number of Jordanian universities they will recognize. *Al-Fanar*.

Ouelhezi, M. (2009, August 31). L'Institut Tunis-Dauphine dans les starting-blocks. Web Manager Center. Retrieved from http://www.webmanagercenter.com.

Patton, M.J. (1992). Constraints to privatization in Turkey. In I. Harik & D. Sullivan (Eds.), *Privatization and liberalization in the Middle East* (pp. 106–22). Bloomington: Indiana University Press.

Pennington, R. (2017, July 22). Pre-university year for Emiratis won't be phased out yet, officials say. *The National*. Retrieved from https://www.thenationalnews.com/.

Perkin, H. (2007). History of universities. In J.J.F. Forrest & P. Altbach (Eds.), *International handbook of higher education* (pp. 159–205). Dordrecht, Netherlands: Springer.

Plackett, B. (2016a, April 26). New foundation seeks to give 15,000 scholarships to Arab students. *Al-Fanar*.

Plackett, B. (2016b, September 22). Arab science needs more respect. *Al-Fanar*. Retrieved from https://www.al-fanarmedia.org.

Plackett, B. (2016c, December 3). Most Arab-world researchers want to leave, a new survey finds. *Al-Fanar*. Retrieved from https://www.al-fanarmedia.org.

Powell, W.W., & Snellman, K. (2004). The knowledge economy. *Annual Review of Sociology, 30*, 199–220. doi:10.1146/annurev.soc.29.010202.100037.

PROPHE (Program for Research on Private Higher Education). (2021). Global private and total higher education enrollment by region and country, 2010. Retrieved from https://prophe.org/en/global-data/.

PSA (Planning and Statistics Authority). (2018). Education Statistics, Chapter 4 – 2018. Retrieved from https://www.psa.gov.qa/.

QU (Qatar University). (2021). QU timeline. Retrieved from http://www.qu.edu.qa/.

Ramirez, F.O. (2010). Accounting for excellence: Transforming universities into organizational actors. In V. Rust, L. Portnoi, & S. Bagley (Eds.), *Higher education, policy, and the global competition phenomenon* (pp. 43–58). New York, NY: Palgrave Macmillan.

Ramirez, F.O. (2012). The world society perspective: Concepts, assumptions, and strategies. *Comparative Education, 48*(4), 423–39. doi:10.1080/03050068.2012.693374.

Ramirez, F.O., & Tiplic, D. (2014). In pursuit of excellence? Discursive patterns in European higher education research. *Higher Education, 67*(4), 439–55. doi:10.1007/s10734-013-9681-1.

Redden, E. (2015, March 18). Persona non grata. *Inside Higher Education*. Retrieved from https://www.insidehighered.com.

Reiter, Y. (2002). Higher education and sociopolitical transformation in Jordan. *British Journal of Middle Eastern Studies, 29*(2), 137–64. doi:10.1080 /1353019022000012641.

Résultats du Bac 2012 au Maroc: 48,96% de taux de réussite. (2012, June 26). Yabiladi. Retrieved from http://www.yabiladi.com.

Richards, A. (1992). *Higher Education in Egypt* (Working Paper 862). Washington, DC: World Bank.

Riddle, P. (1993). Political authority and university formation in Europe, 1200–1800. *Sociological Perspectives, 36*(1), 45–62. doi:10.2307/1389441.

Ridge, N. (2014). *Education and the reverse gender divide in the Gulf States: Embracing the global, ignoring the local.* New York, NY: Teachers College Press.

Robertson, S.L. (2005). Re-imagining and rescripting the future of education: Global knowledge economy discourses and the challenge to education systems. *Comparative Education, 41*(2), 151–70.

Romani, V. (2009). The politics of higher education in the Middle East: Problems and prospects. *Middle East Brief, 36*(1), 1–8.

Rugh, W.A. (2002). Arab education: Tradition, growth and reform. *The Middle East Journal, 56*(3), 396–414.

Sabri, H.A. (2011). The impeding drivers of risks at private higher education institutions in Jordan: An analytical approach. *Journal of Education and Vocational Research, 2*(4), 120–31. doi:10.22610/jevr.v2i4.32.

Sahlberg, P. (2016). The global educational reform movement and its impact on schooling. In K. Mundy, A. Green, B. Lingard, & A. Verger. (Eds.), *Handbook of global education policy* (pp. 128–44). Chichester, UK: John Wiley & Sons.

Said, E.W. (1981). *Covering Islam: How the media and the experts determine how we see the rest of the world.* New York, NY: Random House.

Sakr, N. (2004). UN analysis of aggregate Arab "knowledge deficit." *The Political Quarterly, 75*(2), 185–90. doi:10.1111/j.1467-923X.2004.00602.x.

Salehi-Isfahani, D., & Dhillon, N. (2008). *Stalled youth transitions in the Middle East: A framework for policy reform* (Middle East Youth Initiative Working Paper No. 8). Washington, DC: Brookings Institution. Retrieved from https://ssrn.com/ab.

Salehi-Isfahani, D., Hassine, N.B., & Assaad, R. (2014). Equality of opportunity in educational achievement in the Middle East and North Africa. *The Journal of Economic Inequality, 12*(4), 489–515. doi:10.1007/s10888-013-9263-6.

Salem, O., & Swan, M. (2014, February 4). Foundation year at UAE state universities to be scrapped in 2018. *The National.* Retrieved from https:// www.thenationalnews.com/.

Saniei, M., & Baharvand, H. (2018). Human embryonic stem cell science in Muslim context:"Ethics of human dignity" and "ethics of healing." *Advances in Medical Ethics, 4*(1), 7–21.

Sawahel, W. (2014, March 14). New Arab strategy for science, technology and innovation. *University World News.* Retrieved from https://www .universityworldnews.com.

Sawahel, W. (2017, September 1). Tunisia in new bid to attract Sub-Saharan students. *University World News*. Retrieved from https://www.universityworldnews.com.

Sawahel, W. (2020, January 13). Broader horizons – Universities switch to bachelor degree. *University World News*. Retrieved from https://www.universityworldnews.com.

Sayed, E., & Langsten, R. (2014). Gender, tutoring and track in Egyptian education. *International Journal of Educational and Pedagogical Sciences, 8*(10), 3223–7.

Schofer, E., & Meyer, J.W. (2005). The worldwide expansion of higher education in the twentieth century. *American Sociological Review, 70*(6), 898–920.

Scholars at Risk Academic Monitoring Project. (2019). Retrieved from https://www.scholarsatrisk.org.

Scholz, C., & Maroun, M. (2015). The Bologna Process and higher education reform in the eastern and southern Mediterranean: The case of Israel, Egypt and Lebanon. *IEMed Mediterranean Yearbook 2015*, 297–302. Barcelona, Spain: European Institute of the Mediterranean.

Sebai, N.M. el-. (2006). The Egyptian higher education system: Towards better quality in the future. *Journal of Futures Studies, 11*(2), 75–92.

Sedrine, S.S. (2009). La Tunisie [Tunisia]. In B. Labaki (Ed.), *Enseignement superieur et marche du travail dans le monde arabe* [Higher Education and the Labor Market in the Arab World] (pp. 83–118). Beirut, Lebanon: Institut Francais du Proche Orient.

Shawabke, M. al-. (2012, August 8). *How Jordanian students cheat at high school exams* (Report) [Arab Reporters for Investigative Journalism]. Retrieved from http://en.arij.net.

Sherif, I. (2012, July 3). Ministry of Higher Education announced to the public a list of accredited programmes. *Gulf News*. Shirazi, R. (2020). Being late, going with the flow, always doing more: The cruel optimism of higher education in Jordan. *International Journal of Qualitative Studies in Education, 33*(3), 293–310.

Siddiqi, A., Stoppani, J., Anadon, L.D., & Narayanamurti, V. (2016). Scientific wealth in Middle East and North Africa: Productivity, indigeneity, and specialty in 1981–2013. *PloS One, 11*(11), e0164500. doi:10.1371/journal.pone.0164500.

Sieverding, M. (2009). *The ambivalence of higher education: Class aspirations among women university students in Cairo*. Paper presented at conference of Middle East Studies Association (MESA), 22 November 2008, Boston, MA.

Sieverding, M., Krafft, C., & Elbadawy, A. (2019). An exploration of the drivers of private tutoring in Egypt. *Comparative Education Review, 63*(4), 562–90. doi:10.1086/705383.

Slama, N. (2013, November 27). Student unions a force in Tunisian politics. *TunisiaLive*. Retrieved from http://www.tunisia-live.net.

Slaughter, S., & Rhoades, G. (2004). *Academic capitalism and the new economy: Markets, state, and higher education.* Baltimore, MD: Johns Hopkins Univesity Press.

Sobhy, H. (2012). The de-facto privatization of secondary education in Egypt: A study of private tutoring in technical and general schools. *Compare: A Journal of Comparative and International Education, 42*(1), 47–67. doi:10.1080/03057925.2011.629042.

Souali, M. (2009). Le Maroc [Morocco]. In B. Labaki (Ed.), *Enseignement superieur et marche du travail dans le monde arabe* [Higher education and the labor market in the Arab world] (pp. 13–46). Beirut, Lebanon: Institut Francais du Proche Orient.

Souitaris, V., Zerbinati, S., & Laham, A. al-. (2007). Do entrepreneurship programmes raise entrepreneurial intention of science and engineering students? The effect of learning, inspiration and resources. *Journal of Business Venturing, 22*(4), 566–91. doi:10.1016/j.jbusvent.2006.05.002.

SPHERE (Support and Promotion for Higher Education Reform Experts). (2020a). *Higher Education in Jordan.* Retrieved from https://supporthere.org.

SPHERE (Support and Promotion for Higher Education Reform Experts). (2020b). *Higher Education in Lebanon.* Retrieved from https://supporthere.org.

Stasz, C., Eide, E., Martorell, F., Goldman, C.A., & Constant, L. (2007). *Post-secondary education in Qatar: Employer demand, student choice, and options for policy* (Vol. 644). Santa Monica, CA: Rand Corporation.

Stone, P. (2013). Access to higher education by the luck of the draw. *Comparative Education Review, 57*(3), 577–99. doi:10.1086/670663.

Strangler, C. (2018, July 15). The struggle for democracy in Morocco. *Jacobin.* Retrieved from https://www.jacobinmag.com.

Street, R., Kabbani, N., & Oraibi, Y. al-. (2006). *Responding to weak labor market conditions facing youth: The case of Syria.* Paper presented at conference on Youth in the Middle East and North Africa: Expanding Economic Prospects in Urban Areas (pp. 1–28). Rabat, Morocco: Arab Institute for Urban Development.

Stromquist, N.P. (2002). *Education in a globalized world: The connectivity of economic power, technology, and knowledge.* Lanham, MD: Rowman & Littlefield.

Sukarieh, M. (2016). On class, culture, and the creation of the neoliberal subject: The case of Jordan. *Anthropological Quarterly, 89*(4), 1201–25.

Sukarieh, M. (2017). The rise of the Arab youth paradigm: A critical analysis of the Arab Human Development Report 2016. *Middle East-Topics & Arguments, 9,* 70–83.

Swan, M. (2013, September 18). International branch campuses key role in the UAE. The National. Retrieved from https://www.thenational.ae.

Taha-Thomure, H. (2003). *Academic freedom in Arab universities* Lanham, MD: University Press of America.

Tamari, S. (2009). Between the "golden age" and the Renaissance: Islamic
   higher education in eighteenth-century Damascus. In O. Abi-Mershed (Ed.),
   Trajectories of education in the Arab world (pp. 52–74). New York, NY: Routledge.

Teacher syndicate reports Tawjihi cheating as ministry disputes claims. (2014,
   December 31). *Jordan Times.*

Teferra, D., & Altbach, P.G. (Eds.) (2003). *African higher education: An
   international reference handbook.* Bloomington: Indiana University Press

Tyack, D.B., & Cuban, L. (1995). *Tinkering toward utopia.* Cambridge, MA:
   Harvard University Press.

UAE Open Data Portal. (2021). *Academic Bridge Program completion rates, 2000–
   2015.* Retrieved from http://www.bayanet.ae.

UAECD (United Arab Emirates Cultural Division. (2021). *Education in the United
   Arab Emirates.* Retrieved from http://www.uaecd.org/.

UN (United Nations). (2015). Transforming our world: The 2030 agenda for
   sustainable development. New York, NY: Author. Retrieved from https://
   sustainabledevelopment.un.org/.

UIS (UNESCO Institute for Statistics). (2019). UIS.Stat. Retrieved from http://
   data.uis.unesco.org/.

UNDP (United Nations Development Programme). (2002). *Arab Human
   Development Report: Creating opportunity for future generations.* New York, NY:
   United Nations. Retrieved from http://hdr.undp.org.

UNDP (United Nations Development Programme). (2003). *Arab Human
   Development Report: Building a knowledge society.* New York, NY: United Nations.
   Retrieved from http://hdr.undp.org.

UNDP (United Nations Development Programme). (2004). *The Arab Human
   Development Report 2004: Towards freedom in the Arab world.* Retrieved from
   http://hdr.undp.org.

UNDP (United Nations Development Programme). (2005). *The Arab Human
   Development Report 2005: Towards the rise of women in the Arab world.* Retrieved
   from http://hdr.undp.org.

UNDP (United Nations Development Programme). (2009). *The Arab Human
   Development Report 2009: Challenges for human security in the Arab region.*
   Retrieved from http://www.undp.org.

UNDP (United Nations Development Programme). (2016). *The Arab Human
   Development Report 2016: Youth and the prospects for human development in a
   changing reality.* Retrieved from http://www.arab-hdr.org.

UNESCO (United Nations Educational, Scientific and Cultural Organization).
   (1997, November 11). Recommendation concerning the status of higher
   -education teaching personnel. Retrieved from http://portal.unesco.org/.

UNESCO (United Nations Educational, Scientific and Cultural Organization).
   (1998, October 9). *World Declaration on higher education for the twenty-first
   century: Vision and action.*

UNESCO (United Nations Educational, Scientific and Cultural Organization). (2015). *UNESCO Science Report: Towards 2030*. Paris, France: Author.

UNESCO (United Nations Educational, Scientific and Cultural Organization). (2016, May 23). *More Arab countries are seeking to orient their economies towards knowledge*. Retrieved from https://en.unesco.org.

Vora, N. (2018). *Teach for Arabia: American universities, liberalism, and transnational Qatar*. Stanford, CA: Stanford University Press.

Waardenburg, J. (1966). *Les universites dans le monde Arabe actuel* [The universities of the Arab world] (Vol. 1). Paris, France: Mouton.

Waast, R., Arvanitis, R., Richard-Waast, C., & Rossi, P.L. (2010). What do social sciences in North African countries focus on. *World Social Science Report*, 176–80.

Waast, R., & Rossi, P.L. (2010). Scientific production in Arab countries: A bibliometric perspective. *Science, Technology and Society, 15*(2), 339–70. doi:10.1177/097172181001500207.

Waldow, F. (2018). Commentary to part III: Why is "being international" so attractive? "Being international" as a source of legitimacy and distinction. In C. Maxwell, U. Deppe, H.-H. Krüger, & W. Helsper (Eds.), *Elite education and internationalisation* (pp. 247–53). Cham, Switzerland: Palgrave Macmillan.

Wallerstein, I.M. (1969). *University in turmoil: The politics of change*. New York, NY: Atheneum.

Waterbury, J. (2020). *Missions impossible: Higher education policymaking in the Arab world*. Cairo, Egypt: American University in Cairo Press.

WDI (World Development Indicators). (2021). Washington, DC: World Bank. Retrieved from https://data.worldbank.org/.

Weber, A.S. (2014). Linking education to creating a knowledge society: Qatar's investment in the education sector. In N. Baporikar (Ed.), *Handbook of research on higher education in the MENA region: Policy and practice* (pp. 52–73). Hershey, PA: Information Science Reference.

Weipert-Fenner, I., & Wolff, J. (2015). *Socioeconomic contention and post-revolutionary political change in Egypt and Tunisia: A research agenda* (PRIF Working Paper 24). Frankfurt am Main, Germany: Hessische Stiftung Friedens-und Konfliktforschung.

Wickham, C.R. (2002). *Mobilizing Islam: Religion, activism and political change in Egypt*. New York, NY: Columbia University Press.

Wildavsky, B. (2012). *The great brain race: How global universities are reshaping the world* (Vol. 64). Princeton, NJ: Princeton University Press.

Wilkens, K.A., & Masri, S. (2011). *Higher education reform in the Arab world*. Washington, DC: Brookings Institution Press.

Wilkins, S., & Huisman, J. (2012). The international branch campus as transnational strategy in higher education. *Higher Education, 64*(5), 627–45. doi:10.1007/s10734-012-9516-5.

World Bank, The. (1986). *Staff appraisal report: Kingdom of Morocco Education Sector Reform Program* (Report No. 5923-MOR). Washington, DC: Author.

World Bank, The. (1991). *Project completion report: Education Sector Reform Program (Loan 2664-MOR)* (Report No. 9568). Washington, DC: Author.

World Bank, The. (1997). *Implementation completion report: Republic of Tunisia Education and Training Project* (Report No. 16574). Washington, DC: Author.

World Bank, The. (2000). *Higher education in developing countries: Peril and promise*. Washington, DC: Author.

World Bank, The. (2008a, February 4). Globalization requires education reforms in Middle East and North Africa, report says. Retrieved from https://www.worldbank.org.

World Bank, The. (2008b). *The road not traveled: Education reform in the Middle East and North Africa*. Washington, DC: Author.

World Bank, The. (2011). Reforms needed in higher education to meet the needs of youth in the Middle East and North Africa. Retrieved from https://www.worldbank.org.

World Bank, The. (2013). *Jobs for shared prosperity: Time for action in the Middle East and North Africa*. Washington, DC: Author. Retrieved from http://hdl.handle.net/10986/13284.

World Bank, The. (2015, March 17). *Implementation completion and results report on a loan (IBRD-73920) in the amount of EUR 61.3 million (US$ 76.0 million equivalent) to the Republic of Tunisia for a second higher education reform support project*. (Report No. ICR3297). Retrieved from https://documents.worldbank.org.

World Bank, The. (2016, February 25). *Tertiary education for employability project for Tunisia*. Retrieved from https://www.worldbank.org.

al-Youm 24. (2016, June 7). بالتزامن مع الباكالوريا... مجلس النواب يصادق على قانون جزر الغش. [In conjunction with the Baccalaureat, Parliament approves new law to prevent cheating]. Retrieved from http://www.alyaoum24.com.

Yusuf, M. (2008). Prospects of youth radicalization in Pakistan. The Saban Center for Middle East Policy at Brookings, Analysis Paper, Number 14. Retrieved from: https://www.brookings.edu/wp-content/uploads/2016/06/10_pakistan_yusuf.pdf.

Zeghal, M. (2007). The "recentering"of religious knowledge and discourse: The case of al-Azhar in twentieth-century Egypt. In R. Hefner & M.Q. Zaman (Eds.), *Schooling Islam: The culture and politics of modern Muslim education*. Princeton, NJ: Princeton University Press (pp. 107–30).

Zemni, S. (2017). The Tunisian revolution: Neoliberalism, urban contentious politics and the right to the city. *International Journal of Urban and Regional Research*, *41*(1), 70–83. doi:10.1111/1468-2427.12384.

Zghal, R. (2007). Un équilibre instable entre le quantitatif et le qualitative: L'enseignement supérieur en Tunisie. *Revue Internationale D'éducation de Sèvres*, *45* (September), 51–62. doi: 10.4000/ries.

Zou'bi, M.R., Mohamed-Nour, S., el-Kharraz, J., & Hassan, N. (2015). The Arab States, In *UNESCO Science Report: Towards 2030*, 430–69. Paris, France: UNESCO. Retrieved from: https://en.unesco.org/.

Zughoul, M.R. (2000). Private and privatised higher educational institutions in Jordan. *Mediterranean Journal of Educational Studies*, 5(1), 95–117.

Index

The letter f following a page number indicates a figure. The letter t following a page number indicates a table.

Maghreb. *See* North Africa
makruma (affirmative-action)
  (Jordan), 71–6, 84, 109, 133. *See also*
  access: exam-based
Mamluk Empire, 23
Manthri, Y, al-, 108
Masri, S., 8, 59
Mauritania, 154
Mazawi, Andre, 9, 10, 13, 14–15,
  31, 83
Mediterranean School of Business, 131
medium of instruction. *See* language
  of instruction
Menoufia University (Egypt), 111
meritocracy, 53, 54–8, 71–6, 84. *See*
  also access: exam-based
method: data analysis, 17–18;
  multilevel and comparative
  approach, 10–17, 17f
Meyer, J.W., 115–16
Middle East Studies Association, 199
Ministry for Education and Higher
  Education (Qatar), 48
Ministry of Education (Morocco), 65
Ministry of Education and Higher
  Education (Lebanon), 40, 65
Ministry of Higher Education
  (Egypt), 37
Ministry of Higher Education
  (Syria), 42
Ministry of Higher Education and
  Scientific Research (MESRS)
  (Tunisia), 46
Ministry of Higher Education and
  Scientific Research (MOHESR)
  (Jordan), 38
Ministry of Higher Education and
  Scientific Research (UAE), 50
Ministry of National Education,
  Vocational Training, Higher
  Education, and Scientific Research
  (Morocco), 44

Mohammed V University (Morocco),
  98, 111–12; academic freedom,
  197; branch campus in Doha,
  164; class sizes, 91; founding, 43;
  research, 174
Mohammed VI, King of Morocco, 98
Mohammed VI Polytechnic
  University (Morocco), 44
Moini, J.S., 107
Momani, B., 115
Monjib, Maati, 197
Morocco: academic freedom, 197,
  198t; admission policies, 51, 52,
  55, 58; admission policies and
  program choice, 68–9;
  al-Akhawayn University, 164;
  American model bachelor's
  degree, 106; Arabization, 31–2;
  Arab Spring, 7, 59; cheating and
  connections, 62, 63–5; class sizes,
  90, 91; colonization of, 27–8;
  connections, 70; early Islamic
  education, 23; educational
  reforms, 103–6, 126; European
  influence on education, 26, 27,
  28; free public higher education,
  125; GDP per capita, 43; higher
  education system, 35t, 43–5;
  internationalization, 146, 164;
  international students, 154, 155f,
  156, 157, 157t, 158t; middle-class
  youth, 30; moonlighting by
  faculty, 174; national university,
  31; neoliberal economic reforms,
  34; private higher education,
  128, 129–30, 136; private higher
  education enrolment, 124, 125t;
  private vocational education,
  126; quality assurance, 44, 97–8;
  research, 174, 175, 183, 183t, 191–2;
  research publications, 180, 181t;
  scholarship programs, 149, 150–1;

publications, 180, 181, 181t;
scholarship programs, 149

Zayed bin Sultan al-Nahyan, emir of
Abu Dhabi, 32

Zayed University (UAE), 49, 80
Zeghal, Malika, 26
Zghal, Riadh, 129
Zitouna (Tunisia), 23, 45